Chechnya: The Case for Independence

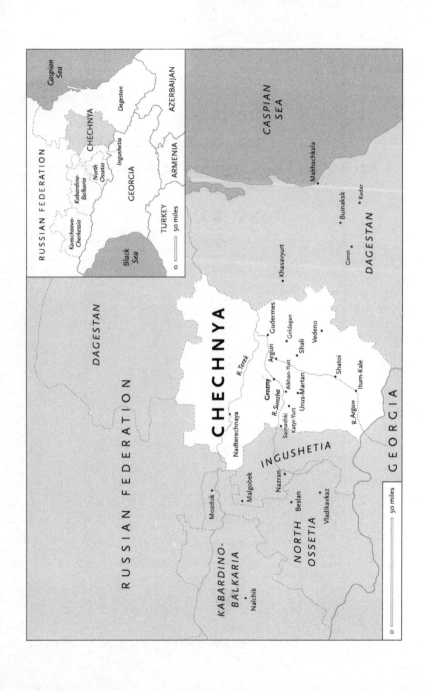

Chechnya:
The Case for Independence

◆

TONY WOOD

VERSO

London • New York

1 3 5 7 9 10 8 6 4 2

Verso

UK: 6 Meard Street, London W1F 0EG

USA: 180 Varick Street, New York, NY 10014-4606

www.versobooks.com

Verso is the imprint of New Left Books

ISBN-13: 978-1-84467-114-4

British Library Cataloguing in Publication Data

A catalogue record for this book is available from the British Library

Library of Congress Cataloging-in-Publication Data

A catalog record for this book is available from the Library of Congress

Typeset in Garamond by Hewer Text UK Ltd, Edinburgh

Printed in Germany by GGP Media GmbH, Poessneck

What happened was what always happens when a state possessing great military strength enters into relations with primitive, small peoples living their own independent lives . . . Either on the pretext of self-defence, even though any attacks are always provoked by the offences of the strong neighbour, or on the pretext of bringing civilisation to a wild people, even though this wild people lives incomparably better and more peacefully than its civilisers, or else on a whole range of other pretexts, the servants of large military states commit all sorts of villainy against small nations, insisting that it is impossible to deal with them in any other way.

Leo Tolstoy, 1902 draft of *Hadji Murat*
(removed from final version)

Contents

Introduction

The purpose of this book is to set out the case for Chechen independence. Many works have examined the historical background and events immediately preceding Russia's two onslaughts on Chechnya since 1994, in which more than 70,000 people have been killed and several times that number displaced from their homes.[1] Journalists and activists have provided vital testimony to the devastating effects of these wars; Anna Politkovskaya, brutally murdered on 7 October 2006, was one of the bravest. The present volume owes a great debt to the courage of such individuals, as well as drawing extensively on the scholarship of others. However, the fundamental issue at stake has generally been absent from public view, especially in the West: whether or not the Chechens have the right to a state of their own.

The question can, I believe, only gain in urgency the longer the killing is allowed to continue. By the time these words are printed, the Russian occupation of Chechnya will have entered its eighth year, with atrocities still being committed against the civilian population by Russian

---

[1] Aleksandr Cherkesov, 'Book of Numbers: Book of the Lost', in Tanya Lokshina, ed., *The Imposition of a Fake Political Settlement in the Northern Caucasus: The 2003 Chechen Presidential Election*, Stuttgart 2005, p. 205.

troops and their Chechen proxies with appalling regularity. Western governments and commentators have repeatedly endorsed the view of successive Russian administrations that war has been waged in Chechnya to prevent the disintegration of Russia, to restore the rule of law in a criminal enclave, and to counter the threat of Islamist terrorism. These justifications have little basis, and only serve to obscure the true substance of the conflict, which remains at root a struggle for national self-determination.

The Chechens' demands are modest – full sovereignty, retaining economic and other ties with Russia. Yet the Russian response has been staggeringly disproportionate: two full-scale invasions, resulting in the deaths of perhaps 10 per cent of the population. The indiscriminate violence unleashed on Chechnya only adds weight to their case for independence, for which, as the following chapters aim to demonstrate, there are incontrovertible historical, moral and legal grounds. These have been almost unanimously dismissed in Russia and the world at large on pretexts that are weak in fact, and shameful in principle. Against the craven consensus that has permitted the crushing of the Chechens' legitimate aspirations to statehood, this book holds that any just and lasting resolution of the war must proceed from a recognition of their legitimacy.

Chapter 1 outlines the specific features of the Chechens as a people, and their particular historical experience. Discussions of the present Russo-Chechen conflict often characterize it as the all-but-inevitable product of a deep-lying ethnic antagonism. But the development of a sense of Chechen nationhood was in fact the cumulative product of external geopolitical and military pressures – from the first confrontations with Cossack settlers in the sixteenth century to the expansion of the Tsarist empire in the nineteenth. It was above all the Soviet period, however, that laid the basis for a modern nationalist movement, and provided traumatic grounds for seeking independence: in 1944, the entire Chechen people was deported to Central Asia, in an officially organized process whose resulting death toll – 30 per cent of the population – puts it firmly in the category of attempted genocide.

The aftershocks of this event reverberate into the present. After a period of exile, the surviving Chechens returned to their homeland in the 1950s – to a life permeated by tensions between returnees and

Russian settlers who had arrived in the interim. It was amid the socio-economic pressures and contradictions of the late Soviet system, described in chapter 2, that the Chechen national movement took shape. Much like other nationalisms on the Soviet periphery, it gathered force under *perestroika* and eventually displaced the old order in 1991, its newly elected leader declaring sovereignty shortly before the USSR's collapse. Chapter 2 also analyzes the broader legal and constitutional dimensions of Chechnya's secession, placing these in international perspective in order to assert its legitimacy.

Chechnya enjoyed de facto independence from 1991–4, but was then invaded by Russian troops and subjected to a level of bombardment that eclipsed the horrors of Sarajevo or Beirut. Chapter 3 examines the build-up to Yeltsin's invasion, and assesses the rationales offered in support of it. These centre on a variety of factors, ranging from a threat to Russia's territorial integrity, the criminal nature of the regime in Grozny, and the potential for a blockade of Russian interests in the region. None of these arguments holds water in constitutional, strategic or logical terms – as was forcefully demonstrated barely three months into the war by Andrei Illarionov, subsequently economic adviser to Vladimir Putin, in a trenchant article in *Moscow News* that is reproduced as an appendix to this volume.[2] The premises of that text – which it would be impossible to publish in Russia today – are still tragically valid, and find many echoes in my own arguments. The military mismatch against which Illarionov spoke out, however, continued for another year and a half – an unnecessary, disproportionate and illegitimate resort to force, by a regime low on credibility and an army keen to reverse defeats in Afghanistan and the Cold War.

The First Chechen War ended in a humiliating withdrawal by Russian forces, and a period of independence for Chechnya from 1996 to 1999 that has routinely been characterized as one of mounting anarchy and crime; Chechnya itself, meanwhile, has been labelled a 'failed state' that deserved to be reined in by Putin in 1999. Chapter 4 seeks to counter this assertion by surveying the actual record: Chechnya's turbulent political scene, its economic woes and social tensions, and above all the colossal task of reconstruction confronting it after the rampages of the Russian army.

---

[2] Andrei Illarionov and Boris Lvin, 'Should Russia Recognize Chechnya's Independence?', *Moscow News*, 24 February–2 March 1995.

Though Chechnya's leaders did largely fail to establish effective authority, the obstacles facing them were immense – and deliberately multiplied by Moscow, whose military demolition of Chechnya, coupled with a refusal to provide assistance in the aftermath, was overwhelmingly responsible for smashing the possibility of a viable Chechen polity.

The invasion launched by Putin in September 1999 propelled him to the Russian presidency. Ostensibly an 'anti-terrorist operation', conducted in retaliation for an incursion by armed Chechen Islamists into Dagestan, the Second Chechen War in reality aimed once again to strangle Chechen independence. Chapter 5 gives an account of the war's murky origins and early stages of combat, before gauging its significance as a factor in the consolidation of a new power elite, predominantly drawn from the ranks of the KGB. I then turn to the corrosive effects of the war on Russian society itself: conscripts return to civilian life corrupted and brutalized by the habits of occupation, while officialdom's grip on the media and unbending hostility to its adversaries has worked to sustain a climate of xenophobia and suspicion. Together, these features of Putin's Russia preclude any genuine democratic freedom; indeed, chapter 5 argues that not only Chechnya's, but Russia's interests would best be served by ending the occupation and recognizing the Chechen people's right to self-determination.

No account of the Chechen wars would be complete without a tally of Western responses – ranging from full-blown endorsement to silent approval of Russian war crimes, for the benefit of a smoother transition to 'liberal democracy'. The utter dereliction of the outside world with regard to Chechnya is a recurrent theme in this book, but receives particular attention in chapter 5. Much of Russia's success in winning overseas assent for its second assault on Chechnya stems, of course, from the priority accorded to the 'War on Terror' since the September 11 attacks. The Russian authorities have consistently sought to portray the Chechen resistance as part of an international Islamist threat, linked not to a nationalist agenda but the programme of al-Qaeda and affiliated groups. Chapter 6 presents an alternative view based on a historical picture of the role of Islam in Chechnya, stressing the interweaving of national and religious identity in local traditions, and the mobilizing function of Islamist discourse during confrontations with external forces.

The Russian invasions of 1994 and 1999 sparked a search for solidarity and funds in the wider world. What little material assistance the Chechens have received comes either from diaspora communities or from Islamist groups in the Middle East, with flows disproportionately benefiting the Islamist wing of the resistance thanks to the presence among them of Arab fighters. Chapter 6 contends, however, that both the number of *jihadi* volunteers and the extent of Islamist funding have been exaggerated by a Russian leadership keen to ascribe any opposition to the designs of shadowy foreign forces. The core motivation of the Chechen resistance, on the contrary, remains a desire for sovereignty that takes precedence over the imperatives of faith.

In recent years, there has been an upsurge in the activity of armed Islamist groups across the North Caucasus, raising the spectre of a regionalization of insurgency. The impetus for this has come substantially from the Chechen resistance itself, which has sought to multiply fronts against its opponent. However, as chapter 7 recounts, the growing instability in the North Caucasus has far deeper roots. Rebellion is fed by local anger with the depredations of regional elites, who have presided over a vertiginous drop in the living standards of the population, while systematically stifling any expressions of discontent with their corrupt and incompetent rule. Russia's attack on Chechen sovereignty has enabled disparate frustrations to be directed at a single adversary. The most rational strategy for its rulers would be to separate these battles from one another: recognition of Chechnya's right to independence would remove the strongest rallying point for regional opposition, and provide better conditions for attempting the longer-term project of reversing the economic and political marginalization of southern Russia's Muslim populations.

Within months of invading Chechnya, Putin had announced the start of a process of 'normalization', a supposed path to peace and stability through the holding of a constitutional referendum and voting for a new parliament. Chapter 8 holds a mirror to the ugly reality: a rapacious, fraudulently elected puppet regime whose militias engage in widespread brutality against the civilian population. From a cruel occupation by a foreign power, Russia's intervention in Chechnya has turned into a combined colonial counter-insurgency and incipient civil war. Far from bringing stability, the Kremlin's strategy has put in place an illegitimate regime whose main function has been to sow enmity within Chechen society. A guerrilla war, however, continues – and it is one neither Moscow and its hirelings, nor the resistance ranged against them, can conclusively win.

The best means of ending the war, in fact, lies in Russia recognizing the Chechens' right to govern themselves. It is a straightforward enough demand, and one that has been accorded to hundreds of peoples across the world. Many of them are smaller, in terms of population, than the Chechens: of the UN's 192 member-states, 41 – more than a fifth – have under one million inhabitants; moreover, 37 states have been admitted to the UN since 1990, giving the lie to any idea than Chechen independence would overstretch the international state-system.

Why, then, have the Chechens been ruled ineligible for statehood? There are three principal claims. Firstly, an appeal to realpolitik, according to which Chechen aspirations for independence must be ruled out of court, merely because Moscow would not accept such an outcome.[3] On these grounds, of course, most of the nearly 200 states the world presently contains would not exist: following the same logic, the British, French, Spanish, Portuguese, Ottoman and indeed Russian empires would have been left intact. The argument that Russia should not be antagonized is also groundless: the Western powers have eagerly expanded NATO right up to its frontiers without concern for such niceties. The oft-cited risks to Europe's energy supplies, meanwhile, should be assessed more soberly: Russia needs markets for its abundant natural resources as much as Europe needs to purchase them.

The second basis for dismissing Chechnya's right to existence is that the country had its chance at independence between 1996 and 1999, and performed so woefully that its sovereignty could justifiably be revoked.[4] Such reasoning is an outgrowth of a worldwide trend among liberals in the 1990s to see national frontiers as little more than a shield

---

[3] Jonathan Steele, 'Doing Well out of War', *London Review of Books*, 21 October 2004.

[4] Anatol Lieven, 'Chechnya and the Laws of War', in Dmitri Trenin and Aleksei Malashenko, *Russia's Restless Frontier: The Chechnya Factor in Post-Soviet Russia*, Washington, D.C. 2004, pp. 209–24; Robert Bruce Ware, 'A Multitude of Evils: Mythology and Political Failure in Chechnya', in Richard Sakwa, ed., *Chechnya: From Past to Future*, London 2005, pp. 79–115.

enabling rogue regimes to commit crimes against humanity; the same notion has served to legitimate military intervention by Western powers, from the Balkans to Iraq, purporting to punish those responsible – though the enormous civilian toll of such 'humanitarian' adventures makes clear the low priority actually accorded to human life. What holds for these places is even more true of Chechnya: the idea that a country already reduced to rubble deserved further pulverization is simply untenable. Whatever the misdeeds and failings of its rulers, the scourge of war was never an appropriate means for redressing them. The existence of a slave trade in Chechnya has also been listed among the subsidiary factors giving cause for an intervention;[5] it is worth noting, however, that the same experts have not cast a concerned eye at Thailand's child prostitutes, for instance, and called for Bangkok to be razed to the ground. Moreover, how many states routinely fail to provide security and livelihood for their citizens, and yet their leaders – many of them not even elected, unlike those of independent Chechnya – are regularly welcomed in the White House, Kremlin or Downing Street?

Thirdly, it has been argued that the war has now mutated into a struggle between a corrupt army, armed criminal gangs and Islamist extremist factions, and that the ideal of independence has simply evaporated from this stinking morass.[6] On this view, the question of sovereignty is irrelevant to the populace's more basic need for security and stability, which should be established by any available means. This rests on a number of false premises. The war has indeed created an atmosphere of arbitrary cruelty and impunity in which corruption and crime thrive, and as the situation in Chechnya grows more desperate, the rhetoric of millenarian religious sects seems more closely to reflect the shattered reality. But if material gain and scriptural dogma were all that was at stake, the fighting would long ago have ceased. Its continuation is due to a substantial pool of popular support for those fighting the invaders, and to widespread rejection of the authorities put in place at gunpoint by their armies. The pro-Moscow regime is utterly

---

[5] Ware, 'A Multitude of Evils', p. 99.
[6] Variants of this position can be found in Anna Politkovskaya, *A Small Corner of Hell: Dispatches from Chechnya*, Chicago 2002; Georgi Derluguian, *Bourdieu's Secret Admirer in the Caucasus*, Chicago 2005; Thomas de Waal, 'The North Caucasus: Politics or War?', *openDemocracy*, 7 September 2004.

devoid of legitimacy, which is not, as one observer has said, 'a political luxury that most Chechens know they cannot afford'.[7] On the contrary, it is the only possible foundation for a government with effective authority over its territory, and hence for a secure and stable future. Such a government, in turn, can only be produced by giving the Chechens the right freely to choose whether they wish to remain under Russian rule, or whether – as they have insisted on the only occasions when they have been asked – they want the state of their own to which they are legally and morally entitled.

There are, of course, grounds for concern at what would happen in Chechnya following a Russian withdrawal. In a country rife with weapons and unslaked vengeance, a generalized settling of accounts could take an immense toll. But this is no reason for allowing the present slaughter and repression to continue. It should rather prompt urgent discussion of how best to demilitarize the republic, and what kind of judicial processes will have sufficient popular legitimacy to pre-empt bloodshed. The extreme social fragmentation Chechnya has undergone since 1994, and the obstacles to economic revival in a context of deindustrialization, pose further vital problems that are not to be scanted. However, all of these matters depend on the establishment of a representative, democratically elected government. This is not possible while Chechnya is under military occupation, and while its population faces torture or death for speaking in favour of independence.

None of the counter-arguments listed above answers the basic question of principle: is Chechnya entitled to independence? The burden of this book is to demonstrate that the Chechens have as much right to a state as any other people, and that their moral case for sovereignty is an increasingly strong one. It is only as a sovereign state that Chechnya will be able to fulfil the wishes of its citizens, and it is as a sovereign state that it must negotiate relations with Russia and resolve its considerable internal problems. As an occupied nation, on the other hand, it will continue to suffer the brutality and impoverishment wrought by great-power domination – and to respond with the sole possession of a proud but dominated people: resistance.

*   *   *

[7] Robert Bruce Ware, Interview, *United Press International*, 29 November 2005.

A word on spellings and transliteration. Much of what is known about Chechnya in the West derives from Russian and Soviet sources, for reasons that will become clear on reading the historical sections of this book. There is also no fully reliable system for transcribing Chechen. Names of Chechen places and people have therefore passed into English usage in one or other variant of their Russian approximations – including the country itself, which many Chechens prefer to call Chechenia, since the stressed Russian ending of 'Chechnya' arguably bears a pejorative connotation. Without wishing to endorse the colonialist perspective through which Chechnya is viewed, I have nonetheless stuck, overall, to commonly accepted spellings and labels, for simplicity and ease of reference. I have adopted a modified version of the Library of Congress system for transcribing Russian, making adjustments for proper nouns that are widely known in a different spelling (hence Gorky, rather than Gor'kii).

This book originated as an article for *New Left Review*, and I am very grateful to colleagues there for their comments and suggestions: thanks to Perry Anderson, Susan Watkins, Jacob Stevens, Emilie Bickerton and Kheya Bag. Family and friends have given me much support and encouragement, which was hugely appreciated: thank you Michael Wood, Elena Uribe, Gaby Wood, Patrick Wood, Chris Turner, Holly Chatham, Andrew Greenall, James Tindal and Bigna Pfenninger; and apologies to those I have omitted. Paul Tumelty, Satanay Dorken and Francis Boyle provided valuable assistance on several points; my conversations and correspondence with Imran Hussein, Sean Guillory and Tom Marston were both enjoyable and instructive. A special word of thanks must go to Georgi Derluguian, who was unfailingly helpful and generous with his time despite disagreeing with the book's central premise; to my editor Tom Penn and everyone at Verso; to Richard Reeve, for his all-round expertise; and to Susan Jones, for her sympathy and sanity. Others whom I would like to thank must remain nameless for their own safety.

25 November 2006

1.

The Chechen Experience

Nokhchi khila khala du.
It is hard to be a Chechen.
Chechen proverb

History is not destiny. Events of the last three hundred years did not render inevitable the two wars waged in Chechnya since 1994, any more than immutable Chechen or Russian ethnic identities laid down battle lines in advance. But in order to understand the nature and origins of the present conflict, we need to grasp the changing character of Chechen resistance to Russian and Soviet rule. Bitter experience has not only conditioned Chechens' expectations, it has served as a catalyst for the emergence of the concept of Chechen nationhood itself, central to the push for independence and the durability of the ongoing war. As we will see, for the Chechens, national consciousness was above all the result of real social, political and military pressure from outside. In that sense, though they have long existed as a distinct people, as a nation the Chechens have been forged under the hammer-blows of history.

The Chechens are one of an intricate patchwork of peoples inhabiting the northern slopes of the Caucasus, a chain of vertiginous, snow-capped mountains stretching for over 600 miles between the Caspian and Black Seas. The region has been known since ancient times as one of unparalleled human diversity: Herodotus, Pliny the Elder and Strabo spoke of the bewildering number of interpreters required to do business in its markets, and the Arab geographers labelled it simply 'the mountain of tongues'. The name 'Chechen' is in fact a Russian designation, after a village where a battle between Cossack settlers and the local people took place in 1732. The Chechens refer to themselves as 'Nokhchii', and claim to be mythically descended, 'like sparks from steel', from the hero Turpalo-Nokhchuo. They are closely related to the neighbouring Ingush and the Kists and Bats in present-day Georgia, the four groups being jointly known as the Vainakh, meaning simply 'our people'. Their languages are mutually intelligible, but form a separate branch of the North Caucasian family, utterly distinct from Indo-European, Turkic or other categories.

The Chechens have been present in the North Caucasus for several thousand years, their livelihood predominantly provided by livestock, subsistence farming and the surrounding forests. There are few written traces of them before medieval times, though some scholars have suggested links to the Hurrian and Urartian civilizations of eastern Anatolia and Mesopotamia. An oblique light is shed on them by Georgian, Arab and Kievan chronicles, which register the sweep of successive invaders towards the mountains from the steppe to the north – Sarmatians, Pechenegs, Khazars, Mongols – or lands to the south: Sassanids, Arabs, Seljuks.[1] Like the mountain peoples around them, the Chechens developed a martial ethos, reflected as much in traditions of horsemanship and weapon-handling as in the defensive towers guarding their compact villages. As elsewhere in the Caucasus, honour and hospitality have a crucial function in Chechen culture, with elaborate networks of norms and obligations – known collectively as *nokhchalla* – reinforced by familial and clan ties. Misdeeds were, and often still are, dealt with through an uncodified system of customary law, known as *adat*. Memory too has a prominent role, not only in the perpetuation of oral traditions – including the epic songs, *illesh*, or mythic Nart sagas – but in the customary duty to remember seven generations of ancestors. In the absence, until relatively recently, of a written culture,

[1] For the pre- and early history of the Chechens, see Amjad Jaimoukha, *The Chechens: A Handbook*, London 2005, ch. 2. The book contains much material that is rarely found in English-language works, and its chapters on Chechen culture are particularly valuable.

folk memory has been the basis of Chechen historical consciousness.[2]

We should resist, however, any vision of the Chechens as an unvarying, primordial people. Contacts with the rising and falling dominions to the north and south engendered shifting alliances and brought social, cultural and linguistic change – as did climatic developments, such as the global cooling of the sixteenth century that forced many Chechens down onto the plains, or the gunpowder revolution of the seventeenth which, in making rifles widely affordable to the mountains' peasants, drastically altered the balance of forces between them and the region's extractive bands of horsemen.[3] The Chechens seem to have repeatedly rejected rule by outsiders, and opted against hierarchies of their own. Though there were short-lived early medieval Vainakh kingdoms, as well as brief periods of overlordship by the Georgians in the tenth to twelfth centuries and by the princes of neighbouring Kabarda in the sixteenth, by the seventeenth century Chechen society had settled into a distinctive social pattern founded on groupings of clans or *taips* living in formal equality – 'free and equal like wolves', as the Chechen saying has it.[4]

The concept of freedom has pride of place in Chechen culture, as the language itself testifies: the most common greeting translates as 'enter in freedom'. Indeed, the word for freedom, *marsho*, also encompasses much broader notions of peace and well-being. Individual liberty is

[2] On Chechen culture's orientation to the past, and the nature of its epics, see the essay by Obkhad Dzhambekov in Kh. V. Turkaev, ed., *Kul'tura Chechni: Istoriia i sovremennye problemy*, Moscow 2002, p. 71; see also the essays in the same volume by Z. I. Khasbulatova on etiquette and traditions of mutual assistance, and on traditional architecture by V. I. Markovin. On myths and legends, see Jaimoukha, *Chechens*, ch. 14 (by JonArno Lawson); and *Skazki i legendy ingushei i chechentsev*, compiled by A. O. Malsagov, Moscow 1983; English version printed in 1996 by the Folklore Society.

[3] Georgi Derluguian, *A World History of Noxchi*, work in progress; my thanks to the author for allowing me to read the unpublished manuscript.

[4] The clan is one link in a chain of social collectivities to which all Chechens traditionally belong, stretching from the extended family (*doezal* or *tsa'*) through sub-clans (*gar* or *neq'i*) and *taips* up to the tribal confederation, *tuqum*. However, Jaimoukha's suggestion that *taip* derives from Arabic *t'a'ifa* (community, group) implies this particular structure may be relatively recent in date: see *Chechens*, p. 83; and Moshe Gammer, *The Lone Wolf and the Bear: Three Centuries of Chechen Defiance of Russian Rule*, London 2006, p. 4. The latter volume is a succinct, scholarly survey of Chechen history, with particularly strong sections on the late Imperial period and 1917–21, though it deals somewhat cursorily with events since 1991.

bound up with ideas of communal equality. Traditionally, Chechen society was divided into only two categories: the *uzden* or free man, and the *lai*, slave. While the latter – often prisoners of war or other outsiders – had no rights, the former lived in an acephalous, semi-democratic structure in which weighty matters were put to the vote at clan councils. In this the Chechens were not dissimilar to highland peoples elsewhere in the world – in Scotland, Albania or the Basque Country, for instance.[5] This anarchic mode of social organization was to have far-reaching implications. Firstly, unlike many other Caucasian peoples, the Chechens lacked feudal structures; there was thus no native elite to be co-opted by external powers, as there was in princely domains such as Kabarda or Avaria. Secondly, although the dispersal of authority could result in fractiousness and feuding, in times of war the clan group-ings – *tuqums* – proved a remarkably solid base for military success. In a sense, the Chechens were already ideally organized for guerrilla warfare long before they engaged the Tsar's armies.

The myriad ethnic groups of the North Caucasus share many customs, myths and practices, and have since the nineteenth century been joined by a common religious tradition: all but one eventually converted to Islam, though the intensity of religious affiliation tends to decrease from east to west. But over the centuries, these peoples have been divided not only by particularities of language and geography, but by divergent historical experiences of foreign dominion. The constant geopolitical tussle over the region between successive empires to north and south created a varying pattern of rebellions against outside rule and accom-modations with it, a fragmentation that echoes the turbulent contours of the landscape. To understand why Chechnya is different from its neighbours, we need first to have a picture of these specificities – a socio-historical map of the North Caucasus as a whole.[6] This will necessarily involve some schematic simplification; I will describe only

---

[5] The analogy is made by Georgi Derluguian, who proposes the formula: mountains + weapons = clan democracy. Derluguian, 'Chechentsy: Proiasnitel'naia zapiska', *Prognozis*, No. 1, Autumn 2004, p. 149.

[6] A model version is provided by the opening pages of John Baddeley's *The Russian Conquest of the Caucasus* [1908], London 1999. This is the classic account of its subject, and Baddeley's occasional lapses into standard imperial prejudice detract only slightly from his brisk, engaging narrative.

the region's larger ethnicities, leaving aside the dozens more that are required to complete the entire jigsaw.

At the western end of the Caucasus range are the Circassians who, along with the Chechens, were historically the most numerous of the peoples in the area. As the *ethnie* closest to the Black Sea, the Circassians had the most frequent contact with the mercantile empires that plied its waters – and were frequently captured by Greek, Genoese or Venetian traders to be sold as slaves in the markets of Constantinople or Venice; others left voluntarily to serve as mercenaries, becoming part of the Mamluk warrior caste that came to rule Egypt in the thirteenth century.[7] In Europe, Circassians – who refer to themselves as Adyghe – came to be synonymous with Caucasians as a whole. They became especially well known in the nineteenth century, when their struggle against Tsarist expansionism earned them the sympathies of Russia's imperial rivals, notably in London, where Lord Palmerston dispatched agents to run guns to the resistance. The rebellion was crushed by 1864, however, and the Circassians punished by mass deportations from which they have never recovered demographically. At present, they number 50,000, constituting a mere 11 per cent of the population of Karachaevo-Cherkessia, the autonomous republic within Russia's borders they now share with the Karachays, who compose 39 per cent.[8]

The Karachays are one of several small Turkic peoples scattered across the Caucasus. These are generally held to be the remnants of former steppe overlords who were pushed into the mountains as their historical fortunes waned. They include the Nogais and Kumyks, who mostly inhabit Dagestan and parts of Chechnya, and the Balkars, whose territory lies further inland from that of the Circassians. Like the Circassians, the Balkars put up strong resistance to Russian rule – contrasting sharply with the Kabardins, to whom they are today jurisdictionally bound in the Russian autonomous republic of Kabardino-Balkaria. With a present population of half a million to the Balkars' 100,000, the Kabardins hugely outnumber their Turkic co-citizens, and have historically played a vastly different role. This is in large measure due to their hierarchical social formation: originally a

---

[7] Neal Ascherson, *Black Sea: The Birthplace of Civilisation and Barbarism*, London 1996, pp. 95–6; and Paul Henze, 'Circassian Resistance to Russia', in Marie Bennigsen Broxup, ed., *The North Caucasus Barrier*, New York 1992, p. 69.

[8] Data on all North Caucasus peoples from 2002 Russian census.

subgroup of the Circassians, the Kabardins have been described as 'neither state nor tribe but a flexible and highly segmented network of aristocratic warriors', who practised a form of feudal extraction on the agriculturalist and egalitarian clan-based peoples around them.[9] The knights of Kabarda aligned with Moscow very early on: in 1557 they professed fealty to Ivan the Terrible, who married a Kabardin princess to seal the alliance. The compact made an important contribution to the growth of the Tsar's empire, and has broadly held ever since.

However, the passes across the high central section of the Caucasus were secured primarily through the loyalty of the Ossetians. Predominantly Christian by tradition, and Indo-Iranian by ethno-linguistic provenance, the Ossetians are widely thought to be descendants of the Alans, a warrior nation whose origins are traced in turn to the Sarmatian horsemen who dominated the steppe from pre-Christian times until the fourth century. Since the establishment of the Russian fort of Vladikavkaz – 'Ruler of the Caucasus' – in the late eighteenth century, the Ossetians have been staunchly loyal to Tsarist, Soviet and post-Communist authorities, and their autonomous republic continues to serve as the Russian army's regional garrison. In the nineteenth century, the Ossetians' dependability played a vital role in aiding the empire's further expansion, and in thwarting attempts to unify the resistance to it: lines of communication between rebellious tribes to the west and east were broken by the Ossetian wedge. Their territory is at present divided between Russia and Georgia, forming an autonomous region in each known respectively as North and South Ossetia; the combined ethnic Ossetian population of both is over 500,000, making them among the most numerous of the Caucasian peoples.

The greatest concentration of ethno-linguistic variety in the Caucasus is found at its eastern extreme, in Dagestan, where wooded mountains give way to more barren, forbidding terrain. Stretching along the western shore of the Caspian, Dagestan is home to dozens of different ethnic groups – over thirty languages are spoken across its territory. Its political fortunes have long depended on the compacts forged by its princelings with powers to the north and south, as Arab, Persian, Ottoman and Russian empires struggled for control of the Caspian littoral. Russia has held sway since

[9] Georgi Derluguian, *World History of Noxchi*, ch. 1.

the nineteenth century, though only after a protracted colonial war against an Islamic resistance that united Dagestan's constellation of *ethnies* with the Chechens to the west. As the place where Islam entered the region in the eighth century AD, Dagestan was the epicentre from which Islamic learning – and missionaries – radiated westwards across the North Caucasus; it was also where pietistic reform movements first became joined with rebellion against the Russian Empire, a nineteenth-century precedent which many of the region's Islamist groups seek to emulate in the present.

A fragile balance between Dagestan's various ethnicities is today under-written by the central authorities in Moscow, on whose subsidies this poor, mountainous republic overwhelmingly depends. The two largest groups, the Avars and Dargins – who today compose 29 and 16 per cent respectively of a total population of two and a half million – have tended to dominate official and clerical posts, creating a certain amount of resentment among Kumyks, Lezgins, Laks and others.[10] These inter-ethnic tensions, and the small size of the various peoples concerned, have made broader unity elusive – as has Dagestan's social structure, founded on civil communities, known as *jamaat*, in which one or several villages hold collective rights to land.[11] These 'small republics', which were shaken free of the feudal order of Avar nobles and Kumyk *shamkhals* by the wars and social upheavals of the nineteenth century, add another layer of complexity to an already kaleidoscopic picture.

Between the fragmentation of Dagestan and the Ossetian centre of the Caucasus range lies the historical territory of the Vainakhs. The Chechens have always been the dominant branch of the *ethnos*, and with a population estimated at 850,000, the Chechens are today the most numerous of the peoples of the North Caucasus.[12] Though often

---

[10] Liz Fuller, 'Daghestan: Anatomy of a Permanent Crisis', *Radio Free Europe/Radio Liberty*, 13 July 2005.

[11] Georgi Derluguian, 'Che Guevaras in Turbans', *New Left Review*, I/237, p. 13 fn. 18. *Jamaat* in this usage should be distinguished from its more recent application to Islamist groups in the region as meaning 'brotherhood'.

[12] Population figures for Chechnya are the subject of much contention. The Russian 2002 census gives a figure of 1,031,647, but this is widely thought to be inflated. Allowing for war casualties, refugees and official manipulation, more cautious estimates range around the 850,000 mark. Aleksandr Cherkasov, 'Book of Numbers: Book of the Lost', in Tanya Lokshina, ed., *The Imposition of a Fake Political Settlement in the Northern Caucasus: The 2003 Chechen Presidential Election*, Stuttgart 2005, pp. 190–97.

interlinked with other Vainakhs by marriage – to the extent that ethnic or even clan boundaries between them are frequently blurred – the Chechens are different from the Ingush and the Kists and Bats in several respects. The Kists and Bats, who presently number no more than a few thousand, have had more prolonged contacts with Georgian people and culture, and are divided from the Chechens and Ingush by the forbidding wall of mountain that forms Chechnya's border with Georgia. The most basic distinction between Chechens and Ingush, meanwhile, is one of scale: the former have historically outnumbered the latter by as much as four to one, though the gap has decreased in recent decades; the total Ingush population was 413,000 in 2002. More crucial, however, have been the two peoples' divergent responses to Russian rule. The attitude of the Ingush has varied between sullen submission and outright rebellion, depending on the mood amongst their neighbours and fellow-Vainakhs – a calculation no doubt motivated in part by their small size and correspondingly smaller chances of success.

The Chechens, by contrast, have an almost unbroken record of struggle against foreign rule. Indeed, it is principally the striking depth and consistency of Chechen resistance that sets them apart from the peoples around them – among whom both admiration and resentment of Chechens are common. It can be ascribed to a number of factors, besides the paradoxical resilience of the Chechens' anarchic social structures. Religion has been an important mobilizing force. Islam melded with local animist traditions from the sixteenth century onwards; in the nineteenth century it was Naqshbandi Sufi brotherhoods, with their aversion to hierarchy and creed of resistance, that proved best able to unite disparate Caucasian peoples under the banner of Islamic solidarity. Topography and demography have also been significant. The plains that comprise the northern third of present-day Chechnya were largely a Soviet-era addition; historical Chechnya consists of the low mountain ridges between the Terek and Sunzha rivers that laterally bisect the country, the fertile rolling plains and hills beyond, and the thickly forested mountains and impassable defiles of the southernmost portion. The dense, lush undergrowth of the highlands provided better cover for fighters than was available in Ingushetia or Dagestan, making Chechnya a natural theatre for guerrilla warfare. Moreover, the Chechens' numerical weight meant that they tended to provide the majority of footsoldiers for rebellions against Russian rule.

These geographical and sociological contingencies were reinforced by the legacy of resistance itself, which has become a key component of Chechen national identity. Starting in the late eighteenth century, the experiences of conquest, colonization and rebellion were added to the features of Chechen society and culture enumerated above, forming a shared tradition that only increased in power and resonance with each subsequent round of revolt and repression.

Russia's southward expansion began in 1552 with Ivan the Terrible's conquest of the khanate of Astrakhan, one of the last remnants of Chingiz Khan's empire. It was around this time that Cossack settlers began to arrive in the region – bands of freed serfs, criminals and runaways who fled to Russia's southern periphery to escape central authority. The word Cossack itself comes from the Turkic word for 'free man', which not only conveys a sense of their collective libertarian ethos, but indicates the inter-mingling of their Russian origins with steppe peoples and practices. Cossacks would indeed occasionally intermarry or become absorbed into local tribes, but just as often the result was an enmity reinforced by cultural distance and frequent raids by both sides. Different as they were from the Russia they had long ago left behind, the Cossacks were gradually transformed from Muscovy's exiles into the Empire's advance guard, colonizing and then policing the frontiers of Siberia and the North Caucasus decades before imperial infrastructure could catch up.

Muscovite interest in the Caucasus subsided after Ivan the Terrible, owing to shifts in geopolitical fortunes and priorities. By the eighteenth century, however, the Tsarist polity had consolidated its position enough to revive its expansionist ambitions, and the Caucasus became the focal point of rivalry between the Ottoman, Persian and Russian empires. Cossack settlements – *stanitsy* – were now joined by military installations, both subject to raids from the 'mountaineers'. Catherine the Great's intensification of attempts to subdue the region provoked an uprising in 1784–91 led by the Chechen Sheikh Mansur. Though he inflicted a stunning defeat on the Russians on the Sunzha in 1785 – becoming a folk hero in the process – Mansur was unable to repeat his success, and died in Russian captivity in 1794.

With the annexation of Georgia in 1801, Russia obtained a foothold on territory to the south of the Caucasus ridge. Far from seeing the Caucasus as an optimal boundary – as forbidding a natural obstacle as one could wish for – Russian imperial strategists had from the time of Peter the Great looked further, to the riches of Persia and India. The conquest of the Caucasus was in that sense merely a way-station on the path to dominance of the zone beyond, where Russia would confront more serious imperial competitors. Advancing across the mountains was a clear bid to shift the balance: a forward base in Georgia would give Russia 'interior lines in Transcaucasia sufficiently short to fight both Ottomans and Persians, either separately or even at the same time.'[13] Even when both these adversaries had been beaten, a Russian grip on lands beyond the Caucasus was deemed essential: as General Rostislav Fadeev was to write in 1860, 'If Russia's horizons ended on the snowy summits of the Caucasus range, then the whole western half of the Asian continent would be outside our sphere of influence and, given the present impotence of Turkey and Persia, would not long wait for another master.'[14]

Georgia's princely court adapted readily enough to life under the Tsars, glad of Russian protection against unstable Islamic principalities to the south; Armenia too largely welcomed the stability promised by Moscow's increasing geopolitical weight, while the absorption of Azerbaijan, long used to foreign overlordship, also proved relatively straightforward. But the mountains over which imperial grand strategy had so easily vaulted still had to be secured – a far more difficult undertaking. The method devised for pacifying the Caucasus was to construct a line of forts along the Terek and Sunzha rivers – including Grozny, meaning 'Terrible', founded in 1818. Russian policy was personified by General Aleksei Yermolov, who from 1816 attempted to subdue Chechnya, where resistance was stiffest, by means of punitive raids on mountain villages, collective punishment, razing of houses and crops, deforestation, forced

[13] John LeDonne, *The Grand Strategy of the Russian Empire, 1650–1831*, Oxford 2004, pp. 24, 99. Geoffrey Hosking has also suggested that the rhythm of Russian imperial expansion was 'shaped by the constellation of power on its frontiers at any given moment. Expansion comes to an end only when Russia fetches up against another power capable of offering effective resistance and of affording a stable and predictable frontier'. See Hosking, *Russia: People and Empire, 1552–1917*, London 1997, pp. 13–14.

[14] Fadeev, *Shestdesiat' let kazkavskoi voiny*, Tiflis 1860, pp. 8–9; quoted in Hosking, *Russia: People and Empire*, p. 18.

mass deportation, and settlement of Cossacks on lands vacated by Chechens. 'Condescension in the eyes of the Asiatics is a sign of weakness, and out of pure humanity I am inexorably severe', declared Yermolov.[15] His actions were hailed as 'the drumbeat Enlightenment' by the playwright Aleksandr Griboedov, one of many Russian writers of the Golden Age to serve in the Caucasus – an imperial proving ground for the *jeunesse dorée* in much the same way as India was for the British; though the Caucasus was also a place of exile for gilded troublemakers. Pushkin, Lermontov and Tolstoy were among those who served in the region or travelled through it, and they are largely responsible for the Romantic lens through which Russians view the region: a domain of sweeping vistas, sheer cliffs, cut-throat but noble natives, and unending ennui.[16]

If Russian colonialism produced a more brilliant literary legacy than its counterparts elsewhere, its tactics in the Caucasus were not dissimilar to those deployed across the globe by Europe's imperial powers. A memorandum circulated to European governments in 1864 by the Russian foreign minister, Aleksandr Gorchakov, appealed to a shared sense of racial superiority to justify Russia's expansion into Central Asia, where Russia confronted 'half-savage, nomad populations having no fixed social organization'. Gorchakov's words could equally have applied to the Empire's dealings with the Caucasus:

---

[15] Quoted by Gammer, *Lone Wolf and Bear*, p. 37. Yermolov's portrait currently hangs in the Russian Army's North Caucasus headquarters in Rostov-on-Don: see Dmitri Trenin and Aleksei Malashenko, *Russia's Restless Frontier: The Chechnya Factor in Post-Soviet Russia*, Washington, D.C. 2004, p. 139. Trenin is a former Russian army officer, and Malashenko one of the country's leading experts on Islam; their book contains thoughtful discussions of the present war's strategic implications and its impact on Russia's armed forces, as well as a sober assessment of the role of religion in the insurgency.

[16] Like Griboedov, Lermontov and Pushkin had few qualms about the subjugation of the mountain peoples. Lermontov's 'Cossack Lullaby' – portraying a 'wicked Chechen' crawling towards the cradle, sharpened dagger in hand – established an imperial trope that has lasted to this day. However, Tolstoy, who served in Chechnya from 1851–4, at the height of the Caucasian War, was far more critical. On 6 January 1853 he wrote in his diary that the war was 'such an unjust and evil thing that those who wage it try to stifle the voice of conscience within them' (*Tolstoy's Diaries: Volume I. 1847–1894*, ed. R. F. Christian, London 1985, p. 65). Similar sentiments appear in 'The Cossacks', written 1852–62, and most powerfully in his last work, *Hadji Murat*, published only in 1912, which provides a striking vision of both the rebels and their Tsarist adversaries.

In such cases, it always happens that the more civilized State is forced, in the interests of the security of its frontier and its commercial relations, to exercise a certain ascendancy over those whom their turbulent and unsettled character make most undesirable neighbours . . . Such has been the fate of every country which has found itself in a similar position. The United States in America, France in Algeria, Holland in her colonies, England in India – all have been irresistibly forced, less by ambition than by imperious necessity, into this onward movement where the greatest difficulty is to know where to stop.[17]

In 1829, Nicholas I entrusted to Field Marshal Paskievich the task of the 'suppression once and for all of the mountaineers or the extermination of the recalcitrant'.[18] Yermolov had been replaced in 1827, but his methods remained in force. Their immediate effect was to dispossess and enrage an entire population; but they also had longer-term sociological consequences that only increased the likelihood of resistance. In their eagerness to drive the Chechens out of the agricultural lowlands and into the mountains where they would eventually starve, Russia's military strategists also blocked the differentiation of Chechen society by landownership, thus cementing the very clan-based order that had made resistance so effective.[19] A series of rapacious tax increases and interference in local affairs sparked further discontent across the region. The Chechens and their neighbours initially responded with armed raids on Russian positions, but in the 1820s this began to take a more organized form, as attempts were initiated to unify all mountain peoples against the Russian advance. By the end of the decade resistance had begun to coalesce around Naqshbandi preachers who rapidly moved

[17] Quoted in Anatol Lieven, *Chechnya: Tombstone of Russian Power*, London 1998, p. 313. Lieven's remains by far the best single book on the subject, full of fascinating information, acute insights and striking historical parallels; it makes a powerful moral and intellectual case against the strategic thinking that informed Yeltsin's decision to invade in 1994.

[18] Cited in John Dunlop, *Russia Confronts Chechnya: Roots of a Separatist Conflict*, Cambridge 1998, p. 18. Dunlop, based at the Hoover Institution and formerly editor of the Jamestown Foundation's *Chechnya Weekly* newsletter, provides a solid historical narrative, and his examination of the events of the early 1990s is judicious and well sourced.

[19] M. M. Bliev and V. V. Degoev, *Kavkazskaia voina*, Moscow 1994, cited in Dunlop, *Russia Confronts Chechnya*, p. 16.

from urging Islamic piety and internal reform to advocating liberation from the foreign yoke. The leaders of the rebellion came from Dagestan, where Qur'anic learning, and hence the theological weaponry available, was far more advanced. After gaining the support of influential clerics, the Avar Ghazi Muhammad was proclaimed Imam in 1829, and declared holy war – *ghazavat* – on Russia the following year.

Ghazi Muhammad was defeated by the Russians in 1832, but in his brief spell in command he introduced a number of innovations in military tactics and organization that were described by Russian observers at the time as a 'well-conceived system of popular war.'[20] His successor, Hamzat Bek, proved more adept at alienating his supporters than organizing rebellion, and in Chechnya the leadership briefly passed to Tasho Hadji, a Naqshbandi adept who further refined Ghazi Muhammad's system, but who was forced onto the defensive by Russian attacks in the mid 1830s. In the meantime, a more formidable figure had succeeded Hamzat Bek, after the latter's assassination in 1834. Shamil, born in 1797 in the Avar village of Gimri, was approved as Imam on Hamzat Bek's death and by 1836 had consolidated his position against his rivals.

Shamil proved a skilful military commander as well as a charismatic preacher and politician, and inflicted huge losses on the far superior forces ranged against him. Though the Russians seemed to have utterly defeated him at the siege of Akhulgo in 1839, Shamil escaped and within a year had recouped enough authority not only to lead the rebellion once more, but also to establish effective authority over large swathes of Chechnya and Dagestan. His ability to operate across ethnic boundaries can be explained in part by the currency of Avar as a military *lingua franca* in the region – Kumyk being used for other purposes – and in part by the expanding influence of the Naqshbandiyya, whose networks bound teacher and disciples in a common language of faith and resistance.[21] There was, moreover, a crucial social component to Shamil's success, as peasants in Dagestan and Chechnya took the opportunity to rebel not only against Russia but also against their own established structures of dominance, from which Shamil's theocratic discipline promised – with Qur'anic qualifications – to liberate them.

---

[20] Gammer, see *Lone Wolf and Bear*, pp. 48–9.
[21] Thanks to Georgi Derluguian for these points.

From 1840–59 the Tsars committed themselves to a full-scale war against Shamil's proto-state, involving tens of thousands of troops in gruelling onslaughts upon an elusive enemy. General Tornau wrote that 'one day is like another; that which happened yesterday will be repeated tomorrow – everywhere are mountains, everywhere forests, and the Chechens are fierce and tireless fighters.'[22] When the Russian victory eventually came in 1859, it was due as much to the strategic clearing of Chechnya's forest cover as to imperial manpower.

But there were factors at work internal to Shamil's domains. The Imamate was founded on the extension of Shamil's version of *shari'a* law at the expense of local customary tradition. Islamic discipline was seen as the best way of securing unity against the Russians, but it required long-standing particularities to be set aside. The conventional narrative has Shamil undone by his own severity, coupled with sheer Russian military might. This is to a large degree correct, but overlooks the social and political character of Shamil's rule, which swept away the feudal order in Dagestan and replaced traditional elites and councils with an entirely novel command structure. This included administrative and military deputies – *naibs* – as well as judges, an inspectorate and secret police, and a professional military corps, known as *murtaziqa*. During the 1840s Shamil also set in place a differentiated tax system, pensions for widows and invalids, and military hospitals. Formal authority was vested in successive councils of religious leaders and *naibs*, who had to ratify all of the Imam's decisions.

In practice, Shamil was constrained by the interests of his *naibs* who, due to land grants in reward for loyalty or success in battle, began to take on the character of a new elite. As Shamil's military fortunes declined during the 1850s – notably with the loss of the grain-fields of lower Chechnya – the exactions of this layer, and the levies required to feed the *murtaziqa*, weighed increasingly heavily on Chechnya's peasantry. By the time of his final defeat in 1859, Shamil's support had dwindled to bare

---

[22] Cited in Baddeley, *Russian Conquest of the Caucasus*, p. 268. More recent scholarly accounts of the war include Moshe Gammer's lucid *Muslim Resistance to the Tsar: Shamil and the Conquest of Chechnya and Daghestan*, London 1994, deservedly the standard reference in the field, and Anna Zelkina, *In Quest for God and Freedom: Sufi Responses to the Russian Advance in the North Caucasus*, London 2000. A less rigorous but more colourful version is that of Lesley Blanch, *The Sabres of Paradise* [1960], London 2004.

hundreds. The Imamate had been undermined from within by fractiousness and exploitation, and battered from without by axe and artillery.[23]

Perhaps the most telling sign of Shamil's weakness, however, was his failure to benefit from the Crimean War. He was unable to secure outside support, and his letters to the Ottoman Sultan and Queen Victoria went unheeded – though committees were formed in support of the mountaineers in England's industrial heartland, where any Russian advance in the direction of India was viewed as a threat to Britain's textile factories.[24] Willing enough to promise arms and assistance when conducting diplomatic intrigues against St Petersburg, the great powers were quick to leave Shamil out of their calculations when battle was joined. Shamil was also, crucially, unable to unite his struggle with that of the Circassians to the west, where fighting continued until 1864; separated by territory loyal to Russia, the two theatres of the Caucasian War remained essentially unconnected.

The longer-term historical significance of Shamil's reign was that it marked the first indigenous attempt at state-formation – made not in the name of nations, but of faith and a common highland identity. Russians and Caucasians alike drew other lessons from Shamil's defeat – many of them applied erroneously today. The latter saw that prolonged resistance was possible, but difficult to sustain without discipline, unified authority and external backing. Shamil Basaev's attempts to forge a pan-Caucasian Islamic front against Russia at the close of the twentieth century should be seen at least in part as an attempt to replicate the strategy of his nineteenth-century namesake. The Russians, meanwhile, saw that persistence, numbers and overwhelming force eventually paid off.

The recurrent unrest on his empire's southern flank, whose weakness was exposed by the Crimean defeat, evidently convinced the new Tsar Aleksandr II to adopt a still more stringent policy. Forced deportations

---

[23] Zelkina, *In Quest for God and Freedom*, has the clearest picture of Shamil's administration. For a Marxist account stressing its social dimensions see N. I. Pokrovskii, *Kavkazskie voiny i imamat Shamil'ia* [1940], Moscow 2000. Shamil lived on in Russian captivity, exiled to the provincial town of Kaluga, until 1870, when he was permitted to go to Mecca; he died in Medina the following year. On Shamil's later years, see Blanch, *Sabres of Paradise*, pp. 424–58.

[24] Blanch, *Sabres of Paradise*, p. 256, mentions concerned meetings in the Midlands and Yorkshire.

of the empire's Muslim peoples, including the Crimean Tatars, began in 1856 and continued until 1865. A total of perhaps 600,000, including 100,000 Chechens, left by land and sea, packed into boats bound for Ottoman ports such as Varna or Trabzon, or else crossing the border on foot. Tens of thousands perished from starvation and disease – 'genocide by forced exodus', in the words of one scholar.[25] The vast bulk of deportees were Circassians, many of whom settled initially in the Balkans, though they were later resettled in Anatolia. Most of the Chechens who survived returned after the 1877–8 Russo-Turkish war; but many remained in Asia Minor and the Middle East, and were later joined by other refugees who formed the basis for significant diaspora communities in present-day Turkey and Jordan, as well as Syria and Iraq.[26]

Rebellion rumbled on even in the months after Shamil's surrender, and broke out more violently in both Chechnya and Dagestan in 1862–3 and 1877–8. This time it was mobilized primarily by Qadiri Sufi brotherhoods. Less austere than the Naqshbandis, the Qadiris practised a more expressive form of the *zikr*, the circular dance and incantatory ritual; moreover, in a form of quietism that the Russian authorities had initially hoped meant reconciliation to their rule, the Qadiris 'emphasized individual rather than communal salvation'.[27] But repression turned the Qadiriyya into an oppositional movement, and the 1877 revolt could only be suppressed with the aid of 24,000 troops. Their commander, Adjutant-General Svistunov, called for the insurgents to be 'exterminated like cockroaches and starved to death'.[28]

---

[25] Marie Bennigsen Broxup, Introduction to Broxup, ed., *North Caucasus Barrier*, p. 9. For a detailed account of the deportations, see Alan Fisher, 'Emigration of Muslims from the Russian Empire in the Years After the Crimean War', *Jahrbücher für Geschichte Osteuropas*, 35 (1987), pp. 356–71.

[26] Dunlop, *Russia Confronts Chechnya*, pp. 29–30; Gammer, *Lone Wolf and Bear*, p. 80. On the diaspora, see Jaimoukha, *Chechens*, ch. 16. Alan Fisher observes that the settlement of Circassians and Chechens in Anatolia created massive upheaval among the peoples already living there, notably the Armenians, and suggests that the exodus of the 1850s and 1860s was 'the first act in a drama that would produce large exchanges of population in the Balkans and Middle East' in the early twentieth century – including the Armenian genocide. See Fisher, 'Emigration of Muslims', p. 371.

[27] Gammer, *Lone Wolf and Bear*, p. 75.

[28] Cited in Gammer, *Lone Wolf and Bear*, p. 93.

A relatively quiescent period followed, in which the Chechens remained on the socio-economic margins, and subject to still more severe land hunger than Russian peasants – by 1912, Chechens and Ingush owned less than half as much land per person as Terek Cossacks.[29] The tradition of raids on Cossack outposts continued after conquest, however, becoming a persistent form of brigandage whose perpetrators – known as *abreks* – were depicted by Russia as simple bandits, but whom Chechens viewed as folk heroes on the model of Robin Hood. The most famous of these, Zelimkhan, was even viewed favourably by Soviet historiography, and a statue of him still stands outside the village of Serzhen-Yurt.[30] But despite their overall marginalization, a tiny minority of Chechens did receive a Russian education, as the empire sought dependable local cadres and soldiers. It was from among these men that the beginnings of a local intelligentsia began to emerge, influenced by the ideas of the Russian Populists and later the Social-Democrats.

Benedict Anderson has noted that 'the key early spokesmen for colonial nationalism were lonely, bilingual intelligentsias unattached to sturdy local bourgeoisies'.[31] The pattern in Chechnya was in certain respects similar to that in nineteenth-century Europe, where national movements initially took root in the recording of folklore and traditions. Umalat Laudaev (1818–83) was the first to pen a monograph on the customs of his people, in 1872; Chakh Akhiev (1850–1914) did the same for Ingush in 1872–3. But here, the numbers of scholars involved were so small and the literate public so reduced that the nationalist momentum required to move from first stirrings of national consciousness to a broad sense of national identification was never generated. The Chechens differed in this regard from other peoples on the fringes of great empires, in Central Europe or, say, Finland.[32] The comparatively small size and agrarian nature of Caucasian societies meant that, while

---

[29] 5.8 and 3 desiatinas respectively, to the Cossacks' 13.6 (1 desiatina = 1.09 hectares). See Richard Pipes, *The Formation of the Soviet Union*, Cambridge, MA 1997 (rev. edn.), pp. 94–6.

[30] Gammer, *Lone Wolf and Bear*, p. 117.

[31] Benedict Anderson, *Imagined Communities*, London and New York 1991 (rev. edn.), p. 140.

[32] See Anderson, *Imagined Communities*, p. 74, and Miroslav Hroch, 'From National Movement to the Fully Formed Nation: The Nation-building Process in Europe', in Gopal Balakrishnan, ed., *Mapping the Nation*, London and New York 1996, pp. 78–97. On Landaev and Akhiev, see Turkaev, *Kul'tura Chechni*, pp. 178-81, 189.

national consciousness was in the ascendant elsewhere, here aspirations for autonomy were still framed in pan-Caucasian terms – and advanced on behalf of a coalition of tribes and *ethnies*, rather than an alliance of distinct national collectivities.

By the first decade of the twentieth century, a set of democratic journalists had begun to write critical articles on the current conjuncture – Akhmetkhan and Ismail Mutushev, Ibragimbek Sarakaev, Danilbek Sheripov.[33] The last of these had four brothers whose fates illustrate the subsequent trajectory of Chechen national consciousness: Nazarbek was Chechnya's first native playwright; Zaurbek compiled a Russian–Chechen dictionary; Aslanbek published a collection of Chechen folk-tales in 1916, joined the Bolsheviks and died fighting the Whites in 1919; and Mairbek was a Soviet public prosecutor, but went into the mountains to join an uprising against Stalin in 1942. The passage from ethnography to insurgency within this single generation indicates a formidable acceleration, which requires some explanation.

The discovery of oil near Grozny in the 1880s – the first well was drilled in 1893 – had brought with it rapid industrial and urban growth, and an influx of Russian migrant workers who dominated the city well into the 1970s. Indeed, the previous division between Cossacks and Chechens was now supplanted by a three-way split between Chechens, Cossacks and *inogorodtsy* – literally 'other-towners', but referring to the ethnic Russians or Ukrainians who began to fill the ranks of the proletariat as Grozny industrialized. The city's oil workers, of whom there were 14,000 by 1914, were to play a vanguard role in the Revolutions of 1917. By that time, the tripartite ethnic schema had been overlaid by class solidarities and religious affiliations, creating a complex fragmentation of forces in the years from 1917–21.[34]

In the wake of the February Revolution a Civil Executive Committee was formed in the Terek region, which included local businessmen and dignitaries such as the Chechen oil magnate Tapa Chermoev, Kabardin landowner Pshemakho Kotsev and the Kumyk prince Rashidkhan

---

[33] Kh. V. Turkaev, 'Rossiia i Chechnia: aspekty istoriko-kul'turnykh vzaimosviazei do 1917g.', in Turkaev, *Kul'tura Chechni*, pp. 164–87.
[34] See especially Gammer, *Lone Wolf and Bear*, pp. 119–40.

Kaplanov. Though these men aimed to secure more autonomy for their region, they remained loyal to the Provisional Government, and entered into an uneasy alliance with the Cossacks against the Bolsheviks – at this stage, overwhelmingly *inogorodtsy* – who seized power in Grozny in October 1917. Meanwhile, a fourth set of actors had entered the scene: in the summer of 1917 the Naqshbandi sheikh and livestock breeder Najmuddin of Hotso was declared Mufti of the North Caucasus, while a Chechen National Soviet, set up in May 1917 to rival Chermoev's structure, was effectively run by the Qadiri sheikh Ali Mitaev. The divergent paths taken by the Islamists were crucial to the further unfolding of the drama: Najmuddin served in Chermoev's government, and was subsequently to play a leading role in a *ghazavat* against Soviet rule, while Mitaev was to back the Bolsheviks against the armies of the old regime.

The initial pact between the elite mountaineers and Cossacks soon unravelled. Raids on Cossack *stanitsy* from land-hungry Chechens and Ingush pushed the Cossacks closer to the Bolsheviks, who, now bolstered by soldiers returning from the front, were eager to move against what they saw as the twin perils of bourgeois nationalism and theocracy. More nuanced positions appeared briefly in March 1918, with the formation of the Terek Republic: a Soviet entity in which all nationalities were represented. Sergei Kirov – later head of the Leningrad Communist Party apparat, but assassinated in famously murky circumstances in 1934 – was a pivotal figure in securing the co-operation of Cossacks, Bolsheviks and radical mountaineers alike.[35] In this he was supported by Aslanbek Sheripov, who in November 1917 had coined the slogan 'Caucasians of all tribes, unite!', and argued for Soviet power as the best means of preserving Caucasian independence from the depredations of European colonialism; not, it turned out, without reason, since the British were to occupy Baku from late 1918 to June 1919.[36] By contrast, the Bolsheviks seemed to have offered precisely what Caucasians had for so long been struggling to achieve. Lenin's 'Appeal to the Muslims of Russia' of 3 December 1917 ran:

---

[35] See Richard King, *Sergei Kirov and the Struggle for Soviet Power in the Terek Region, 1917–1918*, New York and London 1987.
[36] See Aslanbek Sheripov, *Stat'i i rechi*, Grozny 1990 for a brief biography and selection of his speeches and articles.

All you, whose mosques and shrines have been destroyed, whose faith and customs have been violated by the Tsars and oppressors of Russia! Henceforward your beliefs and customs, your national and cultural institutions are declared free and inviolable! Build your national life freely and without hindrance. It is your right.

The national question was intertwined with issues of class. Sheripov's calls for land redistribution, taken up by the Terek People's Soviet, inflamed tensions with the Cossacks, who were in open revolt against Soviet power by the summer of 1918 – leading to a 100-day siege of Grozny from August to November, and a union of forces between the Bolsheviks and the Chechens and Ingush.[37] In May, meanwhile, Chermoev and the elite nationalists had formed a separate North Caucasian Mountain Republic, which was rapidly recognized by the Central Powers but had almost no control over any of its territory, which remained in the hands of the Bolsheviks and their allies. The Terek Republic, however, was undone by the arrival of Denikin's White Army in early 1919, which saw enemies both in forces loyal to Soviet rule and in the Islamists, the most implacable of whom now formed a tactical alliance with the Bolsheviks. Their leader was Uzun Hadji, a Chechen Qadiri sheikh who had been exiled to Siberia prior to the First World War, and who in September 1919 became ruler of an Emirate in eastern Chechnya and Dagestan modelled on Shamil's domain. Denikin in turn replicated the policies of Yermolov from a century earlier, burning down *auls*, razing crops and displacing villagers. The resistance against him was ferocious, occupying fully a third of his armies at a crucial point in the Civil War – and thus contributing greatly to the eventual Red victory.[38]

For a brief time, the Bolsheviks and the warriors of the *ghazavat* were united: in August 1919, Uzun Hadji conducted a joint offensive with the Red partisans of Nikolai Gikalo, and an agreement was forged with Sheikh Ali Mitaev to guarantee Chechen autonomy and religious practices within a Soviet system; the slogan under which Communists

[37] Pipes, *Formation of the Soviet Union*, p. 198.
[38] Abdurahman Avtorkhanov, 'The Chechens and the Ingush During the Soviet Period and Its Antecedents', in Broxup, *North Caucasus Barrier*, p. 153. Avtorkhanov's is one of the few Chechen viewpoints of this period available in English. See also Marie Bennigsen Broxup, 'The Last *Ghazawat*: The 1920–21 Uprising', in Broxup, *North Caucasus Barrier*, pp. 112–145.

and mullahs jointly advanced was 'Shari'a and Freedom'.[39] But after the White withdrawal in the winter of 1919–20, the Red Army moved in and began, in the eyes of the locals, to conduct itself like yet another occupier, enforcing its laws in contravention of the agreements it had signed a matter of months previously. Resistance flared up again in the summer of 1920, this time led by Najmuddin, who declared *jihad* in the name of the '*Shari'a* Army of the Mountain Peoples'. In response, the Soviets repeated the tactics of the Tsars, but with the added advantage of aerial bombardment. Najmuddin was defeated in 1921, but he evaded capture until 1925, and further pacification measures were required in the highlands until his arrest and execution.[40] However, by this time the rebels had been outmanoeuvred: in 1921 Stalin declared an amnesty and pledged full autonomy for the rechristened Soviet Mountain Republic and acceptance of local customary law; then, in 1922 the Mountain Republic's various components were sliced away and incorporated, one by one, as regions of Russia.

The tangled battle lines of the Revolution and Civil War years reveal a number of significant developments in Chechen society. The advance of capitalism under the Tsars had begun a differentiation of Chechens into separate social constituencies, obscuring the path to nationalist solidarity. The bourgeois elite and tiny intelligentsia that first voiced aspirations to sovereignty had done so in pan-Caucasian rather than national terms. But since they lacked a social programme that could mobilize the entire population, the quest for the best means of guaranteeing Caucasian freedoms switched to two other tracks: an attempted reprise of Shamil's theocratic discipline, and the pull of class war – two varieties of internationalism, or better, two refusals of the national. A parallel fragmentation on the Russian side meant that, in this period of turmoil, common ground could be found and alliances forged on the basis of interests rather than ethnicity. For the present, national ideas remained negotiable. It was, in fact, the Soviet period that was to provide the social bases and cultural infrastructure on which the

---

[39] Carlotta Gall and Thomas de Waal, *Chechnya: A Small Victorious War*, London 1997, p. 53; Gammer, *Lone Wolf and Bear*, pp. 129–30. Gall and de Waal provide a thorough and highly readable account of the 1994–6 war and the years leading up to it; the book also contains many illuminating observations on Chechen history and culture.

[40] Gammer, *Lone Wolf and Bear*, pp. 131–6.

Chechen sense of nationhood was built, as well as the collective trauma that cemented it.

Aslanbek Sheripov, as we have seen, viewed Soviet rule as the best guarantee of Caucasian self-determination. Though his hopes quickly proved to be misplaced, many Chechens were well disposed towards the Communist order on both material and moral grounds. Some land redistribution was carried out, placating rural Chechens, and Soviet education and infrastructure provided opportunities and occupations the old social formation had never offered. The egalitarianism of Bolshevik ideology also meshed with Chechen social traditions, to the extent that Qadiri adepts saw no immediate contradiction in joining the Communist Party – most prominently Mitaev, who served on the Chechen Revolutionary Committee.[41]

As elsewhere in the Caucasus and Central Asia, Communism was seen as the path to modernity, and much ambiguity towards the USSR persists to this day, especially among the more educated layers who benefited most from it, and in the lowlands, where contact with Russians was more frequent. In the field of culture, Chechen writers of the 1920s turned away from the Arabic poetic traditions of preceding centuries towards realist fiction in the manner of Gorky; it was the playwright and novelist Khalid Oshaev who devised the Latin transcription for Chechen in 1923 – anticipating Atatürk by five years. The first Chechen newspaper, *Serlo* (Light) appeared in 1927, and radio broadcasts in Chechen began the following year.[42]

[41] Mitaev was arrested in 1924 as a 'clerical bourgeois nationalist' and shot the following year. See Vanora Bennett, *Crying Wolf: The Return of War to Chechnya*, London 1998, pp. 263–4; Bennett's is a vivid eyewitness account of the 1994–6 war, with many interesting historical details.

[42] None of the transcription systems devised for Chechen thus far, however, has been able to render its full range of sounds. Like other Caucasian tongues, it is rich in consonants – there are over thirty – but it also has around fifteen vowels and diphthongs that are more reminiscent of Scandinavian languages. See Jaimoukha, *Chechens*, ch. 13; Iu. A. Aidaev, ed., *Chechentsy: Istoriia i sovremennost'*, Moscow 1996, pp. 287–90; and Valery Tishkov, *Chechnya: Life in a War-Torn Society*, Berkeley/Los Angeles 2004, p. 22. Tishkov – who briefly served as nationalities minister under Yeltsin – presents much invaluable sociological data in this abridged translation of his 2001 *Obshchestvo v vooruzhennom konflikte*. The Russian original, over twice as long, contains more interview materials and scholarly apparatus; also omitted from the English version is a chapter on the hysterical negative stereotyping of Chechens by Russian media and politicians.

However, the Soviet command structure in Chechnya was from the outset marked by Russianizing tendencies – initially due to a simple lack of cadres, but increasingly the product of colonialist mistrust of the natives. By the late 30s, modernization had become unambiguously synonymous with Russification – expressed on a symbolic level by an enforced shift to Cyrillic script in 1937–8. Chechnya and Ingushetia were combined into a single *oblast'* in 1934, and jointly elevated to the status of autonomous republic in 1936 – with a nominal right to secede, under the meaningless Stalin Constitution. Yet at this very moment, the Soviet security apparatus in Checheno-Ingushetia was moving against a fictive 'bourgeois-nationalist centre', and had for several years been engaged in counter-insurgency against a string of armed rebellions.

Much as it did in the rest of the USSR, the onset of collectivization in 1929 had marked the beginning of a qualitatively different phase in Chechnya's Soviet history. In response to arbitrary arrests and confiscations of livestock, armed resistance began once more, led by figures such as Shita Istamulov, a former Red partisan. Archives were burnt, petroleum refineries seized and dozens of GPU agents assassinated, prompting the despatch of the Red Army to Checheno-Ingushetia in December 1929. It suffered heavy losses, and the Kremlin line was softened until 1931, when the GPU arrested thousands of Chechens and Ingush for 'anti-Soviet' activity. The following year saw the beginning of a crackdown on the local intelligentsia, though the 3,000 arrests of 1932 were outdone by the 14,000 – 3 per cent of the population – that took place during the Great Purge of 1937. In 1938, 120 leaders of the 'bourgeois-nationalist centre' – supposedly acting at the prompting of the exiled Tapa Chermoev and backed by Turkey – were tried for treason, subversion and terrorist activity; despite extensive use of torture, only one pleaded guilty. An indirect indication of the toll taken by arrests and repression can be seen in the fact that, between the Soviet censuses of 1937 and 1939, Checheno-Ingushetia suffered a population loss of 35,000.[43]

The Chechen historian Abdurahman Avtorkhanov has observed that 'the link that existed between the people and the authorities was broken when the intelligentsia was destroyed'.[44] Young men left for the mountains

[43] Avtorkhanov, 'Chechens and Ingush'; Dunlop, *Russia Confronts Chechnya*, pp. 49–56.
[44] Avtorkhanov, 'Chechens and Ingush', p. 179.

in increasing numbers in the late 1930s, and by 1940 insurgents had gained control of several mountain regions and formed a 'Provisional Popular Revolutionary Government'. Its leader was the writer and former Party member Hassan Israilov, a product of the Soviet educational system whose critical articles on the 'plundering of Chechnya by the local Soviet and party leadership' got him arrested in 1929, aged nineteen. After spending much of the 1930s in prison, Israilov was offered reinstatement into the Party in January 1940. His reply to the Chechen-Ingush ASSR Party Secretary is striking not only in its boldness, but in its strictly secular and defensive conception of his nation:

> For twenty years now, the Soviet authorities have been fighting my people, aiming to destroy them group by group; first the *kulaks*, then the mullahs and the 'bandits', then the bourgeois-nationalists. I am sure now that the real object of this war is the annihilation of our nation as a whole. That is why I have decided to assume the leadership of my people in their struggle for liberation.[45]

Israilov pointed to the example of Finland, which proved that 'this great empire built on slavery is devoid of strength when faced with a small freedom-loving nation' – though the Finns would only hold out against the Soviet invasion for another two months after he wrote these words. Israilov himself fared slightly better: he continued to mount guerrilla actions against Stalin's troops until he was eventually hunted down by the NKVD and killed in December 1944.[46]

The obstinate refusal of Chechens such as Israilov to bow to Soviet authority was surely one of the reasons behind the genocidal deportations of 1944 – referred to in Chechen as *aardakh,* the 'exodus'. The pretext given by the Soviet authorities at the time was that several North Caucasian Muslim peoples and the Crimean Tatars had collaborated en masse with the Nazi occupying forces. One after another, entire ethnic groups were uprooted and sent to Central Asia by train: the Karachays and Kalmyks in October and November 1943, followed in February 1944 by the Chechens and Ingush, the Balkars in March and April of the same year, the Crimean Tatars in June, and the

---

[45] Avtorkhanov, 'Chechens and Ingush', pp. 181–2.
[46] Gammer, *Lone Wolf and Bear*, p. 163.

Meskhetian Turks of Georgia in November. The choice of which peoples were to be deported seems to have been made according to long-standing imperial notions of their 'unreliability' – hence the Kabardins and North Ossetians were untouched. There is no indication that the mid-nineteenth-century deportations were consciously used as examples, however; the Soviet state in any case had more recent models to fall back on: it had carried out a strategic form of ethnic cleansing on several occasions since 1935, forcibly displacing Germans, Poles, Finns, Iranians and Koreans from its border regions on the grounds that they might ally with the adjacent nation-states housing their ethnic kin. These operations had initially affected only part of the populations concerned, and ambiguously combined ethnic with class criteria; but in 1937, the entire Korean population in the Soviet Far East – a total of 171,781 people – was sent to Kazakhstan and Uzbekistan, setting a chilling precedent.[47]

The strategic reasoning behind the North Caucasian deportations has not been fully recorded, but it is likely to have been analogous: Stalin may have planned to move against Turkey, and wanted to clear the area of peoples who might align themselves with the Kemalist state.[48] The persistence of rebellion in Chechnya would have made its people particularly suspect in the eyes of the Soviet security apparatus, for whom Israilov's aspirations to national sovereignty were merely a continuation of the 'political banditism' that had recurred in Checheno-Ingushetia since the late 1920s. Given the degree of popular support required for guerrilla activities of this kind, and the broad ethnic categories in which the Stalinist state dealt, there is an icy rationality to the identification of the entire nation as 'anti-Soviet'. The Chechens,

---

[47] For a fascinating account of the emergence of ethnic cleansing as a recurrent Soviet policy, see Terry Martin, 'Origins of Soviet Ethnic Cleansing', *Journal of Modern History* 70 (December 1998), pp. 813–61. Martin calculates that 'approximately 800,000 individuals were arrested, deported or executed in the ethnic cleansing and mass national operations from 1935 to 1938. This represents around one-third of the total political victims in that time period' – an observation that seems to demand a re-examination of standard narratives of the Great Terror.

[48] Lieven, *Chechnya*, p. 316. This applies especially to the Meskhetian Turks, all 102,142 of whom were deported from Georgia to Central Asia in November 1944; unlike the other deported peoples, they have still not been allowed to return. In the Soviet period, this could possibly be put down to Turkey's membership of NATO, and since then to the Georgians' unwillingness to accommodate them. Negotiations over their fate continue to this day.

then, were seemingly being punished for betraying a state whose
authority they had never fully accepted.

The official Soviet version, in which the deported peoples were collectively punished for collaboration, is at any rate ill founded. In the case
of the Chechens, it is true that émigré circles had briefly made contact
with the German authorities. But the insurgents in Chechnya had established their provisional government when Hitler and Stalin were officially
allies, and in late 1942, as German propaganda courted the Caucasian
peoples towards whom its troops were advancing, Israilov and his ally
Mairbek Sheripov warned the Ostministerium that 'if the liberation of
the Caucasus meant the exchange of one colonizer for another, then
the Caucasians would only consider this a new stage in the national
liberation war.'[49] That spring, Soviet planes were diverted to bombard
the mountain *auls* instead of Hitler's armies.

In Chechnya itself, moreover, opportunities for working with the
enemy were limited: having taken the southern Russian cities of Rostov,
Stavropol and Krasnodar and the North Ossetian garrison town of
Mozdok by late August 1942, the Reichswehr ground to a halt before
reaching Grozny. The only town in Checheno-Ingushetia over which
the Germans managed to establish control before their retreat began in
late 1942 was Malgobek, which had a predominantly Russian population.
Across the region, the handfuls of collaborators were overwhelmingly
outweighed by the number of Caucasians and Tatars volunteering for
service in the Red Army – 17,413 Chechens alone – or fighting with
partisan bands behind German lines.[50]

The plan for the deportation was drawn up in October 1943, codenamed
'Operation Lentil' – *chechevitsa* in Russian, a word whose first two syllables
point a phonetic finger at the principal targets. A total of 120,000 troops
were moved into the republic early in 1944, on the pretext of mending
roads and bridges; many of them were billeted on local families, taking

---

[49] Avtorkhanov, 'Chechens and Ingush', p. 183; see also Timur Muzaev and Zurab
Todua, *Novaia Checheno-Ingushetiia*, Moscow 1992, p. 33. Gammer, *Lone Wolf
and Bear*, pp. 161–5 and Avtorkhanov does not specify how the Chechen
insurgents contacted the Ostministerium; NKVD papers suggest that Israilov had
a network of agents across the North Caucasus, including in German-occupied
territory; but these documents should obviously be treated with caution.

[50] Aleksandr Nekrich, *The Punished Peoples*, New York 1978, pp. 36–8; Dunlop,
Russia Confronts Chechnya, p. 60.

advantage of local traditions of hospitality. On 23 February 1944, the entire population was summoned to local Party buildings across Checheno-Ingushetia to celebrate Red Army Day. There they were informed of their imminent resettlement as punishment for treason. In a process personally supervised by Beria, all the inhabitants of the republic were crammed into Studebaker trucks. Those who resisted were summarily executed, and in the more remote mountain regions, where deporting the population would have been logistically complicated, the inhabitants were simply rounded up and shot. In the *aul* of Khaibakh, 700 people were herded into a barn and burned alive on the orders of NKVD colonel Gveshiani; Beria offered his congratulations, and promised Gveshiani a medal.[51] By the summer, Checheno-Ingushetia had been erased from the map altogether, the republic dissolved into 'Grozny region' and numerous Chechen place-names replaced with Russian toponyms. Mosques and graveyards were destroyed, along with hundreds of books and manuscripts that were among the Chechens' few written records of their past.[52] Over the next decade, thousands of settlers would move into the homes of those deported or killed by the Soviet authorities.

The brutal process was repeated across the North Caucasus, from which a total of 724,297 people were sent to Central Asia in airless freight trains. The figure includes 412,548 Chechens and 96,327 Ingush; 104,146 Kalmyks, 39,407 Balkars and 71,869 Karachais suffered a similar fate.[53] Food was scarce, disease rife, and many simply died of exposure. There is a sizeable discrepancy between the official tally of Chechens and Ingush deported and the number arriving at their destination – a difference of 96,000, if we compare Beria's final report of July 1944 with a figure cited by Khrushchev in 1956. Moreover, the harsh conditions into which the deportees were thrown amplified the effects of sickness and hunger: NKVD files give a death rate of 23.7 per cent for the deported nations between 1944 and 1948 – a total of 144,704 people – though this is likely to be an understatement. Historians comparing census data for 1926, 1939 and 1959 have noted a steep drop in Chechen population growth, from 28 per cent over the period 1929–39 to 2.5 per cent between 1939 and 1959.

[51] Dunlop, *Russia Confronts Chechnya*, p. 65; Gammer, *Lone Wolf and Bear*, p. 170.
[52] Gammer, *Lone Wolf and Bear*, p. 182; Jaimoukha, *Chechens*, p. 212.
[53] See the scrupulous statistical work by Dalkhat Ediev, *Demograficheskie poteri deportirovannykh narodov SSSR*, Stavropol 2003, Table 109, p. 302.

As a consequence, estimates for indirect population loss among Chechens alone range from 170,000 to 200,000.[54] In terms of direct losses, all nations suffered tremendous casualties, but the Chechens were disproportionately affected, losing over 30 per cent of their total numbers, compared to an average of just under 20 per cent for all deported nations.[55] This disparity goes some way towards explaining why the deportation became a galvanizing national trauma for the Chechens in ways it seems not to have done for the other victims.

Statistics nonetheless fall short in conveying the scale of the disaster, or the depth of its impact. In 1991, one in three Chechens was a survivor from 1944, and will have recalled the pitiless efficiency with which the Soviet state tore them from their homes. The experience of exile and tensions following their return were the catalysts for the emergence of a Chechen national movement, and it is to them that I turn in the next chapter. But the events recounted above are the dark soil in which that movement took root. We should note the pain and fury in the words the Chechen poet Ismail Kerimov devoted to the deportations – as well as his inescapable injunction:

> I am pain,
> I am thousands,
> thousands of tears
> shed under
> the roar of the wheels
> in February of 1944.
> I am a sea.
> I am hundreds, I am thousands
> of discarded bodies
> rotting in obscure stations.
> I am a tombstone,
> I am the tattered despair
> of a mother

---

[54] See Nekrich, *Punished Peoples*; Dunlop, *Russia Confronts Chechnya*, pp. 62-70; and Gammer, *Lone Wolf and Bear*, pp. 166–71.

[55] Ediev, *Demograficheskie poteri*, Table 109, p. 302.

[56] From the Russian translation quoted in Aidaev, *Chechentsy*, p. 274; a slightly different version is quoted in Jaimoukha, *Chechens*, p. 213.

with a frozen prayer [. . .]
I am a voice,
and I command you
'Remember!'[56]

2.

Towards Independence

The deportation became the defining event in Chechen national consciousness – only eclipsed in recent years by the two wars launched against this tiny nation by Russia. It was a collective trauma that permeated the society: every single family was torn from its ancestral lands, and every family spent the years in exile nurturing a desire to return. Their Central Asian purgatory imbued the Chechens with what Anatol Lieven has termed a 'steely national discipline', reinforcing a sense of ethnic particularity on which the nationalist movement was subsequently to thrive.[1] But more than this, the deportation provided proof, to the Chechens, that as a people they would not be safe within the borders of any state but their own. The Chechen Revolution of 1990–1 was in that sense not merely an ethnic backlash against Russian domination, but a push for sovereignty as the best means of collective self-preservation against genocide. This imperative can only have gained more force since 1994, as both Yeltsin and Putin have sought to bury the Chechens' right to a state under a torrent of bombs.

The present chapter charts the rise of modern Chechen nationalism,

[1] Anatol Lieven, *Chechnya: Tombstone of Russian Power*, London 1998, p. 321.

from the hardships of exile to the ferment of revolution and secession. It then turns to the legal and constitutional implications of the Chechen bid for independence. Though questions have been raised about its technical legitimacy, it is clear that it possessed the backing of the overwhelming majority of the population, and there is little more that the Chechens could have done to ensure compliance with international law. The burden of responsibility for the disasters that ensued lies not with the Chechens, who had every moral and legal right to claim sovereignty, but with Russia, which refused to recognize the validity of the Chechens' wishes, and with the outside world, which once again chose not to protect a small and vulnerable people from the aggressions of its neighbour.

The deported peoples arrived in the 'Special Settlements' – most of them in Kazakhstan and Kirghizstan – in the dead of winter. Conditions were harsh: housing was provided for only a fraction of deportees, leaving the rest to face the cold in makeshift shelters or tents. The paucity of food allowances led to widespread malnourishment. Moreover, tight restrictions were placed on the deportees' movements, including monthly registration with the Interior Ministry and a ban on travelling more than three kilometres from their place of residence. The occupations through which the Chechens scraped a living mostly involved agricultural or construction work; but overall, exile was for them a process of 'pauperization'.[2]

In *The Gulag Archipelago*, Aleksandr Solzhenitsyn described the Chechens in exile as 'the one nation which would not give in', referring to their pride and also their contempt for the laws of their jailers. The point is an important one: refusal of the Soviet system as a whole led, on the one hand, to the consolidation of alternative forms of social organization and interaction, including clandestine Sufi brotherhoods that perpetuated a specifically Chechen religious tradition. On the other hand, the Chechens also became increasingly drawn into the shadow economy, as one of few means of generating income free of state scrutiny and official discrimination. These were to be enduring features of Chechen society, transforming the nature of its national movement.

---

[2] Aleksandr Nekrich, cited in John Dunlop, *Russia Confronts Chechnya: Roots of a Separatist Conflict, Punished Peoples*, Cambridge 1998, pp. 68–72.

They also marked the Chechens out from the other deported peoples, who on the whole were to arrive at a *modus vivendi* with Soviet power – perhaps due to their lack of a tradition of resistance comparable to that of the Chechens, and to their inferior numbers, which were depleted still further by the deportation.

After the death of Stalin in 1953, Chechens began to trickle back to the Caucasus, in a largely self-organized fashion that the authorities were powerless to prevent. The trickle became a steady stream after Nikita Khrushchev's 'secret speech' of 1956 repudiated much of the legacy of Stalinism. In March 1957, the Chechen–Ingush ASSR was formally re-established – albeit with three predominantly Russian lowland districts added, to dilute the demographic weight of the titular nationalities – and the exiles officially allowed to return. (This no doubt explains why in the 1990s, the separatist regime named a square after Khrushchev.) The Soviet authorities had hoped for an orderly population transfer, but by September 1957, a total of 140,000 Chechens had returned, joined by another 200,000 by spring 1958; almost the entire Chechen population had returned by the end of that year – instead of 1960, as had been envisaged.[3]

Considerable tensions followed their arrival, since the settlers sent to take their place after 1944 – the vast majority of them ethnic Russians – remained. Violence occasionally erupted, for instance in August 1958 when, following the killing of a Russian at the hands of a Chechen in a drunken brawl in Grozny, thousands of Russians marched on the local party committee building and demanded the expulsion of the republic's titular nationalities.[4] For the most part, a system of uneasy colonial co-existence obtained – though the authorities imposed draconian restrictions on the expression of national identity: there was no Chechen-language schooling until 1990, ensuring what has been one of the Soviet period's most crippling legacies. While two changes of alphabet – to Latin and then Cyrillic scripts – cut Chechens off from their written traditions, the educational chokehold of Russian meant

---

[3] Moshe Gammer, *The Lone Wolf and the Bear: Three Centuries of Chechen Defiance of Russian Rule*, London 2006, p. 180.

[4] For a detailed account of the 1958 disturbances, see Vladimir Kozlov, *Mass Uprisings in the USSR: Protest and Rebellion in the post-Stalin Years*, Armonk, NY 2002, pp. 87–111.

that Chechen to this day remains largely a spoken language, in which all Chechens are fluent, but a good deal fewer literate.

Chechens and Ingush were heavily discriminated against, and largely excluded from skilled employment. Indeed, in the late Soviet period, Checheno-Ingushetia's economy was effectively divided into two spheres, in a situation that the sociologist Georgi Derluguian has compared to Algeria under French settler rule.[5] The predominantly urban Russians – 24 per cent of the republic's total 1989 population of 1.2 million – dominated the oil and machine sectors, health, education and social services. The mostly rural Chechens and Ingush – the former far more numerous than the latter, composing 64 per cent of the ASSR's population – worked in agriculture, construction and in the ever-expanding informal sector.

The parallel economy – migrant work, smuggling, criminal gangs – was both a crucial source of income for Chechens and a significant social mechanism in its own right. By the end of the Soviet period, an estimated 40,000 Chechen and Ingush men were taking part each year in the unofficial labour migrations known in Russian as *shabashka*. Prisons became familiar environments for many: while 'perhaps as many as one in six adult Soviet males spent time behind bars' in the Brezhnev era, the proportion was significantly higher – 'upwards of a quarter' – in the Caucasus, where the informal economy was far larger, and discrimination more active.[6] With this shuttling between precarious employment all over the USSR, prison and their home villages, the Chechens' older social structures undoubtedly lost much of their solidity. *Taip* connections were joined, crossed or supplanted by links forged between members of a labour team or Sufi brotherhood, between cellmates and partners in crime. It could be argued, in fact, that the consolidation of a sense of Chechen nationhood occurred in this period as compensation for the loss of other identifications: the architecture of clan and family

---

[5] Georgi Derluguian, *Bourdieu's Secret Admirer in the Caucasus*, Chicago 2005, p. 244. Combining broad theoretical ambitions with lively, first-hand ethnographic observation, Derluguian's highly original approach posits three classes — nomenklatura, intelligentsia and subproletariat – as the central social actors in the region. He has a tremendous range of references and offers many stimulating historical comparisons, as well as inimitable vignettes of the highly cultured Caucasian intelligentsia.

[6] Derluguian, *Bourdieu's Secret Admirer*, pp. 114, 152, 245.

ties was loosened or dissolved under the pressures of semi-industrialization, but an over-arching commonality, nourished by historical wounds and present grievances, emerged and regathered the rubble. The idea is perhaps most eloquently conveyed in the monument erected by the government of Dzhokhar Dudaev in 1994. It was 'made up chiefly of old Chechen gravestones from cemeteries demolished after 1944', and bore the inscription 'We will not weep; we will not weaken; we will not forget.'[7]

The social imbalance between Russians and Chechens became increasingly accentuated due to the explosive population growth of the latter after their return from exile. The 300,000 who survived deportation in 1944 had become a million by 1989, with the Chechens' rate of growth exceeding 3 per cent, compared to the Russians' 1 per cent. The continued marginalization of Chechens and Ingush from official economic life, meanwhile, in a context of structural unemployment, meant that by 1989, the Autonomous Republic had an estimated surplus labour force of over 100,000, while a quarter of ethnic Chechens were now living outside Checheno-Ingushetia, having left in search of work. The brunt of the economic apartheid was, of course, borne by the rural population – according to the 1989 census, 59 per cent in Checheno-Ingushetia, compared to 27 per cent in Soviet Russia as a whole. Official figures for the mid-1980s estimate that '40 per cent of the rural labour force received wages below subsistence level, while close to 60 per cent of adult women had no formal employment'. Of course, unofficial sources of income and familial support networks meant that Chechens generally did not live in penury; nevertheless, they were at a sizeable structural disadvantage. Like other parts of the North Caucasus, Checheno-Ingushetia had markedly lower wages and poorer social provision than the rest of Soviet Russia: the average wage in 1985 was 83 per cent of the RSFSR average, dropping to 75 in 1991; infant mortality was 23 per 1000 in 1987, compared to a federal mean of 14 per 1000. In 1989, only 5 per cent of the population of

---

[7] Lieven, *Chechnya*, p. 320. The monument was destroyed by Russian bombardment in 1995, rebuilt in 1997, and destroyed again by the same method in 1999; Moshe Gammer notes that this 'perhaps symbolizes best the fate of the Chechens and their country': Gammer, *Lone Wolf and Bear*, p. 176.

Checheno-Ingushetia had higher education, while 16 per cent had no education at all.[8]

This, then, was the chief constituency for the project of national independence in Chechnya: a marginalized, poor, under-educated and largely rural population whose experience of Soviet rule was one of precariousness, mistrust and incarceration. They still had, however, to be mobilized. After 1989, in much of the Soviet Union, local intellectual figures lined up behind the Soviet *nomenklatura* and helped secure a refurbishment of the old regime. The key respect in which Checheno-Ingushetia differed from the rest of the USSR was in the effective closure of its elite ranks to participation from the republic's titular nationalities. The reasons for this are the same as those underpinning the emergence of Chechen nationalism itself. The GPU had picked off pre-Revolutionary leaders and intellectuals; but it was above all the deportation and subsequent discrimination that had 'prevented the Chechens from forming a consolidated, self-confident Soviet elite', who could have conducted a seamless oligarchic restoration of the kind that took place elsewhere in the former Soviet lands.[9]

As in the Baltic states, the origins of Chechnya's national movement lie in informal associations established during *perestroika*, such as the historical society 'Kavkaz', which was set up in 1988. In February of the same year, protests against the planned construction of a chemical plant in Gudermes developed into a series of mass meetings in Grozny and elsewhere in which environmental concerns were rapidly joined by notions of national renewal. Cultural figures were prominent from the start; indeed, as elsewhere in Eastern Europe, many of the leaders of Chechnya's nationalist movement came not from the political elite, but from local artistic and intellectual circles – the poet Zelimkhan Yandarbiev and the actor Akhmed Zakaev, for instance. The reason for this was not simply the virtual Russian monopoly on state posts, but also the fact that, after de-Stalinization in particular, the Soviet cultural bureaucracy allowed for the

---

[8] Demographic information: Lieven, *Chechnya*, pp. 322–3, and Valerii Tishkov, *Obshchestvo v vooruzhennom konflikte: Etnografiia chechenskoi voiny*, Moscow 2001, p. 115. Rural labour-force: Derluguian, *Bourdieu's Secret Admirer*, p. 245. Other socio-economic data: Dunlop, *Russia Confronts Chechnya*, pp. 85–8.

[9] Dmitri Trenin and Aleksei Malashenko, *Russia's Restless Frontier: The Chechnya Factor in Post-Soviet Russia*, Washington, D.C. 2004, p. 16.

cultivation of – suitably folkloric and fraternal – national traditions. All-Union conferences brought together intellectuals from disparate nations who exchanged ideas and, in some cases, programmatic documents, transplanted almost intact from the Baltics to the Caucasus.[10]

In June 1989, Doku Zavgaev became the first Chechen to head the Communist Party in Checheno-Ingushetia, a development which prompted some loosening of restrictions on the informal organizations. The following spring, a number of local party secretaries were removed under pressure from fledgling social movements; but these were replaced by Zavgaev's associates, and the March 1990 elections for People's Deputies were generally won by official candidates. Aspirations for democratic and national renewal were henceforth to be channelled through oppositional forces such as the Vainakh Democratic Party (VDP), the name assumed in May 1990 by the 'Bart' ('Unity') organization founded under *perestroika*.

One of the main targets of the historical societies that sprang up in the late 1980s was the fiction of a voluntary union between Checheno-Ingushetia and Russia – a flagrant lie propagated by leading Soviet ideologues such as Suslov, Brezhnev's *éminence grise*, to cover for the reality of colonial dispossession. The move from registering this fact to remedying it began during 1990, as the notion of sovereignty became central to discussions and more radical forces gained the upper hand. Much of the impetus, however, was provided from the outside, by the Soviet authorities themselves, as Gorbachev and Yeltsin competed for the loyalty of peripheral elites by offering constitutional concessions. In April 1990, the USSR Congress of People's Deputies passed three highly significant laws: on 3 April, 'On the Procedure for Deciding Questions Concerning the Withdrawal of a Union Republic from the USSR'; on 10 April, 'On Principles of Economic Relations of the USSR, the Union and Autonomous Republics'; and on 26 April, 'On the Delimitation of Powers Between the USSR and the Subjects of Federation'. The last of these gave all Russian ASSRs 'the full plenitude of state power on their territory', making them full subjects of the USSR with a status equivalent to that of Union Republics.[11] Implicitly, therefore, they all

---

[10] These points are made by Derluguian, *Bourdieu's Secret Admirer*, p. 150.

[11] James Hughes, 'The Peace Process in Chechnya', in Richard Sakwa, ed., *Chechnya: From Past to Future*, p. 271.

had the constitutional right to secede from the Union, though this remained technically unconfirmed pending a revision of the USSR Constitution to reflect the increased number of its constituent parts; an issue which remained unresolved until the Union's collapse. Yeltsin for his part added to the centrifugal momentum: on a visit to Kazan in August 1990 while campaigning for the RSFSR presidency, he famously told Russia's ethnic republics to 'take as much sovereignty as you can stomach'.

It was only after receiving these encouragements that the nationalist forces in Chechnya, led by Yandarbiev's VDP, began to call for full sovereignty within the USSR. In late November, the first Chechen National Congress was held in Grozny, with the full participation of the local Communist Party. On 25 November the congress declared the sovereignty of the Chechen Republic of Nokhchi-cho. Though this decision had no juridical status, it was taken up on 27 November by the republican Supreme Soviet, which declared the sovereignty of the Chechen–Ingush Republic, adding that the entity would in future sign union and federal treaties with Russia on an equal footing. At this stage, then, the chief differences among Checheno-Ingushetia's political forces concerned the composition of a new national leadership, the form of relations with Moscow and the role of Islam. All the main factions of the Chechen National Congress – the Communists, the radicals of the VDP, the Greens, the secular Popular Front of Checheno-Ingushetia and the Islamic Path Party – advocated full sovereignty 'at a minimum'.[12]

This consensus was broken during the course of 1991, with the local Party clinging to power while the nationalist opposition gathered in strength and stridency. March saw the arrival on the scene of General Dzhokhar Dudaev, elected to head the Executive Committee of the Chechen National Congress. Thought a safe, symbolic choice at the time – he was a Soviet air force pilot, and married to a Russian – Dudaev proved unexpectedly active, and brought about a sharp radicalization of the national movement. For the previous five years, he had commanded a long-range bomber division in Tartu, having served in Afghanistan beforehand. He was strongly influenced by the rising

---

[12] Dunlop, *Russia Confronts Chechnya*, p. 93; Lieven, *Chechnya*, pp. 56–64. For a detailed account of the 'Chechen revolution', see Muzaev and Todua, *Novaia Checheno-Ingushetiia*, pp. 34–43.

fortunes of the Estonian independence movement, and had reportedly prevented Soviet troops on his base from being used against demonstrators in January 1991. Moreover, he had left Estonia just as a referendum there returned a strong majority in favour of secession – an event which doubtless encouraged him to embolden his stance: Estonia's population of 1.6 million was, after all, little larger than Checheno-Ingushetia's, and his republic had a smaller Russian minority than either Estonia or Latvia.

The pace of events quickened considerably in the summer of 1991. The Executive Committee of the Chechen National Congress created an armed National Guard, and by May was openly calling for the dissolution of the Chechen–Ingush Supreme Soviet, claiming legitimate authority now rested with the National Congress. In June, the Congress declared that Checheno-Ingushetia should, as a sovereign country, not participate in the elections for Russian president; these went ahead, though, and the votes went overwhelmingly to Yeltsin, the eventual victor. Zavgaev felt his position strengthened by the service thus rendered to Moscow, and in July began to implement economic reforms. As in Russia proper, these resulted in *nomenklatura*-dominated co-operatives being formed which raised prices and engaged in speculation – pushing the rural standard of living still lower.[13]

The decisive blow to the local Party's authority, however, came with the 19 August putsch against Gorbachev – largely aimed at preventing the signing of a new, more confederal Union Treaty which delegated further powers to the Union Republics. Many of Checheno-Ingushetia's CP officials were in Moscow for the Treaty signing, and slipped back to Grozny without taking a decisive stance. Dudaev's Executive Committee, together with the VDP, Greens and Islamists, staged continuous rallies and called a general strike in defence of Yeltsin. A classic revolutionary situation of dual power ensued. On 22 August, the National Guard seized the television station, broadcasting Dudaev's support for the democratically elected government of Russia, and his own demands for sovereignty. On the 24th, a statue of Lenin in central Grozny was toppled, while the next day the republican Supreme Soviet

[13] Timur Muzaev and Zurab Todua, *Novaia Checheno-Ingushetiia*, Moscow 1992, p. 39.

continued backing Zavgaev. Barricades wents up in Grozny on 29-30 August, and over the next few days Dudaev's supporters, joined by hundreds of people streaming into the city from the countryside, took control of more government buildings. On 6 September the National Guard and the paramilitaries of Bislan Gantemirov's Islamic Path Party seized the Supreme Soviet building; Zavgaev was forced to sign a resignation letter, and a CP official either fell, or was pushed, to his death from a window – the revolution's sole casualty. In a Russian television interview on 7 September, Ruslan Khasbulatov, the Chechen speaker of the Russian Supreme Soviet, welcomed the exit of his longtime rival Zavgaev, and was to congratulate democratic forces on their triumph when he arrived in Grozny a week later.[14]

In mid-September the Russian authorities made two bids to negotiate a compromise with the Chechen national movement, one mission backed by Yeltsin, the other carried out by Khasbulatov in person. Yeltsin's envoys left after four days of fruitless discussion with the National Congress and Chechen Supreme Soviet, while Khasbulatov took a mere forty-eight hours to chair the final session of the latter body, force its dissolution, set elections for 17 November and transfer power to a Temporary Supreme Soviet, which included members of the National Congress. The same day, 15 September, Ingush deputies voted for autonomy within the RSFSR; in a referendum at the end of November, 90 per cent of Ingush were to vote in favour of formally separating from Chechnya – a move motivated in part by an unwillingness to be dominated by their more populous ethnic kin, but probably also by a desire to recover the Prigorodny region, a slice of Ingush land awarded to North Ossetia after the 1944 deportations, which would have been placed definitively out of Ingushetia's reach by separation from Russia.

The Executive Committee of the Chechen National Congress brought the election date forward to 27 October. Khasbulatov, though he may initially have thought Zavgaev's downfall would clear his own path to power in Chechnya, soon realized the strength of popular support behind Dudaev. He now warned against any 'usurpation' of

---

[14] Marie Bennigsen Broxup, 'After the Putsch, 1991', in Broxup, *The North Caucasus Barrier*, New York 1992, pp. 226–7.

power by the informal organizations, and gave his backing to the increasingly inflammatory rhetoric of Aleksandr Rutskoi, the Russian vice-president, who called Dudaev's supporters 'a gang terrorizing the population' and on 8–9 October actively recommended the use of force to 'restore order'. The elections went ahead, though several pro-Russian candidates withdrew in protest. Despite some reported irregularities, there can be no doubt as to the verdict: a landslide victory for Dudaev.[15]

On his inauguration on 1 November, Dudaev declared Chechnya's independence. He had campaigned explicitly on a platform of full sovereignty, which had now been ratified by popular consensus. On 2 November, meanwhile, the RSFSR Supreme Soviet – chaired by Khasbulatov, who had been instrumental in ensuring voting took place at all – declared the elections Dudaev had just won to have been unlawful. Then, on the night of 8–9 November, Russian special forces flew in to Khankala airbase near Grozny in a bid to remove Dudaev from power. But the coup attempt was foiled by a combination of armed Chechen opposition and obstruction from Gorbachev, who was still nominally the commander of the Soviet military, and unwilling to repeat the bloodshed that had taken place in Lithuania that January. Under a deal brokered between the National Congress and the authorities in Moscow, Russian troops left Chechnya on buses without firing a shot. For the next three years, the country gained de facto independence.

Dudaev's declaration of independence was the latest in a series that had begun in Lithuania in March 1990. Armenia followed in August, Georgia in April 1991, and 20–31 August 1991 saw similar declarations from Estonia, Latvia, Ukraine, Belarus, Moldova, Azerbaijan, Kirghizstan and Uzbekistan; Tajikistan followed suit in September,

---

[15] Experts have given different final figures – Dudaev winning 90 per cent of the vote on a 72 per cent turnout, or 85 per cent on a 77 per cent turnout. The anthropologist Sergei Arutiunov has noted that Dudaev had 60–70 per cent support. Khasbulatov claimed the elections contradicted democratic norms, but observers from the International Committee on Human Rights reported no violations. See 'Chronology' in Diane Curran, Fiona Hill and Elena Kostritsyna, eds, *The Search for Peace in Chechnya: A Sourcebook 1994–1996*, Kennedy School of Government, Strengthening Democratic Institutions Project, March 1997; Dunlop, *Russia Confronts Chechnya*, p. 114; and Broxup, 'After the Putsch', p. 236.

Turkmenistan in October and Kazakhstan in December. The contrast between the treatment of these states and Chechnya is striking. On 6 September, for example, the Kremlin recognized the independence of Estonia, Latvia and Lithuania, and on 17 September the three nations were given seats in the UN; Ukraine and Belarus were already members, but the rest of the former Soviet republics were admitted on 2 March 1992 (except Georgia, which had to wait until July for lack of a government).

In Chechnya, however, the Russian government was to pursue a schizophrenic strategy. On the one hand, Moscow on several occasions accepted Chechen independence de jure. On 14 March 1992, after negotiations on a range of legal, economic and security issues, Chechen and Russian representatives signed protocols explicitly referring to the 'political independence and state sovereignty of the Chechen Republic', a formula that was endorsed in further documents signed on 28 May and 25 September of that year.[16] Moreover, every Russian administration since 1991 has accepted the separation of Chechnya and Ingushetia, conducted at the initiative of local forces, and supposedly illegitimate according to the same criteria by which Chechen sovereignty has been ruled unlawful. On the other hand, during 1992–94 the Yeltsin regime actively sponsored several attempts to destabilize or topple Dudaev, before opting for full-scale invasion in 1994.

The full range of arguments offered in favour of Russia's invasion will be examined – and countered – in the next chapter. However, we should address here the question of how Chechnya's secession should be viewed under international law. The international legal instruments governing secession are permeated by a tension between the principle of self-determination and the preservation of territorial integrity. The former, endorsed in different registers by Lenin and Woodrow Wilson, underpinned a wave of national liberation movements in the aftermath of World War One, and saw the emergence of several new states from the ashes of the Austro-Hungarian and Ottoman empires. However, it was only Europeans that were deemed worthy of full sovereignty by the League of Nations, which parcelled out the colonial possessions of the defeated powers among the victors as Mandates or Protectorates –

---

[16] Dunlop, *Russia Confronts Chechnya*, p. 169.

and ignored completely any aspirations to independence in the British or French colonies. The second wave of newly independent states unfurled after 1945, with a massive surge around 1960 as African states gained sovereignty. It was surely the addition of these states to the global scene, coupled to the ongoing appeal of Third World liberation movements, that brought about such landmarks as UN General Assembly Resolution 1514 of December 1960, which states that all people subject to colonial rule have the right to 'freely determine their political status'. This principle has since been reaffirmed: for instance, the 1966 UN Covenant on Civil and Political Rights and the International Covenant on Economic and Social Rights both begin by stating that 'all people have the right of self-determination'.

However, the commitment to decolonization was from the outset counterbalanced by other considerations. UN General Assembly Resolution 742 of November 1953 had listed the 'factors of self-government', circumscribing the criteria – largely at Moscow's insistence – so as to limit decolonization to non-contiguous territories, thus excluding territorial empires such as that of the Soviets. The fiction of voluntary union provided the USSR with a further defence against the principle of self-determination. Elsewhere the world's governing elites largely shared a desire to avoid further fragmentation. The dominant concept here is that of *uti possidetis juris*, 'which holds that new states may be formed on the basis of the highest administrative units and within the established administrative borders of the colonial era, and discourages the unilateral redrawing of boundaries by secession or territorial seizure'.[17] The principle was originally deployed in nineteenth-century Latin America, to ratify the outcome of the wars of liberation from Spain – and as such, simply transferred into local elite hands the administration of territories defined with no reference either to ethnic or linguistic boundaries, or to geographical realities. Nevertheless, the same principle was enshrined in Africa in the wake of decolonization. In 1964, the Organization of African Unity passed a resolution asserting the stability of colonial boundaries, and has allowed only one secession to take place since then: that of Eritrea in 1993, which until 1952 had been a separate colonial state from Ethiopia, and so, it was argued, was simply reverting

---

[17] Hughes, 'Peace Process', p. 269.

to its previous status.[18] It may recognize the secession of Somaliland, a former British colony that is currently part of Somalia, according to the same rationale.

The manifest injustice of such a doctrine is clear: peoples are only allowed to seek self-determination along boundaries determined by their colonial overlords. Nevertheless, Chechnya's bid for sovereignty meets the criteria. According to the three separate laws passed by the USSR Congress of People's Deputies in 1990, Checheno-Ingushetia had the same constitutional status as full Union Republics – the USSR's highest administrative units. The final confirmation of this status by an amendment to the Soviet Constitution admittedly did not take place; but then the Chechens should not be held accountable for Moscow's unfulfilled promises. Moreover, after the collapse of the USSR, relations between Russia and the constituent units of the RSFSR remained unclarified until the drafting of a new federal treaty in 1992 – which Chechnya, having already declared sovereignty under Soviet law, did not sign. Pending the outcome of negotiations, then, the instruments governing relations between Chechnya and Russia after 1991 remained at the very least unclear.

The concern voiced in paragraph 25 of the 1975 Helsinki Accords, to which the Soviet Union was a signatory, that self-determination should be conducted by democratic means can also be allayed: Dudaev had an incontestable popular mandate for independence. Though he had no serious challengers advocating continued union, the pro-Moscow camp actively promoted abstention, making the high turnout in itself a rejection of their programme. Moreover, the Ingush were allowed democratically to express their dissent from the bid for secession and remain part of Russia. The territory that remained after the withdrawal of the Ingush was a clearly defined area where the majority of the population shared language, customs, religion and historical experience – maximally satisfying most of the criteria laid out in UN General

---

[18] Though they are very distinct cases, there are nonetheless some instructive parallels between the Chechen and Eritrean struggles for self-determination – including their total isolation from the outside world, eventual attainment of sovereignty, and subsequent slide once again into war. The key difference is that the Eritreans gained full international recognition, and a UN seat. See Michela Wrong, *I Didn't Do It For You: How the World Used and Abused a Small African Nation*, London 2005.

Assembly Resolution 753, unlike nearly all of the African states admitted to the UN since 1945. The Chechens, then, formed an identifiably distinct population within an agreed set of geographical boundaries, and the majority of them had given their assent to a declaration of sovereignty for which there were solid constitutional grounds according to the legislation of the USSR itself.

Given these facts, why did Chechnya not secure international recognition? Here we must face the total inconsistency of international practice. *Uti possidetis* did not apply to the Partition of India in 1948, nor has it to Palestine at any point since the same year. Though secession *tout court* has often been verbally discouraged by UN chiefs and heads of state alike, there have been so many exceptions as to make its exclusion on principle an entirely empty gesture. Several African states recognized the breakaway Republic of Biafra in 1967–70, while France, Portugal and Israel provided material support. After the fall of the Berlin Wall, the Western powers were only too happy to see the Baltic States escape Soviet dominion. In November 1991, the European Community's Badinter Commission concluded that the secessions of Slovenia and Croatia should be recognized simply because Yugoslavia was anyway 'in a process of dissolution' – a 'radical, if tautological, position' that marked 'an attempt to reconcile EC political interests and international customary law'.[19] The alacrity with which Germany, in particular, recognized Slovenia and Croatia played a crucial role in the further disintegration of that state. The UN Protectorate in Kosovo has produced another de facto independent state, with the full backing of the 'international community', but again in contravention of *uti possidetis*.

The reality is that international validation of secession depends on factors beyond mere legitimacy and popular will. If the doctrine of *uti possidetis* slants the terms for secession in favour of colonial states, it can also be overridden where realpolitik demands. As Tom Nairn has observed, the strictures of international law defend 'the sacredness of every existing frontier' – a principle which, though it 'may sometimes protect the weak from the strong and hungry . . . also defends the strong from the weak and hungry'.[20] In the case of Chechnya, a broadly

[19] Hughes, 'Peace Process', p. 270.
[20] Nairn, 'Internationalism and the Second Coming', in Gopal Balakrishnan, ed., *Mapping the Nation*, London and New York 1996, p. 278.

legitimate and constitutional secession went unrecognized because it ran counter to the interests of Russia, a Security Council member and still a significant player on the world stage, albeit one facing formidable political, economic and social crises after the collapse of the USSR. The willingness of the 'international community' to first deny recognition of Chechen sovereignty, and then overlook or in many cases actually support the Russian invasion of Chechnya, has no basis in international law, and should be seen as a conscious political choice. It is one whose consequences are still echoing in the minds of Chechnya's immiserated citizens, and in the battle-blasted streets of Grozny.

3.

Yeltsin's Vietnam

When Russian tanks rolled into Chechnya on 11 December 1994, few expected the outcome to be a brutal twenty-month war that would kill upwards of 45,000 people, turning Grozny into a scene of post-apocalyptic devastation and leaving the republic's infrastructure in tatters. Announced as an operation to 'restore constitutional order', the Russian invasion rapidly turned into a military disaster, and eventually resulted in a humiliating withdrawal that many saw as heralding Russia's demise as a great power.[1] The Chechens' success in fighting the Russian army to a standstill was one of the most remarkable feats of modern warfare. No less remarkable were the political and strategic miscalculations that led the Russian authorities to opt for military intervention – and the staggering disproportion between the force deployed and the ends supposedly being sought.

The principal justifications offered in support of Yeltsin's assault on Chechnya centre on the need to rein in a rogue enclave, both to restore the rule of law and to maintain Russia's territorial integrity, said to be

---

[1] As conveyed by the title of Anatol Lieven's *Chechnya: Tombstone of Russian Power*, London 1998. The heading for this chapter is taken, with apologies, from David Remnick's *Resurrection*, New York 1997.

at risk of fragmenting into dozens of pieces should Chechnya's bid for independence succeed. Further rationales for the invasion have been sought in geostrategic considerations and criminal conspiracies, while many have focused on more contingent factors of Kremlin politics – the most cynical version being, in the words of Security Council Secretary Oleg Lobov, that 'we need a small, victorious war to raise the President's ratings.'[2] None of these motivations remotely justifies the avalanche of bombs and terror unleashed on Chechnya in 1994–6, which smashed the prospect of a viable Chechen state and effectively prepared the ground for the return of war in 1999. Moreover, all the arguments put forward to legitimize the invasion rest on a series of false assumptions about the political and economic situation of Dudaev's Chechnya, the character of the Chechen resistance, and the potential for secession of Russia's federal components. In order to assess the scale and degree of deliberation behind Yeltsin's disastrous error, we need to tackle these three aspects in turn.

Journalists visiting Chechnya in the years of de facto independence under Dudaev reported from a 'twilight zone, neither inside Russia nor outside it'. The rouble was still the currency, people still carried Soviet passports, and there were no signposts at the border announcing arrival in a separate state – and yet there were no Russian flags anywhere, nor Soviet troops, the last Red Army units having been withdrawn in June 1992.[3] This ambiguous state of affairs was the product of Chechnya's liminal status as an unrecognized territory operating beyond the reach of Moscow, a condition which had serious political, economic and social consequences.

Chechnya under Dudaev had a contested political scene, with a highly mobilized population taking part in numerous demonstrations and counter-demonstrations. The parliament 'proved a lively debating

---

[2] Reported by the liberal Duma member Sergei Yushenkov, in Carlotta Gall and Thomas de Waal, *Chechnya: A Small Victorious War*, London 1997, p. 161. Lobov apparently added that Clinton had recently done the same in Haiti and succeeded. The phrase echoes Interior Minister Viacheslav Pleve's advice to Nicholas II prior to the Russo-Japanese war of 1904–5, which should have given Lobov pause.

[3] Gall and de Waal point out that at this time Russian troops were still in place in the rest of the Eastern bloc: *Small Victorious War*, p. 106.

chamber and the press was vigorous and uncensored'.[4] Support for Dudaev came above all from rural areas, where ethno-nationalist appeals to tradition resonated more strongly, and where religious practices marked the culture more than in Grozny. It was doubtless with a view to his highland constituency that Dudaev in 1994 renamed Chechnya the Chechen Republic of Ichkeria, after a mountain region that had been the centre of resistance to Russian rule in the nineteenth century.

Opposition to Dudaev, however, had begun even before the November 1991 declaration of independence. Parallel to the demonstrations that had powered him to the presidency, there were large public gatherings in central Grozny, which continued up until the Russian invasion. Dudaev's opponents from the outset included much of the Chechen middle class, especially Grozny's more educated layers, many of whom rejected his maximalist approach in favour of more gradualist tactics for separation from Russia. Together with Chechens from the northern lowlands, they had generally benefited more from the Soviet system than their rural countrymen, and hence stood to lose more from its dismantling. But it is worth noting that even those vehemently opposed to Dudaev in this period insisted on independence. A *Moscow News* reporter asserted in November 1992 that 'at present there are no forces in Chechnya supporting federative realations with Russia nor are there any who want to restore the republic's former autonomous status.' In 1995, Khalid Delmaev, an anti-Dudaev Chechen liberal, told readers of the same newspaper that 'Chechnya's statehoos may be postponed . . . but it cannot be avoided'.[5]

The opposition to Dudaev stemmed largely from factors other than his stance on sovereignty. His considerable personal eccentricities played a part: he often made bizarre statements and brash gestures, such as decreeing Chechnya should be one hour behind Moscow time, to be closer to Europe, or offering asylum to Erich Honecker. He was also prone to bouts of paranoia, announcing on one occasion that Moscow intended to destabilize Chechnya by artificially creating earthquakes. More significant were his criminal connections: two of his key early supporters were Bislan Gantemirov, a former black marketeer who was

---

[4] Gall and de Waal, *Small Victorious War*, p. 106.
[5] *Moscow News*, 22–29 November 1992; 1–7 September 1995.

appointed mayor of Grozny, and Yusup Soslambekov, who had been imprisoned for rape; the wealthy gangster Khozh-Akhmed Nukhaev provided financial backing, while the convicted murderer Ruslan Labazanov joined Dudaev's Presidential Guard in 1992. These and other leading figures who had initially been Dudaev's allies split from him one after another, as political tensions grew and Chechnya's economic slide led to heightened competition over limited spoils.

Dudaev's choice of economic policy was largely determined by the priority he gave to the question of sovereignty. He had attempted to set an independent course, placing his hopes, according to his Finance Minister Taimaz Abubakarov, in a romantically exaggerated notion of Chechnya's resources.[6] Some of his decisions were based on ideas that were becoming outmoded elsewhere in the former Soviet Union: for instance, he resolved that the price of bread in Chechnya should remain at a symbolic 1 rouble – which led to widespread speculation in this basic commodity when prices were freed in Russia in January 1992, as Chechen traders could make enormous profits simply by driving to a market across the border. Setting prices in Chechnya made little sense when most goods had anyway to be purchased in roubles in Russia. But the shortages Dudaev's policy created were exacerbated by a Russian blockade that, though easily circumvented, worked in favour of black marketeers and stretched ordinary Chechens' meagre resources still further.

Statist allegiances also partly explain Dudaev's resistance to pressure from Chechen elites – notably Salambek Khadzhiev, former Soviet petrochemicals minister – to privatize state property. According to Dudaev, who observed events in Russia after Anatoly Chubais's 'voucherization' with alarm, privatization would not only disperse the few resources his newly sovereign state possessed, but would also unleash turf-wars among powerful political players in Chechnya. The instability wrought in Russia by the 'shock therapy' of the early 1990s, meanwhile, led Dudaev to push for a separate Chechen currency – against the advice of Abubakarov, who pointed out that Chechnya lacked the reserves to back it.[7] But, propelled by the notion that a sovereign state should have its own currency, Dudaev

---

[6] Taimaz Abubakarov, *Rezhim Dzhokhara Dudaeva: pravda i vymysel*, Moscow 1998, p. 18. Dudaev apparently had visions of Chechnya as the Kuwait of the Caucasus.

[7] Abubakarov, *Rezhim Dzhokhara Dudaeva*, pp. 36, 49, 118–20.

had *nakhar* notes in several denominations printed, and they were only prevented from coming into circulation by the outbreak of war.

Dudaev's insistence on maximum sovereignty led to severe economic problems. Stressing the need to maintain Chechnya's independence, he refused any accommodation with Moscow on tax revenues, leading to a banking blockade as of early 1992 – as a result of which the Chechen National Bank was unable to conduct any legitimate transactions with the outside world.[8] The same blockade meant payments for Chechnya's industrial products became a complicated matter, and surely accounts for much of the drop in industrial production in Chechnya, which fell by 30 per cent in 1992 and by 61 per cent in 1993.[9] Some of this decline was also due to the emigration of tens of thousands of ethnic Russians, many of them key specialists in the oil industry, who left out of fear of ethnic antagonism – of which there was a regrettable amount, since non-Chechens were unprotected by clan networks and hence more vulnerable to crime.[10] But oil continued to flow in and out of Grozny's refineries during the Dudaev years, at the rate of 15m tonnes in 1991, falling to 9.7m in 1992 and 3.5m in 1993.[11]

With the official economy deadlocked and awash with unbankable cash, informalized trade and corruption expanded exponentially. Dudaev lifted all taxes on profits and eased restrictions on the small trade many engaged in to make ends meet. Grozny became a commercial hub, its market drawing people from across the Caucasus and giving rise to a wealth of 'shuttle traders', who would take one of two flights leaving Grozny daily for Dubai, Turkey or even China, and return with electronic goods on which they would pay no duties – as compared to the 20–30 per cent due in Russia.[12] There was also a lucrative trade in armaments, many of them purchased or looted from the retreating

---

[8] Abubakarov, *Rezhim Dzhokhara Dudaeva*, p. 151. Gall and de Waal report that the chairman of Chechnya's Central Bank had to cash a cheque in Istanbul and return carrying $4m in cash in two cardboard boxes: *Small Victorious War*, p. 135.

[9] Dunlop, *Russia Confronts Chechnya*, p. 126.

[10] According to the Russian Federal Migration Service, 90,000 people left Chechnya in 1991–3, the bulk of them ethnic Russians or Ukrainians. Valery Tishkov, *Chechnya: Life in a War-Torn Society*, Berkeley/Los Angeles 2004, p. 65.

[11] Sebastian Smith, *Allah's Mountains: The Battle for Chechnya*, London 2001, p. 131.

[12] Gall and de Waal, *Small Victorious War*, p. 132.

Soviet Army – the former arrangement famously agreed to by the then Deputy Defence Minister Pavel Grachev. Other criminal activities flourished – including train robberies and, most notoriously, a case in 1992 where Chechens forged 60bn roubles' (then $700m) worth of promissory notes (*avizos*) and managed to collect 40m roubles in cash from Russian banks before the authorities were alerted. The most profitable racket to be run in Grozny involved the sale of oil for export. The official profit from oil sales for 1993 was estimated at $800–900m, much of which may well have disappeared into the pockets of ministers to whom Dudaev delegated control of the industry – suspicions fell on Gantemirov and the businessman Yaragi Mamodaev – though the actual figures could in any case be higher.[13]

Such were the activities the Russian invasion of 1994 was supposed to curtail. But a crucial feature of nearly all of them is that they required the collusion of officials in Russia. Flights in and out of Grozny would have needed clearance to cross Russian airspace; export licences for oil would still have to be granted in Moscow; arms trading would not have been possible without commanders willing to part with weapons for cash. In the case of the *avizo* scandal, Stephen Handelman has observed that 'the volume of promissory notes required for the swindle implied collusion with bankers and businessmen elsewhere in the country'; sure enough, four Russian Central Bank officials were arrested in connection with the case in 1993.[14] It is worth noting that, when all other Russian representatives had withdrawn, the Trade Ministry kept an envoy in Grozny. When asked in 1996 to what extent Chechnya's 'free economic zone' was nurtured in Moscow, Sergei Shakhrai, who had been Russian Deputy Prime Minister at the time, said '100 per cent'.[15] Despite official protests from Moscow at the concentration of lawlessness in Chechnya, it was a convenient gap in the fiscal fence for criminals, businessmen and officials from across the former Soviet Union, and the larceny taking place within its boundaries was an outgrowth of the orgy of theft then gripping Russia itself.

Russian complaints about Chechnya's 'free economic zone' are further

---

[13] Gall and de Waal, *Small Victorious War*, p. 128.
[14] Stephen Handelman, *Comrade Criminal: The Theft of the Second Russian Revolution*, London 1993, p. 119.
[15] Gall and de Waal, *Small Victorious War*, p. 125.

undermined by the fact that, as pressure was ramped up on Dudaev, Moscow awarded precisely this status to neighbouring Ingushetia. Thanks to Decree No. 36 of 19 June 1994, dozens of companies could freely avoid taxes and launder money through commercial banks located on Russia's Caucasian periphery.[16] Moreover, the Caucasus was not the only region where Russia's laws proved as porous as its borders. There were frequent train robberies and hold-ups in the northwest, and metals and minerals were regularly smuggled into the Baltic States. According to one estimate, 10 per cent of all the metals and oil smuggled out of Russia in 1992 went through the Baltics, and in 1993 over $35m worth of non-ferrous metals crossed into Estonia, most of it illegally. Trainloads of oil heading through Lithuania to the Russian enclave of Kaliningrad disappeared almost daily.[17] Public attention in Russia, however, was focused on the Caucasus as the fount of criminality – empirically verifiable, for many, in the prominence of Azeri, Armenian, Georgian and Chechen gangs in Russia's major cities. The Chechens were neither the most numerous nor most successful of these; but their tight-knit discipline and fearful reputation magnified them into the archetype of the gangster in the contemporary Russian imaginary. Such popular preconceptions proved a powerful ally in the Russian authorities' propaganda offensive against Dudaev.

Dudaev's government was certainly guilty of economic mismanagement. But set in regional context, Chechnya's economic nosedive and burgeoning criminality after 1991 come to seem part of a wider catastrophic trend. Many of its woes stemmed directly from the Russian blockade, and from structural problems common to several post-Soviet states. With the fall of the Soviet Union, the links between factories and their raw materials and markets were broken, leaving many sovereign states with only fragments of a real economy. In these conditions, and with inflation rampant, the informal sector came to account for a vast proportion of economic life. This was particularly true in the southern tier of the Union, which was less industrialized, suffered large-scale

[16] Mark Whitehouse, 'From War Zone to Tax Haven', *Moscow Times*, 4 March 1997.
[17] Svetlana Glinkina, 'Privatizatsiya and Kriminalizatsiya' (1994), in Mark Galeotti, ed., *Russian and Post-Soviet Organized Crime*, Aldershot 2002, p. 253.

structural unemployment and hence had a far larger informal sector than other parts of the USSR. In Transcaucasia, which includes the Soviet successor states most comparable to Chechnya, there were abrupt shrinkages of GDP: 35 per cent in Azerbaijan between 1991–2, and 23 per cent in 1992–3; 40 and 32 per cent respectively in Georgia, 52 and 15 per cent in Armenia. Industrial production decreased by 44 per cent in Georgia in 1992, and the relevant figures for Armenia and Azerbaijan are 48 and 24 per cent.

The Transcaucasian region provides further, telling points of comparison. Both Georgia and Azerbaijan elected nationalist leaders uncongenial to Moscow – Zviad Gamsakhurdia took office in Tbilisi in 1991, and Abulfaz Elchibey in Baku in 1992. Both were nationalists of a populist bent, Elchibey being especially threatening to Russian interests, since he planned to exclude Russia from oil deals being signed by his newly independent country. Gamsakhurdia was deposed in a 1992 coup in which Russian involvement is widely alleged; Elchibey was toppled in 1993 by a rebellion which happened to coincide with the withdrawal of Russian troops from a base in the city of Ganja. Even with Gamsakhurdia gone, Russia continued to undermine the new Georgian government of Eduard Shevardnadze by supplying arms and weapons to the secessionist region of Abkhazia, where many of the Chechen field commanders who would fight the Russians in 1994–6 – among them Shamil Basaev – received training from Russian military intelligence (GRU) and gained vital combat experience. Again, in this regional context, Chechnya's political instability becomes part of a pattern of post-Soviet turmoil, much of it inspired and directed by Moscow.

The first overt move against Dudaev came in late March 1992, with an attack on the national TV centre that was repelled after a day, with five casualties. The putsch had been announced in advance by Russian media, and Moscow's involvement seems likely.[18] The ramping up of dissent during 1993, however, emerged as part of a struggle between

---

[18] Gall and de Waal, *Small Victorious War*, p. 114; Robert Seely, *Russo-Chechen Conflict, 1800–2000: A Deadly Embrace*, London 2001, p. 118. Seely, a former Kiev correspondent for the London Times, devotes the middle third of his book to the period 1991–4, giving a crisp, well-informed account of the Dudaev regime.

rival centres of power, gathered around the presidency on the one hand, and parliament on the other. After an opposition demonstration in mid-April openly called for his departure, Dudaev dissolved parliament and declared presidential rule – leading his opponents to name an alternative government under Mamodaev. The opposition called a referendum for 5 June on Dudaev's presidency, and held rallies in central Grozny outside the Town Assembly building – Gantemirov's power-base. Pro-Dudaev gatherings took place a few hundred metres away, and both turned into permanent demonstrations. On 2 June, Dudaev arrived to address his opponents, and was greeted by catcalls and shots fired into the air; as he departed the scene, one of his bodyguards was shot in the back. The next day he dissolved the Constitutional Court, which had backed Mamodaev, and on 4 June moved to disperse the opposition by force. Fighters led by Shamil Basaev seized the Town Assembly building, with tanks and machine-gun fire taking at least twenty lives, though the opposition puts the tally at sixty. As Gall and de Waal observe, 'whatever the real death toll, it was the first mass bloodshed in Chechnya and destroyed the hope of democratic dialogue. From now most overt opposition to Dudaev was violent.'[19]

Dudaev clearly deserves much blame for crushing dissent by these means – and for such scenes as followed in Sheikh Mansur Square, where a bonfire was made of voting slips for the opposition's referendum. But those who view this as a unique and intolerable infringement of democratic prerogatives should note the parallel between Dudaev's actions and Yeltsin's only a few months later. In October 1993, confronted with a hostile Supreme Soviet and facing political deadlock, he ordered tanks to shell his elected opponents into submission. The ensuing violence killed at least 150, and Yeltsin used the hushed aftermath to ram through an ultra-presidential constitution, approved by a rigged referendum – to general applause from the West.

Moreover, the Chechen opposition had armed its supporters and made the first move in what rapidly became a physical rather than polit-ical battle. It should also be recalled that, unlike Yeltsin's opponents Rutskoi and Khasbulatov, the Chechen opposition to Dudaev was being

---

[19] Gall and de Waal, *Small Victorious War*, p. 120. See also Bennett, *Crying Wolf*, p. 286.

actively funded and encouraged by an aggressive foreign power. There can be little doubt that Russia had a hand in Chechnya's rising political turbulence. Violence escalated in the autumn of 1993, with grenade attacks on transformer stations in October, unclaimed bombs in government buildings in November, and armed opposition gunmen surrounding the presidential palace in December. Attempts to assassinate Dudaev failed, but several areas of the republic moved into open defiance of his rule, and it was clear the stakes were being raised.

As noted earlier, the forces ranged against Dudaev were generally in favour of independence; the parliament which opposed him, for instance, still protested when the new Russian Constitution approved in December 1993 included Chechnya as part of federal territory.[20] All the more appallingly shortsighted, then, the opposition's strategy of collusion with the Kremlin in order to dispose of Dudaev. The risks posed to Chechen sovereignty by Russian involvement should have been apparent by the summer of 1993, given that Moscow had twice previously threatened an invasion. On the first occasion, in November 1991, it was foiled by a combination of popular mobilization and foot-dragging by Gorbachev. The second came in the autumn of 1992, when a dispute between Ingush and North Ossetians over the Prigorodny region – awarded to the latter when Stalin deported the Ingush in 1944 – turned into open conflict. Russian troops moved in ostensibly to keep the peace, but in fact merely presided over the expulsion of over 60,000 Ingush from land they had re-settled on their return from exile, in what was 'in essence a Russian-managed pogrom'.[21] In November, under cover of this deployment, Russian tanks rumbled towards the as yet undemarcated Ingush–Chechen border, hoping to provoke Dudaev into an attack. Dudaev declared neutrality in the dispute and organized his forces defensively, and after a tense stand-off Moscow backed down.[22]

At the beginning of 1994 Umar Avturkhanov, head of the administration of Nadterechny region in the northern plains of Chechnya, formed the Chechen Provisional Council. It spent the next few months

---

[20] Seely, *Russo-Chechen Conflict*, p. 154.
[21] Seely, *Russo-Chechen Conflict*, p. 135.
[22] Seely, *Russo-Chechen Conflict*, p. 136–7; Gall and de Waal, *Small Victorious War*, p. 117.

skirmishing with Dudaev and lobbying Moscow to be recognized as the legitimate government of Chechnya, and by the summer of that year had begun to be provided with money and weapons by the Russian Federal Counter-Intelligence Service (FSK). Russia was at this point pursuing a dualistic, if not duplicitous strategy towards Dudaev, with one arm of the state proposing negotiations over a federal treaty while another engaged in covert operations aimed at disposing of him. The rival factions of Yeltsin's government each seemed to have a different approach, which each was implementing at the same time. Thus while the Kremlin responded positively, if vaguely, to the idea of a Russian–Chechen summit in the spring of 1994, in May of that year a car-bomb narrowly failed to kill Dudaev in Grozny. Attempts by officials of the Nationalities Ministry to establish contact with Dudaev were thwarted by Ruslan Khasbulatov, until October 1993 chairman of the Supreme Soviet, and a longstanding foe of Dudaev.[23]

Much has been written about the intricacies and intriguing behind the Kremlin walls in the run-up to war. For some, the sidelining of the liberals in Yeltsin's team in favour of more hawkish figures in November 1994 accounts for the abrupt shift towards the use of force – Yeltsin having decisively ruled out military intervention as late as 4 October. But this is to overlook the immediate trigger for the invasion: the failure of yet another covert attempt to topple Dudaev. Responsibility for this lies with the FSK, whose initial plan of simply arming Avturkhanov to the teeth and letting his militia topple Dudaev had to be revised, once it became clear that their proxy had no popular support. Russian assistance gradually increased: when Avturkhanov's forces advanced on Grozny in August 1994 and were beaten back by Chechen government troops, the Russians provided helicopter support to cover his retreat.[24] The first Russian casualty of the war died on 28 September, when his helicopter was fired on during an attack on Chechen government forces; Moscow denied the event took place.[25] But Russian involvement was stepped up: the FSK secretly recruited Russian soldiers for a tank column, which entered Grozny on 26 November 1994 – and was

[23] Gall and de Waal, *Small Victorious War*, pp. 114-5.
[24] Seely, *Russo-Chechen Conflict*, pp. 155, 162; Gall and de Waal, *Small Victorious War*, pp. 151–2.
[25] Gall and de Waal, *Small Victorious War*, pp. 151.

immediately captured by pro-Dudaev forces, the FSK's erstwhile Chechen allies having scattered to loot the city.

The Russians again denied involvement, but the appearance of the soldiers on television, held captive in Dudaev's presidential palace, provided incontrovertible proof. The covert strategy had proved a fiasco; Yeltsin reportedly opted for all-out war only two days later, and in the meantime delivered an ultimatum to Dudaev's forces to surrender.[26] Bombing began at the end of November, though once again the Kremlin denied the planes were Russian. Rallies against the war took place in Grozny, and there were last-minute attempts to mediate, not least a meeting between Dudaev and Defence Minister Grachev on 6 December, after which Dudaev agreed to release the captive soldiers. But on 7 December the Security Council gave final approval to the invasion, and four days later, 40,000 Russian troops entered Chechnya.

The Russian analysts Dmitri Trenin and Aleksei Malashenko have called the 26 November incursion 'Yeltsin's equivalent of the Bay of Pigs'.[27] More than a military blunder, it revealed fundamental errors at the heart of Russian policy towards Chechnya. The FSK's analysis, for instance, focused on the Chechens' decentralized *taip* structures, and saw political developments before and after 1991 as the playing out of inter-clan rivalries – almost as if in echo of Moscow's own Byzantine convolutions. Apart from treating *taips* as fixed primordial units, 'the FSK picture completely ignored the immense uniting power of Chechen nationalism'.[28] As noted earlier, even Dudaev's opponents were in favour of independence, and though he may not have been a universally popular or even competent leader, the bulk of the Chechen population would sooner tolerate his faults than welcome a Russian invasion. The strength of popular support for independence was what nourished the formidable Chechen resistance; Russia's refusal to recognize the magnitude of that support was what cost so many lives.

*   *   *

[26] The Security Council met on 29 November simply to approve the decision. The vote was unanimous, though Justice Minister Yuri Kalmykov – an ethnic Circassian – resigned immediately afterwards. See Gall and de Waal, *Small Victorious War*, pp. 157–60.

[27] Dmitri Trenin and Aleksei Malashenko, with Anatol Lieven, *Russia's Restless Frontier: The Chechnya Factor in Post-Soviet Russia*, Washington, D.C. 2004, p. 21.

[28] Lieven, *Chechnya*, pp. 335–9.

The Russian invasion force encountered resistance even before it had reached Chechnya. Two of the three tank columns planning to converge on Grozny from the west, north-west and east were blocked by civilian protestors in Dagestan and Ingushetia, where clashes resulted in the death of the Ingush Health Minister. Major-General Ivan Babichev's men were delayed by a crowd of Chechen women, on whom he refused to fire. Russian forces slowly advanced towards Grozny, but a fortnight had elapsed before they were ready to move into the city. When they did, they met resistance of a ferocity they had clearly not expected. The battle for Grozny began on New Year's Eve. Russian conscripts, poorly trained, ill-equipped and badly organized, were picked off by highly mobile and well-armed Chechen groups, many of them spontaneously generated and reporting to no central command. Russian losses were enormous: as many as 1,500 were killed in the assault on Grozny, in which, according to one estimate, they lost more tanks than in the 1945 capture of Berlin.[29]

It took two months for federal forces to take full control of the city. During this time, Grozny was subjected to a terrifyingly intense bombardment: one observer counted 4,000 detonations in one hour, compared to around 3,500 a day in Sarajevo.[30] The amount of ordnance dropped on a city with an estimated Russian population of 200,000 makes a mockery of subsequent Russian solicitude for their ethnic kin; whatever the ills of Dudaev's rule, they pale into insignificance beside the 27,000 civilians reportedly killed in the taking of Grozny.[31] The city's population halved as its inhabitants fled to the countryside – or left Chechnya altogether: Ingushetia took in 90,000 refugees, and Dagestan also provided shelter for many.

Chechen government forces finally withdrew from Grozny on 7 March, but instead of heading for the mountains, began to organize resistance village by village. The Russians responded to this surprisingly dogged opposition with a massive escalation of violence against the entire population. Early in 1995 a series of 'filtration camps' was established to detain combatants, or indeed any males of fighting age; it developed into a network with centres in Mozdok, Grozny, Pyatigorsk and Stavropol, with smaller camps scattered across the Chechen

[29] Gall and de Waal, *Small Victorious War*, pp. 16, 18.
[30] Gall and de Waal, *Small Victorious War*, pp. 219, 395–6 n. 14.
[31] Gall and de Waal, *Small Victorious War*, pp. 197, 227.

countryside.[32] Thousands disappeared into torture cells and mass graves. As Gall and Waal observe, 'the "constitutional order" the Russians had promised to impose on Chechnya had turned into a horrible orgy of violence against the civilian population.'[33]

The most searing instance of what had become a war against the Chechen people came on 6–8 April 1995 in the village of Samashki, where Russian Interior Ministry troops killed over 100 civilians, many of them at point-blank range, in a drug-fuelled rampage.[34] Such brutality served only to ignite further resistance, and for many Chechens the war became a struggle for national self-preservation. Audio cassettes with recordings of resistance songs – 'Freedom or Death', 'Chechnya in Flames', 'Wolf Trails' – began to circulate.[35] The core of active fighters during the 1994–6 war may not have been very large; possibly as few as 1,000 conducted the defence of Grozny. But the Chechens could not have fought for as long as they did without consistent material and moral support from the populace at large. With no real backing from any external power, the Chechen resistance was an entirely self-sustained entity: weapons were acquired in battle or else by purchasing them from corrupt or hungry Russian servicemen; logistical help came at village level, and command structures often mapped onto clan allegiances. The Russian invasion provided the stimulus for a largely spontaneous national military mobilization.

Nevertheless, superior Russian firepower was having its effect, and in the spring of 1995 the Russians crossed the strategically vital Argun river and took the towns of Shali and Gudermes. By the end of May they were in control of the plains and, with the Chechen government holed up in the mountains, a decisive military breakthrough began to look possible. It was at this point that Shamil Basaev undertook his raid on Budennovsk, seizing a hospital on 14 June and taking over a thousand hostages. A busload of heavily armed Chechens had apparently bribed their way 100 miles into Russia, and now demanded a cessation of hostilities and the withdrawal of Russian troops. A bungled attempt to storm the hospital resulted in the death of 121 hostages, and Prime Minister Viktor Chernomyrdin began negotiations with Basaev which

---

[32] Bennett, *Crying Wolf,* p. 400.
[33] Gall and de Waal, *Small Victorious War,* p. 233.
[34] Gall and de Waal, *Small Victorious War,* pp. 242–7.
[35] Bennett, *Crying Wolf,* p. 510.

provided vital breathing space for the Chechens. The raid's audacity was matched only by its ruthlessness. Many of the freed Russian hostages, however, aimed their anger not at their captors but at the government overseeing the devastation that had now been brought so close to them.

The bloodshed in Budennovsk was followed by a strange period in which some disarmament took place, and there were even joint patrols between Chechen and Russian forces as senior figures on each side kept to a truce – although a political settlement remained out of view. Good will began to evaporate, however, when Russian planes started to bomb the mountains in August, and hostilities resumed in full in the autumn. According to Russia's Human Rights Commissioner Sergei Kovalev – a strong critic of the war – the prime aggravating factor was Moscow's insistence on holding elections in Chechnya in December 1995.[36] That spring, the Kremlin had set up a puppet government under Khadzhiev, with Avturkhanov as his deputy and Gantemirov once again mayor of Grozny. By the autumn they had decided to replace Khadzhiev with their old favourite Doku Zavgaev, who was duly installed after a ballot in which few Chechens participated – though Russian soldiers did vote, as did many Western journalists. Chechen resistance attacks aimed at disrupting polling in Russian-controlled Urus-Martan and Gudermes turned into pitched battles, and the war rumbled into life once more.

Zavgaev's puppet regime had no support besides that of the occupying power. Indeed, he was nicknamed Doku Aeroportovich because he spent so little time outside the Russian airbase at Khankala.[37] More importantly, his administration was so larcenous as to make Dudaev's seem a paragon of virtue: in the first two months, Zavgaev was allocated 12.3 trillion roubles, 11.2 trillion of which could not legally be accounted for, according to a subsequent report by the Russian Audit Committee.[38] Claims that the invasion was aimed at restoring the rule of law crumble before the reality of Russian policy: its first allies were the very criminals and corrupt officials responsible for the Dudaev regime's shady reputation, and the men Moscow put in charge of administering Chechnya stole more money than Dudaev could have even imagined.

Dudaev remained a potent symbol of Chechen independence, and

[36] Gall and de Waal, *Small Victorious War*, pp. 287–8.
[37] Bennett, *Crying Wolf*, p. 467.
[38] Gall and de Waal, *Small Victorious War*, pp. 314–15.

came to represent far more than his questionable talents justified. Likewise his Presidential Palace, focal point of the initial defence of Grozny. In early February 1996, tens of thousands came to Grozny from villages and towns across Chechnya to protest against the war, camping out for a week outside the ruins of the Palace and demanding the withdrawal of Russian troops. It was 'a remarkable, spontaneous demonstration which thoroughly alarmed Zavgaev'.[39] He had to call in masked riot police, who killed ten people in dispersing the crowd. The remnants of the Presidential Palace were razed to the ground a few days later.

By the spring of 1996 the Chechens had established a single command structure, set in place by the Chief of Staff Aslan Maskhadov, a former Soviet artillery colonel who had served in Hungary, the Baltics and the Soviet Far East, and returned to Chechnya in 1992. With their fighters much more disciplined and better organized, the Chechens began to infiltrate the plains once more, and from 6–9 March carried out a daring raid on Grozny, virtually taking control of the city before melting away into the hills. The attack demonstrated that, for all their manpower, the Russians had been unable to choke off the resistance. The high Russian casualty rate had sapped morale in the military, and Russian media coverage of the war consistently presented the public with images of worn-down, teenage boys being sent to a senseless death. A small but persistent anti-war movement took root, amidst widespread public discontent. The notion of withdrawal from Chechnya became increasingly popular – something Yeltsin could ill afford to ignore, with electoral disaster looming: a presidential poll was due in June, and his popularity rating was in the single figures.

In the run-up to the election, Russian policy once again swerved between offers of dialogue and all-out assault. A day after it was announced that either Yeltsin or Chernomyrdin would meet with Dudaev for talks, Yeltsin ordered the assassination of the Chechen president, carried out by rocket attack on 22 April. The acting President Zelimkhan Yandarbiev went to Moscow to agree a ceasefire and exchange of prisoners on 27 May; the next day Yeltsin appeared in Chechnya on the campaign trail, telling troops that the war was won, and that the 'bandit groups' had been 'annihilated'. Though he fell short of the

---

required 50 per cent in the first round of voting on 16 June, Yeltsin won the run-off on 9 July, and aerial bombardment of Chechnya recommenced almost immediately.

The Russians were forced to the negotiating table, however, by the Chechen offensive on Grozny, Gudermes and Argun of early August – timed to coincide with the specially abridged inauguration ceremony through which Yeltsin stumbled on 9 August. With the Chechens now once again in control of much of the capital, the Russian military had been forced back to its positions of December 1994. On 14 August Yeltsin dispatched General Aleksandr Lebed – his defeated rival in the presidential race, whom Yeltsin had brought into his government to secure his support for the second round – to open discussions with Maskhadov. Despite some last-minute brinkmanship by the hawkish General Pulikovsky, who gave the inhabitants of Grozny 48 hours to leave the city, Maskhadov and Lebed agreed a ceasefire on 21 August. By the end of the month, Russian troops had pulled out of Grozny, and on 31 August 1996 Lebed and Maskhadov signed the Khasavyurt Accords, which rejected the use of force to settle future disputes between Russia and Chechnya and recognized Chechnya as a subject of international law, but postponed a final decision on its status until the end of 2001.

The first Russo-Chechen war was a humiliating defeat for the Russians and, despite their victory, a cataclysm for the Chechens. Conservative estimates record 7,500 Russian military casualties, 4,000 Chechen combatants and no less than 35,000 civilians – a minimum total of 46,500; others have cited figures in the range of 80,000 to 100,000.[40] Little remained of central Grozny except rubble, and the countryside had been devastated by warfare of a ferocity unmatched in these lands since the Second World War. The subsequent fortunes of Maskhadov's Chechnya, de facto independent after 1996, will be the subject of the next chapter. But what of the argument that Chechnya's secession had to be crushed, lest it set off a chain of separatist moves in the rest of Russia? In Chechnya, the war produced precisely the outcome it was supposed to avert. The price of the Chechens' success has arguably dissuaded any of Russia's

[40] John Dunlop, 'How Many Soldiers and Civilians Died During the Russo-Chechen War of 1994–1996?', *Central Asian Survey*, vol. 19, nos 3–4 (September 2000), pp. 329–39.

other ethnic territories from attempting the same. But had further bids for independence been likely in the first place?

The idea that Russia would unravel were one of its constituent parts to secede is essentially an internal version of the Cold War trope of the 'domino effect'. It rests on precarious foundations. Robert Wade has suggested that the likelihood of secession increases 'the more that three conditions are met: location on a non-Russia border; population with non-Russian majority; a plausible export revenue base'.[41] To take the second of these, demography: of Soviet Russia's thirty-one titular ethnic republics, in 1991 only four had an absolute majority of the titular groups – North Ossetia, Tuva, Checheno-Ingushetia and Chuvashia – while three had a simple majority: Tatarstan, Kabardino-Balkaria, Kalmykia. Russians formed the majority of the population in the rest. Economically, all but two of the seven republics listed above were heavily dependent on the federal budget; only Tatarstan, a major manufacturing centre which produced 25 per cent of the country's oil, and Checheno-Ingushetia, which produced 90 per cent of Russia's kerosene, were net contributors.[42] Only these two republics refused to sign federal treaties with Russia in 1992.

Tatarstan is frequently cited as a positive model, the peaceful road not taken in Chechnya. The two are superficially comparable in certain respects: a population with Islamic traditions, a nationalist movement emerging from the informal organizations of the *perestroika* period, plentiful oil and guns. But the differences are far more significant. Geographical location is one – Tatarstan is entirely surrounded by Russia, making a bid for total separation extremely impractical. Second, the Tatars did not have a historical tradition of resistance to Russian rule, or a traumatic event of such recent memory as the deportations of 1944. Thirdly, the Tatars were much more integrated into the Soviet order than the Chechens, having similar levels of education and population growth to their Russian co-citizens. Most importantly, the *nomenklatura* in Tatarstan retained their grip on the republic's political life into the post-Soviet period, with the veteran apparatchik Mintimer Shaimiev easing into the presidency in 1991; he has since been re-elected twice, in 1996 and 2001. The Tatars did adopt a Declaration of State Sovereignty in 1990, much like others of the RSFSR's

---

[41] *Financial Times*, 8 September 2004.
[42] James Hughes, 'Managing Secession Potential in the Russian Federation', *Regional and Federal Studies*, vol. 11, no. 3, autumn 2001, pp. 41–3.

sub-units. But Tatar nationalism presented no urgent reasons for withdrawing from Russia altogether, and sovereignty was largely used as a bargaining chip in negotiations with Moscow. The main issue was the distribution of revenues between a central *nomenklatura* and a peripheral one, and a deal was eventually reached early in 1994.[43] Even this compromise, however, has unilaterally been redrawn since 2000 by the Russian authorities, as part of Putin's drive toward re-centralization – indicating the vulnerability of such compacts to Moscow's will.

Chechnya was the only one of Russia's ethno-territorial units in which the cause of independence gathered significant mass support, backed by a democratic movement combining a range of political forces. Some have suggested that a deal along the lines of Tatarstan could also have been reached in Chechnya, and that a meeting between Yeltsin and Dudaev would have sufficed.[44] Given the latter's insistence on full sovereignty, this seems doubtful. But it is clear that Dudaev wanted to maintain links with Russia and other former Soviet states. In October 1993, he sent a telegram to Chernomyrdin stating that 'we do not see strategically a place for the Chechen Republic outside the single economic, political and legal space which covers the current Commonwealth of Independent States'.[45] A looser version of the Soviet Union would also have suited the majority of Chechens – but one in which Chechnya had equal rather than subordinate status.

What of Russia's geostrategic objections to Chechen independence? Chechnya sits athwart a section of the Baku–Novorossiisk oil pipeline, then the sole means for Caspian oil to enter Russia's distribution networks. There were lucrative deals to be made for Azeri oil, and some have suggested the need to secure the pipeline before a particularly juicy contract was signed in 1995 – lest Dudaev cut off supplies – as a factor behind the

---

[43] See Valentin Mikhailov, 'Chechnya and Tatarstan: Differences in Search of an Explanation', in Richard Sakwa, ed., *Chechnya: From Past to Future*, London 2005, pp. 43–66, who observes that in 1994, 88 out of 96 members of Tatarstan's political and administrative decision-making elite were members of the former *nomenklatura*. See also Matthew Evangelista, *The Chechen Wars: Will Russia Go the Way of the Soviet Union?*, Berkeley/Los Angeles 2002, pp. 96–109, which contains admirably clear-headed discussion of the comparative and strategic aspects of the Chechen Wars.

[44] According to the former Kremlin advisor on nationalities policy Emil Pain: see Gall and de Waal, *Small Victorious War*, p. 169.

[45] Gall and de Waal, *Small Victorious War*, p. 122.

Russian invasion. But Chechnya had just as much interest in keeping the pipeline open as Russia: without it, Chechen refineries would have no purpose, and Chechnya's principal source of income would dry up. The issue here was one of transit rights, not strangulation of Russian industry.

In political terms, the Russian authorities frequently raised the spectre of an independent Chechnya galvanizing other Caucasian peoples to form a single state that would spread instability in order to threaten vital Russian geopolitical interests. The region's patchwork of particularities, and the dependence of most of its republics on federal funds, made such a development unlikely: the Chechens' neighbours lacked a national movement of comparable impetus, and have historically preferred some form of accommodation with Russia to the risks of separation. In the early 1990s, the prospect of pan-Caucasian unity rapidly waned after an early surge of solidarity, and especially so in the wake of the Ingush–North Ossetian conflict of 1992. By 1994 the Chechens were entirely isolated, and the Russians had already removed Gamsakhurdia in Georgia and Elchibey in Azerbaijan, the two regimes most likely to help.

The idea that Russia moved to stave off instability on its frontiers, meanwhile, is a breathtaking piece of hypocrisy. In 1992, Moscow sent arms and men to support secessionist movements in Transdnistria, Abkhazia and South Ossetia; the coups in Georgia and Azerbaijan were engineered with Russian help. Russian 'peacekeepers' to this day ensure the de facto autonomy of South Ossetia and Abkhazia, whose citizens have been awarded Russian passports in a creeping extension of Moscow's territorial sway. Much of Russia's policy towards the 'near abroad' seems designed in fact to increase instability rather than damp it down.

None of the justifications advanced for the 1994 invasion of Chechnya – restoring order, preventing Russia's disintegration and protecting its strategic interests – had a solid basis in fact. The threat presented to Russia by Chechen independence was magnified out of all proportion by a military establishment eager to reassert itself after defeat in Afghanistan and the US victory in the Gulf War. The Russian government was also able to take advantage of the juridical limbo in which Chechnya remained after 1991, having refused to sign a new federal treaty, but lacking the full Union Republic status that would have guaranteed international recognition. Amid an upsurge in Russian nationalism,

Yeltsin's clique thought a brief military intervention might consolidate their endlessly corrupt and increasingly unpopular rule. That they survived in power after deliberately instigating a disastrous war which killed tens of thousands of people was an astounding turn of events, for which the West bears a large share of the responsibility.

Throughout the 1990s, the US and leading European states backed Yeltsin to the hilt, fearful of a Communist revival. Their preference for free-market capitalism over democratic prerogatives led them to support Yeltsin when he sent tanks onto the streets of Moscow to subdue his opponents in 1993, and to endorse the 'shock therapy' of privatization and monetary reform which immiserated millions. But the blackest stain on the West's post-Soviet record was its acquiescence in the havoc wrought in Chechnya. While bombs rained down on Grozny in their thousands in December 1994, Western leaders were silent; it took until 13 February for Clinton to even raise the issue. In April 1996 Clinton compared the situation to the US Civil War, imputing to Yeltsin the status of an Eastern Lincoln. Sebastian Smith has pointed out that 'perhaps the most hypocritical act was the vote by the Council of Europe – a pan-European organization which is meant to promote respect for human rights – to admit Russia as a member in January 1996.'[46]

The West's guilt was not merely rhetorical. Yeltsin's victory in the 1996 election was due in no small part to its massive political and monetary support, orchestrated primarily by the Clinton administration. In March 1996, the IMF extended a $10.3bn credit, while the World Bank loaned $200m; in February, Helmut Kohl provided a mostly unconditional $2.7bn, and Alain Juppé stumped up $392m.[47] In bailing out Yeltsin's flyblown administration, these funds effectively subsidized the destruction of thousands of Chechen lives. The same lesson was drawn from this in Grozny and in Moscow: the Chechens could expect no help from the West. The Russian authorities were greatly emboldened by international silence over Chechnya, a state of affairs put to grim use once again after 1999. In the interim, Chechnya's wartime isolation if anything increased. Its disappearance from the world's conscience was to have a determining impact on its fate.

[46] Smith, *Allah's Mountains*, p. 226.
[47] Fred Weir, 'Betting on Boris: The West Ups the Ante for the Russian Elections', *Covert Action Quarterly*, Summer 1996.

4.

Ichkeria

Their war kills
Whatever their peace
Has left over.
Bertolt Brecht, 1937

The Chechen state that emerged from the rubble left by the war has
been portrayed as an entirely lawless land, blighted by crime and religious
extremism. The government of Aslan Maskhadov, elected president in
January 1997, proved incapable of dealing with the challenges facing
it from warlords and material circumstances alike. On this view,
Chechnya was another of the world's 'failed states', its social and political
structures proving insufficiently advanced to handle sovereignty in a
responsible manner. Russia was therefore entitled to bring it into line
in 1999 – the armed incursion into Dagestan led by Chechen former
field commanders in early August of that year dealing the final blow
to Russian patience.

Between 1996 and 1999 Chechnya was indeed an extremely
dangerous place. An epidemic of kidnapping meant that very few foreign
reporters or aid workers operated on its territory, reducing to an inter-
mittent trickle the information reaching the outside world.[1] Reports
increasingly highlighted only upsurges in violence or particularly

---

[1] By 1998 only three NGOs were operating in Chechnya, as compared to 100 in
Bosnia: Thomas de Waal, 'Grozny's Thankless Task', *Moscow Times*, 8 August 1998.

shocking events, such as the beheading of four hostages in December 1998, or the number of public executions carried out in central Grozny. These and other gruesome facts are incontrovertible. But as with a great deal of Western reporting on poor, marginalized parts of the world, much of the real substance of the country – its social traumas and economic problems, its political struggles – is omitted from such a picture. Independent Ichkeria needs to be seen for what it was: a deeply damaged, destitute country beset by crises and conditions it could not overcome. The principal reasons for this are to be sought in its unresolved status, the damage wrought by the 1994–6 war, and the unwillingness of the Russian authorities to meet their obligations to the country they had virtually destroyed.

The Khasavyurt Accords of 31 August 1996 – a single page of text – postponed a final decision on Chechnya's status until the end of 2001. But significantly, they also recognized Chechnya as a subject of international law, implying de facto Russian recognition of Chechnya as a sovereign entity. A treaty agreed by Maskhadov and Yeltsin on 12 May 1997 reaffirmed this point. On signing the 'Treaty on Peace and the Principles of Interrelations Between the Russian Federation and the Chechen Republic Ichkeria', Yeltsin declared an end to 400 years of hostilities, and referred to his counterpart as the president of the Chechen Republic of Ichkeria – the first time a Russian official had used the separatists' name for their country.[2] More important, however, was the commitment made by both sides in Article 2 'to build our relations corresponding to the generally accepted principles and norms of international law'. International law does not apply to relations between a state and one of its components. It applies to sovereign states, and the fact that the Russian authorities agreed once again to be bound by international law in their dealings with Chechnya implied de facto recognition of its separate, sovereign character.[3]

Yet despite this, the Russian authorities worked assiduously to ensure that the Chechens remained in a juridical limbo: in January 1997, the then Foreign Minister Yevgeny Primakov warned that Russia would cut ties with any state establishing diplomatic relations with Chechnya.

[2] *Moscow Times*, 13 May 1997.
[3] I am indebted to Francis Boyle for these points.

Though Maskhadov invited several foreign delegations to his inauguration as president on 12 February 1997, none attended; Lithuanian MPs were denied visas to enter Russia. His later trips to Saudi Arabia, Turkey, Britain and the US proved fruitless in this regard, and he was required to travel on a Russian passport, Moscow insisting that permitting the use of Ichkerian documents was tantamount to recognition. Official Islamic solidarity was – and still is – non-existent: 'not a single Arab country ever recognized Chechen independence, and their rulers consistently voiced support of Russia's territorial integrity.'[4]

Unable to gain international recognition, Chechnya was also prevented from securing loans or aid from international bodies. Its lack of sovereign currency or foreign reserves kept it firmly in the rouble zone, and therefore unable to raise bonds or credits. With its infrastructure shattered and almost a third of its arable land out of commission thanks to war damage or land mines,[5] Chechnya's economic existence was entirely dependent on Russian funds – which the Chechens viewed as reparations, but which Moscow saw as allocations from the federal budget. Money was repeatedly promised – $93.5m in June 1997, $105m in July 1997, for instance – but just as often failed to materialize, routinely embezzled before reaching its destination. As early as 1996, the Russian State Control Chamber found that $4.4 billion worth of 'reconstruction funds', supposed to be channelled to Chechnya by commercial banks, had vanished into the pockets of government officials.[6] By August 1997, however, Yeltsin still managed to profess amazement that of $130m reportedly sent to the Chechen National Bank, only $20m ever arrived.[7]

Oil had been identified as the obvious path to recovery, and in January 1997 Acting President Yandarbiev announced an ambitious

[4] Dmitri Trenin and Aleksei Malashenko, *Russia's Restless Frontier: The Chechnya Factor in Post-Soviet Russia*, Washington, D.C. 2004, pp. 191, 198.
[5] Valery Tishkov, *Chechnya: Life in a War-Torn Society*, Berkeley/Los Angeles 2004, p. 184.
[6] Donald Jensen, 'The Abuses of "Authorized Banking"', Radio Free Europe/Radio Liberty, January 1998. Among the government's favoured banks for these transactions was Menatep, owned by the oligarch Mikhail Khodorkovsky, who became a *cause célèbre* for Western liberals after his arrest for tax evasion in October 2003.
[7] *Moscow Times*, 11 June and 15 July 1997; Trenin and Malashenko, *Russia's Restless Frontier*, p. 37.

plan for the construction of a pipeline to Tbilisi, designed to branch onto the Baku–Tbilisi–Ceyhan project then under way with the backing of oil majors such as BP. Investors shied away from the considerable political and practical risks involved, however, and the Chechens were left dealing only with Moscow and the existing Baku–Novorossiisk pipeline. As noted in chapter 3, since Chechnya controlled only a section of the latter and had a vital interest in keeping it open, the issues discussed were transit rights and the costs of repairing the pipeline. In July 1997 Russia agreed to meet the latter, and in September promised to pay $845,000 for the right to pump 200,000 tons of oil through Chechnya; but the Kremlin then continued to haggle over the method of payment, and by June 1998 had still not paid a kopeck.[8]

Faced with an appalling scarcity of resources, the Chechen government could do little towards social provision. Access to health services was minimal, and infant mortality was estimated to stand at an incredible 100 per 1000.[9] The war had taken a massive toll not only on the living, but the unborn: according to the Chechen doctor Khassan Baiev, 'paediatricians around the republic reported that from 1995 to 1996 a quarter of newborns suffered birth defects like cleft palates, harelips, stunted limbs, extra limbs and missing internal organs'. Much of this may have been due to sheer trauma; but there are many indications that Russian forces used toxic weapons in Chechnya, 'judging by the shrivelled foliage, the respiratory diseases and the lesions on the faces of children.'[10]

The society that emerged from the war was divided in new ways, with traditional frictions between the more Sovietized lowlands and inward-looking highlands sometimes overlaid by distinctions between resistance fighters and 'National Traitors', as pro-Moscow Chechens became known. After the Chechen victory, a heroic mythology of the resistance fighter developed which found official expression in preferential treatment for war veterans. A state commission was set up to register former resistance fighters, their widows and orphans; a total of

---

[8] *Moscow Times*, 15 July, 10 September 1997; 16 June 1998.
[9] Tishkov, *Chechnya*, p. 189.
[10] Khassan Baiev, *The Oath: A Surgeon Under Fire*, London 2003, p. 185. Baiev provides many insights into everyday life and culture in Soviet Chechnya, as well as striking testimony of the two wars.

1,347 people were entitled to free public transport and reserved places in the fragile educational system.[11] Many more than this claimed veterans' privileges, however, and competition over the meagre rewards led to further tensions.

Economic life was at a low ebb. In April 1997, Nazhmudin Uvaisaev, chairman of the National Bank, stated that 'our monetary policy is that the Chechen people are hardworking'.[12] But work was in short supply. Where 20,000 had staffed Grozny's refineries before the war, by 1997 only 9,000 were employed there. Out of forty-four industrial concerns operating across Chechnya in 1994, a mere seventeen were running in 1999, and many of them had switched from making industrial goods and equipment to more basic, household items. By 1999, production stood at 5–8 per cent of the pre-war level. Unemployment had reached 80 per cent by 1998, while it was estimated that legitimate sources of income could only reach a third of the way to the poverty threshold.[13] In these circumstances, barter, woodcutting and metal salvaging became important means of subsistence.

Grozny's markets did a surprisingly brisk trade, full of cheap goods and agricultural products from across the Caucasus. But it was above all crime that flourished, from arms dealing to small-scale pirate oil-processing operations – in 1999 there were an estimated 800 mini-refineries run by armed factions siphoning off oil from pipelines.[14] With unemployment stratospherically high, and a large number of combat-trained men seeking any work that might pay a wage, the rule of law was increasingly displaced by that of the gun. The most lucrative business was kidnapping, which grew to epidemic proportions. Several former field commanders, including Salman Raduev and Arbi Baraev, as well as some senior members of the Ichkerian government are alleged to have profited from the trade in human lives – the sole thing of value left to many Chechens, though the foreign hostages taken were obviously far more likely to bring in significant ransoms. Various sources point to the existence of two markets, one in Grozny and one in Urus-Martan,

[11] Tishkov, *Chechnya,* p. 192.
[12] *Moscow Times,* 26 April 1997.
[13] Refineries: *Moscow Times,* 1 July 1997. Industry: Tishkov, *Chechnya,* p. 188. Unemployment, income: I. G. Kosikov and L. S. Kosikova, *Severnyi Kavkaz: sotsialno-ekonomicheskii spravochnik,* Moscow 1999, pp. 188–90.
[14] Kosikov and Kosikova, *Severnyi Kavkaz,* pp. 188–90.

where captives could be traded like slaves; indeed, many of them were made to perform manual labour for their jailers.[15]

This trafficking in living souls was the most poisonous feature of Chechnya under Maskhadov, and remains a shameful stain on the nation's record. Several considerations need to be borne in mind, however, before passing any final judgement. Firstly, the sale of captives began during the war; Valery Tishkov, a former Yeltsin minister and no friend to the separatist regime, reports broad agreement that 'the federals initiated the practice by making Chechens pay ransoms for their arrested relatives'.[16] Many of those taken hostage in Chechnya after the war were intended to be exchanged for Chechen prisoners, over 1,000 of whom had disappeared without trace into the network of 'filtration camps'. Secondly, instead of working with the Chechen police, both the Russian authorities and foreign governments chose to negotiate the release of hostages directly with the kidnappers, and time after time paid out large ransoms – thus giving further impetus to the trade. The Chechens achieved several arrests through offering smaller, but still substantial, rewards for information; a strategy not without corrupting effects of its own, but still less likely to actively encourage further kidnappings. As it was, Carlotta Gall reported in 1998 that 'the amount of money involved is now buying the collusion of ordinary people and members of the law enforcement agencies'.[17]

A third point concerns the scale of the kidnappings. Though obviously too large simply by virtue of existing at all, the figures issued to Western media by the Russian authorities marched in convenient lockstep with the political needs of the moment. Ordinary Chechen victims were often left out of calculations, with the result that the true number of captives is hard to gauge. Nevertheless, official Chechen statistics for the number of those being held roughly coincided with those of the Russian Interior Ministry up until 1999. In November 1997 the deputy

[15] Tishkov, *Chechnya*, pp. 114–15; Robert Bruce Ware, 'A Multitude of Evils: Mythology and Political Failure in Chechnya', in Richard Sakwa, ed., *Chechnya: From Past to Future*, London 2005, p. 99. The *Moscow Times* carried a report on 7 April 1999 of a Russian soldier purchased by a Chechen family for $16,000 in order to swap him for their son, sitting in a St Petersburg prison. Sergei Leont'ev had apparently already been sold and re-sold a number of times, and had been made to dig pits and carry bricks.

[16] Tishkov, *Chechnya*, p. 107.

[17] *Moscow Times*, 7 March 1998.

prosecutor in Grozny said 200 had been taken hostage that year, of whom 137 had been freed, and another 54 were known to be alive and still being held. In October 1998 Russian law enforcers said 176 people had been abducted that year, of whom 97 remained captive; Chechen authorities put the figure at 103.[18] By May 1999, however, as political tensions increased, the MVD said that 1,500 – almost ten times its previous figure – had been kidnapped in 1998, 1,140 in 1997 and 272 in 1996. By August the MVD had scaled this back to a total of 1,094 taken hostage between the beginning of 1997 and the end of June 1999. But the phenomenal escalation in the numbers is difficult to explain unless we allow for some deliberate exaggeration on the part of those compiling them.[19]

Moreover, as with the criminal activities taking place in Chechnya under Dudaev, there was extensive participation in the hostage business beyond Chechen borders. This included the Russian military: *Kommersant* newspaper reported in February 1999 that forty-six men from the 136th Motorized Brigade based in Dagestan had been sold into captivity in the previous two years.[20] The connections apparently stretch beyond the Caucasus: according to Tishkov, Arbi Baraev 'established close links with powerful figures in Moscow and became the partner of several top Russian politicians and businessmen – all of them profiting from the trade in hostages.'[21]

This brings us to a final observation about Chechnya's kidnapping industry. Many of the most high-profile incidents coincided with crucial junctures in Chechen politics. On 3 July 1997, for instance, an agreement was signed in Moscow, with Azeri President Aliev also among the signatories, permitting the flow of Caspian oil through Chechnya. The next day, two British aid workers were abducted. On 1 May 1998 Yeltsin's envoy Valentin Vlasov was taken from his plane at Grozny airport as he arrived for discussions with Maskhadov; Vlasov was reportedly held in the same location as the two British hostages.[22] Given Russia's previous history of covert action in Chechnya, and the

---

[18] *Moscow Times*, 21 November 1997, 14 October and 20 October 1998.
[19] *Moscow Times*, 25 May and 4 August 1999.
[20] 'Soldaty prodavali chechentsam svoikh', *Kommersant*, 27 February 1999.
[21] Tishkov, *Chechnya*, p. 120, citing a report in *Argumenty i fakty* from June 2000.
[22] Matthew Evangelista, *The Chechen Wars: Will Russia Go the Way of the Soviet Union?*, Washington, D.C. 2002, pp. 52, 55.

allegations of high-level involvement in the kidnapping trade, it does not seem far-fetched to suggest Moscow might have encouraged those seeking to undermine Maskhadov's authority. The gradual attrition of the latter between 1997 and late 1999 occurred in different forms and for a variety of reasons, which are best examined through an account of Chechnya's fragmented political scene.

Presidential elections were held in Chechnya on 27 January 1997, described by the OSCE as 'exemplary and free' – and, in an ambiguous phrase, by Kremlin Security Council Secretary Ivan Rybkin as 'a sovereign affair of the Russian region'. Aslan Maskhadov won by a comfortable margin, with 59.3 per cent of the votes on a turnout of 79.4 per cent. His nearest rivals were Shamil Basaev, with 23.5 per cent, and Zelimkhan Yandarbiev, with 10.1 per cent.[23] The results – far more evenly distributed than those in Georgia's 1995 elections, or the farcically one-sided contests in Kazakhstan in 1994 or Azerbaijan in 1998 – register the country's principal political faultlines, which divided Maskhadov's project for an independent secular Chechnya from the uncompromising stance of some of his field commanders, who in several cases advocated a pan-Caucasian Islamic state as the sole guarantee of Chechen independence.

Maskhadov's initial attempts to rule by consensus – he included several of his rivals in his first cabinet of March 1997 – foundered as independence merged into immiseration. His inability to secure international recognition or funds through negotiations with Moscow prompted many to take against such dialogue altogether, and opposition mounted throughout 1998 and 1999. Powerful players such as Yandarbiev and Raduev were vocal in their criticism from the outset, Raduev in particular proving a frequent political irritant through his repeated threats to unleash a bombing campaign in Russia. By the beginning of 1998 Raduev had begun to organize demonstrations of veterans against Maskhadov. These might have died down into a marginal phenomenon

---

[23] See 'Chronology', in Diane Curran, Fiona Hill and Elena Kostritsyna, eds, *The Search for Peace in Chechnya: A Sourcebook 1994–1996*, Kennedy School of Government, March 1997. For an engaging portrait of Chechnya during the election, see Georgi Derluguian, *Bourdieu's Secret Admirer in the Caucasus*, Chicago 2005, chapter 1.

had Maskhadov managed to forge a solid bond with Shamil Basaev, the field commander who at that time had the most military prestige and public standing. Basaev had two short spells in government, the second as prime minister from January to July 1998, during which he attempted economic liberalization by slashing the government apparatus and bringing the Chechen minimum wage down into line with Russia's.[24] But, having been unable to make a significant impact either on Chechnya's economic woes or the crime rate, Basaev resigned and devoted himself instead to the Congress of the Peoples of Chechnya and Dagestan – an organization that aimed to unify the two territories into a single state, echoing the imamate of Basaev's nineteenth-century namesake. Basaev soon moved into opposition to Maskhadov, joining with other former field commanders who repeatedly staged rallies calling for the president to step down.

The focal point of political contention in Ichkeria was the role of religion. Islam has played a complex role in Chechnya, with different rites and traditions varying in importance and intensity of adherence. What was new about the period after 1996 was the salience of the militant strand commonly referred to as 'Wahhabism', which had consolidated its presence in Chechnya during the war with the arrival of volunteer fighters from the Arab world. The 'Wahhabites' gained greater influence in the austere conditions that followed the war, and were a significant source of armed opposition to Maskhadov; they also played a destabilizing role in Dagestan. The scale and nature of Islamist activism in Chechnya and the North Caucasus is a topic that deserves separate treatment, and I will return to it in chapters 6 and 7. For the present, we should stress the political function of Islamism as a pole towards which opponents of Maskhadov gravitated.

The constitution Chechnya had adopted in 1992 was secular. When asked by Chechen elders to move towards *shari'a* law in 1993, Dudaev had refused, saying 'Let us put our souls in order according to the Qur'an, and our lives according to the constitution'.[25] However, with large portions of the urban and educated population joining the opposition to him, Dudaev began to use religious slogans as a means of

---

[24] Moscow Times, 24 February 1998.
[25] Quoted in Tishkov, Chechnya, p. 169.

mobilizing his support base; thus, after the attempted coup against him in 1993, Dudaev decreed that Islam was the state religion. Sufi rituals began to play a more active role in public life, notably the *zikr* of the Qadiri brotherhood, which increasingly became less an act of devotion than an affirmation of ethno-national identity.[26]

The public role of Islam increased during the 1994–6 war, as a means of galvanizing resistance by imposing discipline on troops and asserting a common national bond that would distinguish Chechens from Russians. It was during the war that the first *shari'a* courts were set up, in April 1995, functioning parallel to the secular ones. In 1996, Acting President Yandarbiev took this a step further by introducing a new penal code for Chechnya, modelled on that of Sudan, and disbanding the secular courts. Once installed as president in 1997, Maskhadov decreed the formation of a Supreme Shari'a Court, which began to implement the harsh punishments stereotypically associated with *shari'a*. The first public executions took place in September of that year in central Grozny, and were condemned as a 'medieval orgy' by the then Interior Minister Sergei Stepashin (though Russia itself had yet to abolish the death penalty).

The increasing 'Islamization' of Ichkeria was the product of political circumstances. The Chechen social scientist Musa Iusupov notes that, since Russo-Chechen relations had not been regularized, 'the Islamization of political and legal life was seen by the Chechen leadership as a move towards self-determination' – adding that this was 'to a certain extent an enforced response to the federal authorities' neglect of the problems created by the 1994–6 war.'[27] Maskhadov also made overtures to the Islamists in order to fend off criticism of his negotiations with Russia – seen by his opponents as opening the way to a compromise on sovereignty. Ironically, their active role in destabilizing Maskhadov's rule only had the effect of making such compromises more likely, as Chechnya's central authorities struggled to rein in the kidnappers and renegade field commanders.

With talks failing to produce results and conditions growing ever more desperate, by the summer of 1998 Maskhadov's opponents had

---

[26] See Musa Iusupov, 'Islam v sotsial'no-politicheskoi zhizni Chechni', *Tsentral'naia Aziia i Kavkaz*, No. 2 (8), 2000, pp. 164–71.
[27] Iusupov, 'Islam v sotsial'no-politicheskoi zhizni Chechni', p. 171.

taken up arms. Several days of fighting took place in July between government forces and two Islamic paramilitary units in Gudermes, and the same month saw the failure of an attempt to assassinate the president by car-bomb. Demonstrations against and in support of Maskhadov took place in the autumn, but early in the new year he made a misguided attempt to undercut his adversaries' support: on 3 February 1999 he ordered parliament to draft a new Islamic constitution and suspended the existing constitution in the interim, moving to presidential rule.

Maskhadov could still command sizeable numerical support, judging by the rallies several thousands strong held in Grozny in February and March 1999. But his opponents now included not only opportunist warlords such as Baraev or the loose cannon Raduev, but more canny operators such as Basaev, Yandarbiev and the former Foreign Minister Movladi Udugov. Pointing to the union of secular and spiritual power advocated by certain strands of Islamic political theory, they called for the abolition of the presidency and parliament, and on 9 February several former field commanders, including Basaev and Raduev, joined with Yandarbiev and Udugov to form an alternative government called the Mekhk-Shura.[28]

The establishment of a rival government was followed by events which further undermined Maskhadov's by now tenuous authority. On 5 March the MVD envoy Gennadii Shpigun – responsible for running a 'filtration camp' during the 1994–6 war – was kidnapped in Grozny. Two days later Stepashin declared that Russia would take 'adequate measures' to destroy 'criminal formations', and moved to seal the border. On 21 March there was a second assassination attempt on Maskhadov, and further killings of Chechen government figures continued through the spring and summer, while skirmishes with Russian troops began to occur along the border with Dagestan from May onwards. Maskhadov denounced these as provocations from Moscow, and it is highly significant that, according to Stepashin himself, planning for a military invasion of Chechnya had begun as early as March 1999.[29] From June onwards, a 'slow, linear build-up of forces' took place as the Russians

[28] *Moscow Times*, 5 and 10 February 1999.
[29] Interview with *Nezavisimaia gazeta*, 14 January 2000, quoted in Evangelista, *Chechen Wars*, p. 61.

moved military hardware and personnel into areas adjacent to Chechnya, with 7,000 men in place by September.[30]

At the beginning of August 1999, a group of Islamist fighters led by Basaev and the Saudi *mujahed* Khattab moved across the border into Dagestan, supposedly going to the aid of fellow Islamists who had established '*shari'a*' communities outside the reach of the Russian federal authorities in the villages of Chabanmakhi, Karamakhi and Kadar. They were repulsed by a combination of locals and Dagestani police, with the Russian Army joining the fray in mid-August, after the newly installed Prime Minister Vladimir Putin had been charged with restoring 'order and discipline' in Dagestan. Basaev and Khattab's force withdrew to Chechnya on 22 August, defeated but without significant losses. Russian planes bombed the towns of Vedeno and Urus-Martan on 25 August, while Maskhadov condemned the incursion and sought to distance himself from the perpetrators.

Many theories have been proposed regarding Basaev's incursion, whose ostensible purpose was to contribute to the creation of a single Islamic Chechen–Dagestani state. *Nezavisimaia gazeta*, a newspaper owned by the oligarch Boris Berezovsky, alleged that Basaev was lured into Dagestan in an operation planned by Russian intelligence to furnish a pretext for invading Chechnya; others have suggested it was a pre-emptive strike to distract the Russians from an invasion which was in any case imminent.[31] Whatever the real motivations, it is clear that in invading Russian territory, Basaev prepared the way for retaliatory action, and bears a great responsibility for the disaster that ensued a month later, as Russian planes began once more to rain bombs on Chechnya.

Who is to blame for Ichkeria's failures? According to some observers, the problem lies in the structures of Chechen society itself, whose 'endemic fragmentation . . . prevented the consolidation of an over-arching political structure capable of supporting the rule of law and the development of legitimate economic activity.'[32] Valery Tishkov

---

[30] David Satter, *Darkness at Dawn: the Rise of the Russian Criminal State*, New Haven 2003, p. 270 n. 28.

[31] See Georgi Derluguian, 'Che Guevaras in Turbans', *New Left Review*, 1/237, September–October 1999, pp. 3–27; Satter, *Darkness at Dawn*, pp. 63–4; Evangelista, *Chechen Wars*, pp. 75–80.

[32] Ware, 'Multitude of Evils', p. 90.

points to the overlaying of new political rivalries onto *taip* cleavages, and to the 'self-destructive' role played by the new-formed Chechen mythology of victory.[33] The collapse of consensus under Maskhadov, and the desertion from the central government of one field commander after another, were indeed the product of factional struggles, for which many leading figures can rightly be criticized. But the primary source of division in Ichkeria was not a primordial aversion to unity.

The tasks facing Maskhadov on his election in 1997 would have been forbiddingly daunting even with a unified domestic political scene and vast quantities of international aid. As it was, Chechnya was left entirely to its own devices by the outside world, which had sat on its hands during the 1994–6 war and now willingly brushed Chechnya under the carpet of realpolitik. This was the case from the outset: at the time of Maskhadov's election, one Western diplomat stressed the need not to antagonize Moscow while NATO expansion was being pushed through: 'We are playing for stakes this year that are much higher than Chechnya.'[34] By 1999 the priority was to gain the Kremlin's acquiescence in NATO's bombing of Serbia; while British ministers deliberately exaggerated the extent of atrocities in Kosovo to legitimate 'humanitarian intervention', they totally neglected hundreds of thousands living in desperate circumstances in Chechnya, a country shattered by a war far more brutal than anything perpetrated by Milosevic.

In failing to pressure the Russian authorities over Chechnya, the West has a share of the blame both for the war, and for the isolation that blocked Chechnya's chances of rebuilding in the aftermath. There were no UN programmes here offering stipends to former fighters and incentives to return to the land, as in Mozambique, nor offers of matching funds to encourage the Kremlin to meet its promises.[35] There was no international arbitration on the reparations due to Chechnya for war damage, and no tribunals for atrocities committed by federal forces, such as have since been established for Rwanda, Sierra Leone and the former Yugoslavia. Any number of measures might have been implemented to assist Chechnya, but none were attempted. This was

[33] Tishkov, *Chechnya*, p. 222.
[34] *Moscow Times*, 25 January 1997.
[35] Carlotta Gall, 'The Great Game: Basayev Aims at Unification with Dagestan', *Moscow Times*, 17 July 1998.

a matter of political expediency, rather than material practicability; the world simply chose once again to forget the Chechens.

Outside neglect contributed greatly to Ichkeria's misery. But the direct cause was the utter devastation wrought upon it by the Russian military in the preceding years – compounded by a refusal to compensate the Chechens for the senseless destruction that had taken place. Commenting on the disarray in Chechnya in March 1999, the Russian columnist Andrei Piontkovsky knew where to look for the real culprits: 'We are the ones who bombed Chechnya back to the Stone Age, who placed it under an economic blockade and created a situation in which thousands of armed people have no work whatsoever.'[36] Having taken thousands of lives and destroyed the country's infrastructure, the Russian authorities kept Chechnya in an economic and political stranglehold, and simply watched as its tattered social fabric was rent by crime and conspiracy – sometimes actively participating in the undermining of its elected leader.

Many Western commentators have seen the failures of Maskhadov's regime as grounds for including Chechnya in the ever-expanding category of 'failed states' which deserve to have their sovereignty revoked, to be replaced by the custodianship of more civilized great powers.[37] This argument should be rejected as decisively in Chechnya as elsewhere. Few states would have been able to establish a peaceful, prosperous society in three years given the physical ruin, economic collapse and countless political and social fractures wrought by two years of war with a vastly more powerful neighbour. That it was never given a chance to do so was the result of a vindictive intransigence on the part of Russia, and the complete moral dereliction of the 'international community'. Both factors were grotesquely amplified after federal forces invaded Chechnya for the second time in 1999.

---

[36] Andrei Piontkovsky, 'Learning the Lessons of Chechnya', *Moscow Times*, 18 March 1999.
[37] See Anatol Lieven, 'A Western Strategy for Chechnya', *International Herald Tribune*, 9 September 2004.

5.

Putin's War

In September 1999, a series of bombs ripped through apartment buildings in Moscow and the southern Russian cities of Buinaksk and Volgodonsk. Timed to go off in the early morning so as to ensure maximum casualties, the explosions killed nearly 300 people in total and injured scores more. With federal forces massed on the borders of Chechnya, the explosions added to an atmosphere of extreme tension in Russia and were immediately attributed to Chechen 'terrorists'. Prime Minister Putin, nominated to the post on 9 August, appeared on television on 16 September after the Volgodonsk bombing and, using the coarse language of the Russian criminal underworld, spoke of the need to 'wipe them out in the shithouse'. The sentiment was shared by much of the Russian population, for whom the steely determination of this little-known former KGB operative seemed to herald a welcome change from the drunken incompetence of Yeltsin.

Vladimir Putin's ascent to the presidency in 2000, and total dominance of Russia's political scene since then, has undoubtedly marked a transition from the oligarchic capitalism of Yeltsin to a more authoritarian mode. Putin has, notably, installed dozens of former KGB personnel in key positions throughout government, and brought the powerful plutocrats of the 1990s to heel or else driven them into exile. High commodity prices have clearly been crucial to his success, with some of the vast sums pumped into the Russian economy reaching the pockets of appreciative citizens. But it is the war in Chechnya that has been Putin's principal means of consolidating power, paving the way for a second victory in the presidential elections of 2004 and a frictionless extension of his term to 2008. The war has played on a wider sense of wounded national pride, after a decade of military, political and economic defeats for Russia, from Chechnya to NATO expansion, from shock therapy to the rouble collapse of 1998. In contrast to Yeltsin's blundering intervention, it has enjoyed considerable public support, and brought Putin a staggering degree of compliance from political elites and intelligentsia alike.

The pretext for the assault on Chechnya that began at the end of September 1999 – billed as an 'anti-terrorist operation' – had been provided by the incursion into Dagestan by Basaev and Khattab in August. But the apartment bombings of September did the crucial work of preparing domestic opinion for all-out war. No proof of Chechen involvement in the attacks has ever emerged, and the rubble was cleared within days, preventing a thorough forensic investigation. Four Dagestani Islamists were convicted for the Buinaksk bombing in 2001, but there are considerable grounds for suspecting something far more sinister with regard to those in European Russia. On the night of 22–23 September, residents of an apartment block in Riazan', 200 km south-east of Moscow, reported suspicious activity in their basement, and local police arrived to find three sacks of hexogen explosive, a detonator and a timer set to go off at 5 a.m. Riazan' law enforcement soon caught up with the culprits – who turned out to be FSB agents. After a delay of two days, the FSB explained that this had merely been an exercise, and that the substance found had actually been sugar. A string of contradictory statements, lies and misinformation issued from the mouths of the Russian authorities, while Riazan' residents and ordinary Russians elsewhere began to ask themselves if their own government could really have toyed with the lives of its own citizens in this way – or indeed whether it had actually intended to kill them.[1] And if such suspicions could be raised about Riazan', why not about the other bombings? Aerial bombardment of Chechnya began on the evening of 23 September, and all such questions were swept away by the tide of militarism and xenophobia that accompanied the start of the 'anti-terrorist operation'.

The Riazan' incident captures several essential qualities of Putin's Russia: at the very least, the government had manipulated the fears of the populace and placed a breathtakingly low value on the security of its own citizens. The truth could be more monstrous still: a regime driven by cold calculation and bottomless cynicism, willing to murder its own people to further the goals of an authoritarian, kleptocratic elite. In either case, the Second Chechen War has served to cement further the position of this elite, resulting in a vicious occupation which is destroying countless Chechen lives and corroding the social fabric of Russia itself. It is in the interests of both peoples to bring to an end the stream of casualties, to dismantle the atmosphere of mistrust and ethnic hostility the war has engendered, and to remove the weapon of fear from the hands of those who have wielded it to their own profit.

A range of justifications was offered for the new assault on Chechnya: concern for Russia's territorial integrity, the need to rein in a lawless periphery, the battle with Islamist terrorism. Once again, none of them could remotely account for the terror unleashed on Chechnya that autumn, a full-scale invasion whose brutality from the outset exceeded even that of the 1994–6 war. On 29 September Putin had ruled out a 'replay' of that conflict, citing the risk of 'unnecessary casualties among troops'. But the next day, Russian forces moved into Chechen territory to 'solve the main task' – in Putin's words, to 'destroy the bandits, their camps and infrastructure'.[2] Russian planes bombed dams, bridges and oil wells, and it rapidly became clear that the civilian population was the real target of the 'anti-terrorist' operation.

---

[1] David Satter presents an account of the Riazan' incident that demolishes the official version, and argues that the degree of technical knowledge and planning required for the other bombings points to specialists trained by the security services; the explosive used was produced in only one factory in Russia, closely guarded by the FSB. See *Darkness at Dawn*, New Haven 2003, pp. 24–33, 66.

[2] Matthew Evangelista, *The Chechen Wars: Will Russia Go the Way of the Soviet Union?*, Washington, D.C. 2002, p. 69.

On 1 October, Russian forces – 93,000 strong this time, compared to the 40,000 Yeltsin had initially deployed – entered Chechnya, and Putin announced that Russia no longer recognized Maskhadov's government as the legitimate authority there, backing instead the puppet parliament that had been fraudulently elected in 1996, most of whose members lived in Moscow. A range of prominent figures in Russia's political establishment – including former Prime Ministers Yevgeny Primakov, Sergei Stepashin and Sergei Kirienko, as well as the former deputy premier Boris Nemtsov – had suggested an effective partition of Chechnya at the Terek river, behind which Chechen forces withdrew in early October.[3] But Russian generals, bent on reversing the humiliations of 1994–6, rejected the idea. Their troops secured the lowlands that autumn, reaching the outskirts of Grozny on 18 October. Three days later, a missile hit Grozny's central market, killing over 130 people in broad daylight. Putin's response was repellent: 'I can confirm that an explosion did take place in Grozny in a marketplace. But . . . it is not just an ordinary market . . . Actually it is a weapons warehouse, an arms supply base. This place is one of the headquarters of the bandit detachments.'[4] A second missile attack on the city's centre on 27 October killed 112. Bombardment of the city was stepped up, reaching 150 strikes a day by the end of the month, as Russian artillery pulverized the few buildings left standing by their guns five years earlier.[5]

On 6 December Grozny's residents were given an ultimatum to leave the area by 11 December, or face certain destruction. Refugees flooded out of the city, many joining the 250,000 who had already arrived in the neighbouring republic of Ingushetia by the end of November. They were admitted by the then Ingush president, Ruslan Aushev, in direct contravention of an order of 25 September 1999 from General Vladimir Shamanov not to allow Chechen refugees across any of Russia's borders.[6]

[3] Dmitri Trenin and Aleksei Malashenko, with Anatol Lieven, *Russia's Restless Frontier: The Chechnya Factor in Post-Soviet Russia*, Washington, D.C. 2004, pp. 120, 155.

[4] Quoted in Aleksandr Cherkasov, 'The War in the Caucasus and Peace in Russia', in Tanya Lokshina, ed., *The Imposition of a Fake Political Settlement in the Northern Caucasus: The 2003 Chechen Presidential Election*, Stuttgart 2005, p. 267.

[5] Evangelista, *Chechen Wars*, p. 70.

[6] Cited in Aleksandr Cherkasov, 'Book of Numbers: Book of the Lost', in Lokshina, *Imposition of a Fake Settlement*, p. 197.

The flight to safety was scarcely less perilous than staying behind: a column of refugees headed towards Ingushetia was bombarded by Russian planes on 29 October. Fighting continued in Grozny, with the Russians raining huge quantities of ordnance on the city and suffering heavy casualties before finally taking control in early February 2000. On 6 February, Putin announced that 'the operation to liberate Grozny is over'. One month later he was in the city to declare a planned reduction of the garrison from 93,000 to 23,000. On 26 March, buoyed by the apparent success of his 'anti-terrorist' campaign, Putin strolled to victory in the first round of the presidential election, winning 53 per cent of the vote. Chechen government troops retreated to the mountains, where they were pounded by Russian artillery and air-strikes.

Federal forces carried out numerous attacks on civilians in the territory they now controlled, often in the course of 'clean-up' operations or *zachistki*. Ostensibly a simple process of checking identity papers, these became infamous as the occasion for rampages of murder, rape and wanton violence on the part of Russian troops. Serving alongside conscripts were thousands of hardened mercenaries – *kontraktniki* – many of whom had been recruited from Russia's prisons, and who were responsible for several of the war's worst outrages. In early December 1999, 23 inhabitants of Alkhan-Yurt – men, women and children – were killed in a *zachistka*, while over 100 died after a similar operation in Novye Aldy on 5 February 2000.[7] The previous day, the village of Katyr-Yurt had been shelled throughout the morning. Journalists who subsequently visited the village confirmed that the Russians used vacuum bombs in this attack. These float down by parachute, releasing a cloud of petrol vapour when they are a few metres above the ground. The vapour is then ignited, and the oxygen in the surrounding air suddenly explodes, literally sucking the air from any living person in the vicinity and rupturing their lungs. Their use against civilians is banned by the Geneva Convention. On the afternoon of 4 February, the Russians told the surviving inhabitants of Katyr-Yurt they would be able to leave in a convoy of buses bearing white flags. This convoy was then bombed after it left the village. A total of 363 people died in the events, the worst single atrocity of a war replete with barbaric acts.[8]

---

[7] Politkovskaya, *Dirty War*, pp. 116, 309–15.
[8] John Sweeney, 'Revealed: Russia's Worst War Crime in Chechnya', *Observer*, 5 March 2000.

By the beginning of 2000, the Russian authorities had once again put in place a system of 'filtration camps' like those set up during the 1994–6 war. As before, these were the site of torture, murder and summary execution, with males between the ages of ten and sixty, as well as many women, rounded up in *zachistka* after *zachistka*. According to Human Rights Watch, 853 illegal executions had taken place by February 2001; in three documented massacres, a total of 130 had been killed, and there were confirmed reports of 'at least one verified mass grave' near the detention camp at Khankala airbase.[9] The most infamous camp was at Chernokozovo, which apparently had 'Welcome to Hell' written on its gates. The Russian journalist Andrei Babitsky, whose reporting for Radio Svoboda during the first war had been an important source of independent information (albeit funded by the US Congress), was imprisoned by the Russian army in early 2000 and held for a time at Chernokozovo. Beaten repeatedly himself, he was released in late February and reported hearing the screams of a woman being tortured in another cell.[10] An FSB officer, referring to claims that the Chechen resistance had been galvanized by Islamists, was later to admit that 'Chernokozovo did more to turn ordinary Chechens into rebels than anything the Wahhabists could say.'[11]

In June 2000 Putin appointed Akhmad-Hadji Kadyrov as the head of the pro-Moscow administration. Kadyrov was the chief mufti in Chechnya, and had been on the separatists' side in the 1994–6 war; but now he dismissed talk of independence, saying that 'freedom is something the ordinary man does not need'.[12] Kadyrov commanded little respect in Chechnya prior to his elevation. He had organized the first *hajj* from Chechnya, from which he made a large personal profit: funds for the trip were collected from the faithful, but when the Saudi government paid the bill, Kadyrov never returned the money.[13] Other figures to whom

[9] Anatol Lieven, 'Chechnya and the Laws of War', in Trenin and Malashenko, *Russia's Restless Frontier*, p. 218.

[10] Politkovskaya, *Dirty War*, pp. xv, 327; Peter Truscott, *Putin's Progress*, London 2004, p. 130.

[11] Mark Galeotti, 'Beslan Shows Growing Islamist Influence in Chechen War', *Jane's Intelligence Review*, October 2004. See also John Sweeney, 'Cries from Putin's Torture Pit ', *Observer*, 15 October 2000.

[12] Politkovskaya, *Dirty War*, p. 194.

[13] Politkovskaya, *A Small Corner of Hell: Dispatches from Chechnya*, Chicago 2003, p. 140; the book gives an unflinching account of daily life in Chechnya under the occupation, and is searingly critical of the authorities responsible for the war's conduct.

Moscow turned included Beslan Gantemirov, the former mayor of Grozny and a convicted embezzler, who was released from a Russian prison in 1999 to head an armed group, and Arbi Baraev, one of the key players in the kidnapping trade that flourished between the wars.[14]

The presence of these people on the side of the occupiers makes a mockery of arguments that the war was designed to rein in lawlessness. It underscores instead the intent to establish a puppet regime that could be relied on to turn a blind eye to Russian atrocities while it lined its pockets. As in 1995, the quislings Moscow appointed did little to improve the lives of their countrymen: according to Putin's own human rights envoy to Chechnya, of 14.7 billion roubles ($500m) allocated to Chechnya in 2001, only 10 per cent had been used on reconstruction; in 2002, FSB director Nikolai Patrushev admitted that 700 million roubles had been 'misused'.[15] By mid-2002, Grozny was a lunar landscape of ruins and bomb craters. Its population had dropped to 200,000 – half its 1989 level – and those remaining in the city eked out a living in cellars, with no running water or heating, running the gauntlet of mines and snipers every time they emerged into daylight. A network of Russian checkpoints provided further occasions for soldiers to brutalize civilians.

Kadyrov's appointment was the first stage in an alleged process of 'normalization'. In January 2001, Putin passed control of the 'anti-terrorist operation' to the FSB, and in August 2003 to the Interior Ministry, in an attempt to indicate the declining severity of the situation. In reality, the war continued as before. Chechen resistance forces remained able to infiltrate Russian lines, both from bases in the mountains and from hiding places on the plains, sheltered by a civilian population increasingly enraged by the conduct of the occupiers. The massed troops of the Russian Defence Ministry, MVD, FSB and special forces (OMON) – numbering 100,000 in 2005, contrary to Putin's assertions in 2000 of an imminent reduction – controlled the plains by day, but Chechen forces conducted guerrilla operations by night, picking off convoys or patrols before melting into the forest.[16] The

---

[14] Sanobar Shermatova, 'The Secret War between Russian Intelligence Agencies in Chechnya', *Moscow News*, 8 August 2000, cited in Politkovskaya, *Dirty War*, p. xxiv.

[15] Trenin and Malashenko, *Russia's Restless Frontier*, p. 38.

[16] Figures from *Nezavisimoe voennoe obozrenie*, 20 May 2005, cited in *Chechnya Weekly*, 1 June 2005.

conflict became one between 'an elephant and a whale, each invincible in its own medium'.[17]

Casualties had begun to mount. According to official figures, by January 2000 the Russians had lost 1,200 troops; by March it was 1,991. By June 2000 an average of fifty federal troops were being killed every week. The rate of losses dropped as the war entered the phase of guerrilla operations and counter-insurgency, but in late 2004, the Russians' average monthly casualties were still slightly higher than those of US forces in Iraq – fifty-nine per month compared to fifty-eight.[18] Official figures from the Ministry of Defence covering the period from September 1999 to January 2006 give a total of 3,501 Russian servicemen killed in Chechnya, and 32 missing; this does not include personnel from other state agencies such as the FSB, which in late 2005 had 20,000 troops in Chechnya, or the MVD which, according to one military correspondent, had lost 1,600 men by the summer of 2005. The real figures are likely to be far higher, since many of the thousands of wounded later died from their injuries, and the number of missing is several hundreds out from the Defence Ministry's own previous figures.[19] No such regular estimates are available for civilians, but given the devastation inflicted on Grozny, the early stages of the war must have taken the lives of several thousand people.

It was this combination of military stalemate and a casualty rate as high as that experienced by the Red Army in Afghanistan that pushed Putin into a change of strategy: from 'normalization' to 'Chechenization'. The outward sign of this was a sham 'political process'. In March 2003, a referendum was held on a new made-in-Moscow constitution that declared Chechnya to be part of the Russian Federation. It was duly approved by a thunderous 96 per cent, though the vast majority of ordinary Chechens stayed away from the polls. In another rigged ballot in October 2003 – in which 30,000 occupying troops were eligible to vote – Kadyrov was elected president with a supposed 83 per cent of the vote.[20] In practical terms, operations were increasingly put into the hands of Kadyrov's private army, run by his son Ramzan, who rapidly

---

[17] Trenin and Malashenko, *Restless Frontier*, p. 42.
[18] Evangelista, *Chechen Wars*, p. 8; *Nezavisimaia gazeta*, 25 October 2004.
[19] *AP*, 26 February 2006; *Novaia gazeta*, 10 August 2005.
[20] Lokshina, *Imposition of a Fake Settlement*, Stuttgart 2005, pp. 16, 36–7.

acquired a reputation for psychotic brutality. Now it would be Chechens themselves who would be tasked with crushing pro-independence forces, creating the conditions for an incipient civil war. This ushered in one of the blackest periods in Chechen history, to which I will return in chapter 8.

The occupation of Chechnya produced a chilling degeneration among Russian troops. Sheltered by an official policy of impunity – many Russian officers, for instance, were permitted to have several different identities, ostensibly to protect them from 'revenge attacks' by Chechens – federal forces engaged in an orgy of theft and arbitrary cruelty. This now often took the form of simple extortion: during *zachistki* Chechens would have to pay a ransom to prevent the 'filtration' of the men or the rape of the women. By 2002, 'ransom for living goods ranged from five hundred to three or four thousand rubles [between $16 and $130], depending on the age – the younger, the pricier – and on the soldiers' visual appraisal of the home.'[21] There are dozens of reported instances of soldiers returning the bodies of civilian casualties only for a fee – sometimes higher for a corpse than a living person, because of the importance to Chechens of burial on clan lands.

The case of Colonel Yuri Budanov provided perhaps the most striking indication of what Chechens could expect from Russian soldiers and officials. On 26 March 2000, the day Putin won the presidency, Budanov celebrated by getting drunk, kidnapping an eighteen-year-old Chechen girl, then raping and killing her. He was tried by a military court in Rostov-on-Don, headquarters of the Russian army's southern command, in February 2001, and eventually sentenced to ten years' imprisonment after official support for his insanity plea provoked outrage. On 31 December 2002, however, he was acquitted on those very grounds, and his request for a pardon was initially approved by Vladimir Shamanov, veteran of the Chechen campaign and at that time governor of Ulyanovsk, who hailed Budanov as 'a talented commander' and 'honest citizen'. The pardon was withdrawn after a 10,000-strong public demonstration in Grozny prompted protests even from the puppet regime in Chechnya, and Budanov was re-imprisoned

---

[21] Politkovskaya, *Small Corner of Hell*, p. 105.

after a retrial in July 2003. But in February 2006, it was announced that Budanov would likely be released in November, for model behaviour.[22] In a similar case, a group of special forces soldiers led by Captain Eduard Ulman killed six Chechens at a checkpoint in January 2002. They were acquitted by a jury in Rostov-on-Don, a verdict overturned by the Supreme Court in August of 2004; they were re-tried, and acquitted once again, with the Supreme Court again overturning the acquittal in August 2005.

In November 1999, Anatoly Chubais, architect of the crooked privatizations of the Yeltsin years, announced on television that 'the Russian army is being reborn in Chechnya'.[23] If so, a monster has emerged from the Caucasian womb. The violence inflicted on Chechen civilians and fighters has frequently been turned inwards: in 2001, a Russian military newspaper estimated that half of Russian casualties had come in non-combat situations, mostly due to systematic bullying of demoralized teenage recruits – a practice known as *dedovshchina*, literally 'rule of the grandfathers'.[24] Early in 2006, the case of Private Andrei Sychev, a conscript at a tank academy in the Ural city of Chelyabinsk, once again drew public attention to this grisly phenomenon: on New Year's Eve, Sychev was beaten so badly that his legs and genitals subsequently had to be amputated.[25] According to official figures, there were 276 suicides in the Russian army in 2005, along with 857 non-combat deaths; given the culture of impunity nurtured by *dedovshchina*, the numbers are probably much higher. But this is far from the only reason

---

[22] See Politkovskaya, *Small Corner of Hell*, pp. 153–60; 'Chechen Murder Case Colonel Acquitted', *Institute of War and Peace Reporting, Caucasus News Update*, 9 January 2003, available at www.iwpr.net; 'FSIN podtverzhdaet, chto Budanov mozhet byt' dosrochno osvobozhden v noiabre', *Kavkazskii uzel* website, 21 February 2006, available at kavkaz.memo.ru.

[23] Quoted in Emil Pain, 'The Chechen War in the Context of Contemporary Russian Politics', in Richard Sakwa, ed., *Chechnya: From Past to Future*, London 2005, p. 68.

[24] *Nezavisimoe voennoe obozrenie*, no. 37, 2001, cited in Trenin and Malashenko, *Russia's Restless Frontier*, p. 141.

[25] Claire Bigg, 'Russia: Brutal Hazing Incident Rocks Army', *Radio Free Europe/Radio Liberty*, 27 January 2006. In the first stages of the trial of one of Sychev's assailants, it emerged that the Russian army had been accused of 'intimidating witnesses and trying to bribe the victim's family to have the case shelved'; five witnesses withdrew testimony, apparently under pressure from their superiors: Mark Franchetti, 'Witnesses Scared Off in Scandal of Russia's Tortured Conscript', *Sunday Times*, 23 July 2006.

for low morale. The young men sent to Chechnya are largely those without parents rich enough to buy exemption from service. They are given little or no combat training, receive substandard equipment and rations, and are pressed into the service of an occupation loathed by the Chechen civilians among whom they must live. Their fear, as they patrol Grozny clinging to their armoured personnel carriers, is palpable.

Corruption is a systemic feature of the occupation, and one which works to sustain it by making the disaster inflicted on Chechnya profitable. Each of the ministries operating in Chechnya runs its own fiefdom, with corresponding rackets in oil, kidnapping and other contraband. Arms are frequently sold to the Chechen resistance fighters themselves, who then turn them on the occupiers. Moreover, those returning to Russia from tours of duty in Chechnya often bring with them the vicious habits learned there: MVD troops go back to patrolling Russia's streets inculcated with a hatred of Caucasians, and with a sense that violence towards them will be tolerated. Many more return with missing limbs or psychological trauma, unable to rejoin civilian life. In all of these ways, the ugly symptoms of Russia's aggression towards Chechnya have metastasized into a cancer that threatens to consume Russian public and private life.

The Russian media had played a key role in conveying something of the horrors of the 1994–6 war. This time, the authorities have not made the mistake of allowing them the freedom to operate, requiring all journalists to register with the Interior Ministry and be ferried in and out of Chechnya by helicopter – 'embedding' their coverage of the war in the official perspective. This has been reinforced by the regular Friday 'grey briefings', at which 'members of the presidential staff express their wishes (in the form of demands) as to what they want covered and how'. At one such meeting in autumn 2005, journalists were given a helpful glossary of terms, listing preferred designations to be used in coverage – not 'Chechen separatists', but 'Chechen terrorists'; not '*jihad*' but 'subversive terrorist activity'; not 'field commander' but 'leader of an illegal armed formation', and so on.[26]

Official intervention has not been confined to terminology. The two

---

[26] Gazeta.ru, 3 November 2005.

most critical sources of news, the independent TV channels NTV and
TV6, have been silenced: NTV, formerly owned by the media magnate
Vladimir Gusinsky, was taken over in 2001 by the state gas monopoly
Gazprom, which has close links to the government; in 2002, TV6, in
which billionaire oligarch-turned-Kremlin critic Boris Berezovsky held
a sizeable stake, was forced to shut down by a court acting on the orders
of LUKOil, another company with connections to the Kremlin.
Although many crucial and courageous reports have been filed from
Chechnya by Anna Politkovskaya for the liberal bi-weekly *Novaia gazeta*
and Andrei Babitsky for Radio Svoboda – the Russian branch of Radio
Free Europe/Radio Liberty – the influence of radio and especially print
are negligible compared to that of television, now dominated by the
government line.

The treatment Babitsky and Politkovskaya have received indicates
what critical journalists can expect. Babitsky was described by Putin as
'working directly for the enemy', and his reporting as 'much more
dangerous than firing a machine gun'.[27] Politkovskaya on several occasions received abuse and death threats from soldiers in Chechnya, and
was very likely poisoned while travelling to Beslan in an attempt to
mediate in the hostage crisis of September 2004. On 7 October 2006,
as she was preparing to file a story on the torture of Chechen civilians
by Ramzan Kadyrov's militias, she was gunned down in the lift of her
apartment building in Moscow, a contract killing whose prime bene-
ficiaries are those whose brutality and corruption she worked so tirelessly
to expose. It took Putin a full three days to even comment publicly on
the murder, which he condemned in a few stock phrases before
dismissing Politkovskaya's influence on political life in Russia as
'minimal'; claiming that her death 'causes the current authorities far
greater losses and damage than her publications', he went so far as to
suggest that her killing was carried out in an attempt to 'create a wave
of anti-Russian feeling in the world'.[28] Such distortions laid bare once
more the base cynicism of Putin's regime, painting itself as the victim
while yet another of its opponents was being buried. At the time of
writing, there seemed little chance that Politkovskaya's killers would be

---

[27] Putin's autobiography, *First Person*, quoted in Truscott, *Putin's Progress*, p. 130.
[28] Grani.ru, 10 October 2006, quoted in *Chechnya Weekly*, 12 October 2006.

apprehended, since the most likely suspects are backed to the hilt by the Kremlin. Her death removes from the scene one of the few journalists to report directly from Chechnya without regard for official restrictions, and as such represents an enormous loss both to the Russian public and to the Chechens.

Government pressure and the stifling of any alternative view of the conflict have resulted in a dismal convergence of official discourse and journalistic commentary. Rebels – referred to by Russian soldiers as *dukhi*, 'spirits' – are 'destroyed' rather than killed, the adversary either dehumanized or assimilated to a virulent stereotype, to the point where 'terrorist' and 'Chechen' have indeed become virtually synonymous. The poisonous social repercussions of this can be seen in the way that generalized antipathy to 'persons of Caucasian extraction' has often flared up into outright xenophobia, resulting in both official and spontaneous public persecution not only of Chechens but also of other peoples from the region. In September 1999, for instance, 15,000 Caucasian residents of Moscow were expelled from the city by the authorities in 'Operation Foreigner', and another 69,000 compelled to re-register. In September 2003, fifty-four Chechen students were beaten by a skinhead mob in Nalchik, capital of Kabardino-Balkaria; in April 2004, a ten-year-old Armenian boy was set on fire in a market in the central Russian city of Kostroma; in September 2004, a gang of twenty youths ransacked cafes belonging to Caucasians in Yekaterinburg in the Urals; in September 2006, after a brawl involving Chechens, Azeris and Russians resulted in the deaths of two locals, angry mobs rampaged through the town of Kondopoga in Karelia, near the Finnish border, and rallied to demand the expulsion of all Caucasians living in the town; other examples abound.[29]

This widespread public hostility to the Chechen cause partly explains the absence of a cogent movement against the war. As was the case in 1994–6, parliamentary opposition was confined to the liberal parties, above all the centre-right Yabloko, whose leader Grigorii Yavlinsky had been a prominent advocate of free market reforms in the early 1990s;

[29] See Amnesty International report, 'For the Motherland', December 1999; *Chronicle of Higher Education*, 15 October 2003; *Moscow Times*, 23 April 2004; *Moscow News*, 9 September 2004; *International Herald Tribune*, 4 September 2006.

some figures from the Union of Right Forces (SPS) also spoke out occasionally. But these are extremely marginal voices, the two parties each gaining less than 5 per cent of the vote in the Duma elections of 2003. There have been some stirrings outside parliament: human-rights organizations have staged several small demonstrations in Moscow, and on 6–7 November 2004 the Union of Soldiers' Mothers' Committees held the founding congress for a new political party. But dissent has thus far focused largely on the war's brutality rather than its political roots. Chechnya has all but vanished as an issue on which the government's appalling record could be challenged, and the notion of independence is regularly sidelined even by Putin's critics. In 2004, the leftist commentator Boris Kagarlitsky wrote that 'the central issue . . . is not Chechen independence or Russia's territorial integrity, but democracy in Russia and Chechnya'.[30] On the contrary: any truly democratic vote on Chechnya's future would hinge precisely on the question of sovereignty, and any genuine realization of democracy in Russia would depend on ending its oppression of the Chechens, and recognizing their right to a sovereign state.

There are some fragile grounds for optimism on this score. Putin's 'anti-terrorist operation' initially proved popular, gaining the approval of 70 per cent of the Russian population by February 2000. But since then, its popularity has declined, dropping to 44 per cent in favour in October of the same year; it has not risen above 50 per cent since. Opinion polls by Russia's most reputable independent research institute indicate a consistent majority in favour of negotiations, averaging over 60 per cent since 2003. By mid-2005, 77 per cent of those questioned would have been prepared to see Chechnya separate from Russia, or thought this was de facto already the case. By May 2006, only 18 per cent were in favour of continued military operations.[31] It is a long way from here to active opposition to the occupation, however, and the prospects of such a peace being put forward have been dimmed by the reconfiguration of Russian politics that has taken place under Putin.

The hardships and disappointments of the 1990s resulted in a general political atomization and increasing apathy in Russia, electoral turnouts

---

[30] Boris Kagarlitsky, 'Where is Chechnya Going?', *Moscow Times*, 3 June 2004.
[31] Data from the Levada Centre, available at www.levada.ru/chechnya.html; see also *Chechnya Weekly*, 20 July 2005.

dropping and political debate becoming steadily more sterile. Despite much polemical sound and fury, disagreements between the major parties have long been minimal in substance. But the rise of Putin brought a qualitative change in this landscape. Reversing the chaotic, centrifugal tendencies of the Yeltsin years, Putin has worked to consolidate what he famously termed the 'vertical of power'. This has involved a formidable re-centralization of authority, with what had already been a pliable parliament under Yeltsin effectively converted into a branch of the Presidential Administration. The 'United Russia' faction, which has not ventured a single independent opinion since its formation in 2001, is fast becoming a new *nomenklatura* on the model of the Communist Party. Winning 222 of 450 Duma seats in the 2003 elections, it has rapidly developed a nationwide membership and administrative infrastructure, providing careerists with a path to bureaucratic power and economic comfort in exchange for their rubber-stamping of any initiative descended from on high.

More significantly, state structures have been flooded with former and current security services personnel, known as *siloviki*, from the Russian *sila*, 'force'. The sociologist Olga Kryshtanovskaia calculated in 2003 that 58 per cent of those occupying senior posts in the Putin administration had previously been in the security services, compared to 5 per cent under Gorbachev.[32] The Chechen war has been a crucial source of cadres for Putin's neo-authoritarian project: of the seven presidential plenipotentiaries appointed in May 2000 to run Russia's newly devised administrative super-regions – whose boundaries coincide with those of Russia's military districts – two were veterans of Chechnya, and another three were generals. Several more who had commanded forces in Chechnya moved into other senior government posts.[33]

This organizational mutation has been accompanied by a clampdown on dissent and civil liberties in Russia. The muzzling of opinions contrary to those of the government has been carried out not only through the

---

[32] Cited in Arkady Ostrovsky, 'Putin Oversees Big Rise in Influence of Security Apparatus', *Financial Times*, 1 November 2003.

[33] Trenin and Malashenko, *Russia's Restless Frontier*, pp. 152–4. Viktor Kazantsev ran the Southern District until 2004, and Konstantin Pulikovsky the Far Eastern till 2005; Anatoly Kvashnin was appointed to head the Siberian District in 2005. Other uniformed appointees to high office have included Ivan Babichev, Anatoly Kulikov, Lev Rokhlin, Vladimir Shamanov and Gennady Troshev.

takeover of media outlets, but also by legislative means. In June 2002, a law on 'extremism' was adopted which banned any attempt forcibly to alter the constitution or undermine national security. Any organizations the authorities deemed extremist could now be disbanded – with no criteria specified, thus opening the way to à la carte repression. In late 2005, a law was adopted bringing the operations of NGOs on Russian soil under tighter control, prompting a flurry of protest from the West, whose funding for 'civil society' organizations Putin perceived as a variant of espionage. One of the new law's provisions required NGOs to provide the names, addresses, passport numbers and contact details for everyone attending meetings, including those held abroad; this combination of ludicrous bureaucratism and veiled threat seems an apt summation of the Putin regime's use of administrative power.

Foreign-funded NGOs were the particular target of the NGO legislation, which allowed for the closure of organizations deemed to pose 'a threat to the sovereignty, political independence, territorial integrity, national unity, unique character, cultural heritage and national interests of the Russian Federation' – a net broad enough to entangle almost any activity to which the authorities object. It would certainly affect many of the charities and aid organizations which carry out vital humanitarian work in the rubble-strewn vacuum left by state authority in Chechnya. Alongside such administrative pressures, there have been cases of more active persecution: in February 2006, the head of the Russian–Chechen Friendship Society was given a two-year suspended sentence for inciting ethnic hatred by publishing on the internet appeals for peace by Maskhadov and the London-based separatist envoy Akhmed Zakaev; on 13 October 2006 the local court in Nizhnii Novgorod, where the Friendship Society is based, officially ordered that the organization be closed down – silencing another critical voice on Chechnya only days after Politkovskaya's murder.

Russia's authoritarian turn since 2000 has been driven by a coalition between *siloviki* and business and political elites, with the three groups increasingly overlapping. As such, the Putin phenomenon indicates a deeper-lying structural transformation of the Russian state. However, the mechanism for consolidating this neo-KGB system has been Putin's elevation as the man supposedly responsible for bringing order to Chechnya. The utter devastation wrought by Russian troops there since 1999, the ongoing terrorization and murder of civilians, the smashing of livelihoods and infrastructure all point to the total failure of the 'anti-terrorist operation', whose only success has been to sow the seeds of war for generations to come. If there is to be any accounting for the most recent crimes of the Russian state in Chechnya, it will surely have to centre on the man who owes his political existence to the Chechens' suffering. On assuming the presidency at a ceremony in the Kremlin on 7 May 2000, Putin said that 'in Russia, the head of the government was always and will always be the person who answers for everything'.[34] That he seems likely to escape any such judgement is largely the consequence of the outside world's complicity in his genocidal war.

Western responses to Putin's assault on Chechen statehood have involved either eager complicity or mute acquiescence, above all since the launching of the 'War on Terror' after the September 11 attacks. Putin's success in painting the Chechen resistance as part of an international Islamist insurgency partly explains the marginalization of Chechnya from the world's agendas; the actual role of religion in the war and extent of Chechen connections with overseas *mujahideen* requires separate treatment, and forms the subject of chapter 6. But we should note that governments and multilateral institutions proved willing to set Chechnya aside long before September 11. Their responses since then have merely marked the deterioration of an already abject record.

While cynical neglect has been the dominant international attitude, the Blair government from the outset played a more destructive role. The Prime Minister's early embrace of Putin, and consistent support since then, demonstrates the hypocritical selectivity of his 'humanitarian interventionism'. Robin Cook, proponent of New Labour's short-lived 'ethical foreign policy', met Putin in February 2000 and said, of the man who in October 1999 had proposed dispatching with a single shot to the head anyone wanting to negotiate with the rebels, that 'I found his style refreshing and open, and his priorities for Russia are ones that we would share.'[35] The following month, Blair visited Putin in St

---

[34] Quoted in Satter, *Darkness at Dawn*, p. 71.
[35] Sweeney, 'Russia's Worst War Crime in Chechnya'; Satter, *Darkness at Dawn*, p. 269 n. 25. The Russian expression for a single shot to the head is *kontrol'nyi vystrel*, literally 'control shot' – another piece of criminal slang.

Petersburg – providing active international endorsement for a candidate just over two weeks before an election. British priorities were made clear: a spokesman for Blair said 'Russia is too important a country to ignore or isolate over Chechnya.' Besides, as Blair himself pointed out, 'it is important to realize that Chechnya isn't Kosovo.' One British official went still further, declaring that 'there is a terrorist insurrection on their territory'.[36] Even before Putin became president, then, the UK government had surrendered any notion of an independent policy, entirely adopting the position of its new ally. Blair's shoulder-to-shoulder stance with Bush in Afghanistan and Iraq has rightly attracted criticism from many quarters; his fulsome support for Putin demonstrates that New Labour's subservience is not confined to the Special Relationship. On 27 March 2000, Blair rushed to be the first to congratulate Putin on his electoral victory, but was beaten to it by Jiang Zemin and Clinton. He made amends by trying to develop a rapport with Putin: his visit to Moscow in November 2000 marked their fifth meeting in ten months.[37]

In Europe, bodies such as the Organization for Security and Co-operation in Europe (OSCE) and the Parliamentary Assembly of the Council of Europe (PACE) initially criticized the ferocious attack on Grozny; the PACE suspended Russia's voting rights on 6 April 2000. However, protests were soon toned down and dismissed by European governments as counter-productive amid attempts to welcome Putin to the European fold. On 25 January 2001 the PACE restored Russia's voting rights, and the criticisms that have been raised at its meetings by figures such as Andreas Gross, Rudolf Bindig and Frank Judd have been blithely ignored by their respective governments. In September 2001, while state-sanctioned murders were being committed with impunity in Chechnya, Putin received a standing ovation in the Bundestag. In the summer of 2002, Chirac endorsed the Russian view of the 'anti-terrorist operation', and he and Schroeder reiterated their support at Sochi in August 2004. In November 2004 Schroeder went so far as to call Putin a 'flawless democrat', urging a more 'differentiated approach' to Chechnya. Schroeder's support did not go unrewarded: on leaving office in November 2005, he took up a position chairing the shareholders' committee of the North European Gas Pipeline

36 Truscott, *Putin's Progress*, pp. 137–41.
37 Truscott, *Putin's Progress*, pp. 151, 258.

consortium, a joint venture between Gazprom, BASF and E.ON to transport gas under the Baltic Sea.

Germany's increasingly close ties with both Russian business and government undoubtedly played some part in preventing a co-ordinated EU response. But it had become clear within months of the Russian invasion that European threats on this front were toothless. In December 1999, the EU had raised the prospect of sanctions as a result of the ultimatum issued to Grozny's residents to flee the city or face destruction. The Russians simply repeated the ultimatum, and no sanctions ensued. Collective EU efforts have been limited to humanitarian aid for the refugee camps in Ingushetia. A visit to one of them by the future Finnish prime minister Tarja Halonen in 1999 provided an illustrative vignette: Halonen repeatedly insisted 'I represent the European Union, I'm here to help you' and asked what the refugees' problems were; but when confronted by replies such as 'We want a political resolution, not war' and 'Tell them to stop bombing us, to stop killing our children', Halonen seemed at a loss, and could only offer around tangerines.[38]

Despite repeated approaches from Maskhadov's envoys, the UN, for its part, refused to meet with Chechnya's legitimately elected leaders – though Kofi Annan was quick to express his grief at the assassination of the puppet Kadyrov in May 2004. On a visit to Moscow in 2002 Annan even praised Putin's efforts at conflict resolution – doubtless appreciative of Putin's prior backing for his bid to secure a second term as secretary-general. Questions about Russia's actions in Chechnya have routinely been sidestepped at meetings of the UN's Human Rights Committee. Indeed, the spineless reaction of the 'international community' to Putin's war on the Chechens reached a new nadir in October 2003 when Kadyrov, newly installed by rigged polls, attended a meeting of this very body in Geneva. Since 2000, Kadyrov's thousands-strong private militias, commanded by his son Ramzan, had been assisting Russian troops in their assault on the civilian population. The over-

---

[38] Anne Nivat, *Chienne de Guerre*, New York 2001, p. 54. Nivat is the only Western journalist to have reported on the Second Chechen War from behind Chechen lines, disguising herself as a Chechen woman and running the gauntlet of Russian checkpoints and bombardments for six months before being arrested by the FSB and deported in 2000. Her forceful depiction of the Chechens' experiences of the war makes her book an invaluable corrective to embedded accounts – as is her subsequent work, evocatively titled *La guerre qui n'aura pas eu lieu*, Paris 2004.

whelming responsibility of *kadyrovtsy* for the torrent of abductions in Chechnya has been thoroughly demonstrated by eyewitnesses, reporters and human-rights activists operating there. In 2002 and 2003 alone, there were over 1,000 documented disappearances, with at least 100 subsequently found dead and over 650 lost without trace.[39] Kadyrov assured his UN audience, however, that 'no one is more concerned about the citizens of the Chechen Republic today than I am . . . It is true that we have had violations and abductions. But it is wrong to subject me to any sort of inquisitorial process here.' Instead of demanding the removal of this poisonous figure and the holding of democratic elections, or at the very least refusing him permission to attend the Committee, let alone address it, the UN merely 'expressed concern', and acknowledged the 'difficult circumstances under which the presidential election was held'. Further, the UN gave a green light to the continuation of this atrocious war, asking only that 'the state party should ensure that operations in Chechnya are carried out in compliance with its international human rights obligations'.[40]

Nor has criticism been forthcoming from elsewhere. In 1999 the Iranian foreign minister Kamal Kharrazi insisted the Russo-Chechen war was strictly an internal affair, and in December 2005, after a report in the *Sunday Telegraph* claimed that Iran was training Chechen fighters, Tehran issued a statement saying that 'the IRI regards the issue of the Republic of Chechnya as being in the competence of Russia and its internal matter'.[41] China, meanwhile, saw in Yeltsin's and Putin's suppression of Chechen aspirations for independence a useful precedent for its own dealings with Tibet and Xinjiang.[42] Arab governments for their part have at various times emphasized their support for Russia's territorial integrity. In February 2006 the newly elected Hamas even sent delegates to Moscow to meet with Putin. While Chechnya's Islamists saw this as an act of treachery, Akhmed Zakaev pointed out that one can only be betrayed by friends or allies, adding bitterly that Hamas's

---

[39] Figures from the human-rights NGO Memorial, reproduced in International Helsinki Federation report, 'Unofficial Places of Detention in the Chechen Republic', 12 May 2006,.Appendix 2. Note that Memorial only covers 25–30 per cent of the country; the real figures are likely to be far higher.

[40] Lokshina, *Imposition of a Fake Settlement*, pp. 225, 230.

[41] *Chechnya Weekly*, 8 December 2005.

[42] Trenin and Malashenko, *Russia's Restless Frontier*, pp. 191, 205.

embassy 'does not surprise or anger us more than the visits and friendly conversations with Putin of the Iranian, Qatari and Saudi leaders'.[43]

During the 1994–6 war, the Chechen resistance received considerable support from its diaspora in Turkey, with the tacit permission of the authorities, while Azerbaijan accepted many refugees and gave medical treatment to wounded fighters. The second war has seen significant policy shifts in both countries. As one analyst noted, 'Turkish support for the Chechen cause during this war has been significantly limited. The Turkish government has impeded, and at times banned, pro-Chechen rallies, restricted the ability of pro-Chechen organizations to operate and raise funds, and forced a number of Chechen activists to leave the country.'[44] Perhaps other factors took precedence: Prime Minister Ecevit signed several agreements with Moscow 'on the eve of the Russian storm of Grozny in 1999', including the 'Blue Stream' deal for a gas pipeline under the Black Sea. In Azerbaijan, though the number of refugees from the second war was far higher – at one stage reaching 10,000, compared to 3,000 in 1994–6 – the Azeri authorities willingly echoed the Russian clampdown, extraditing Chechen Islamists to Russia to prevent the radicalization of their own populace, and pressuring the Chechen Cultural Centre in Baku into closing. A police sweep among Chechen refugees in January 2001 obligingly coincided with a state visit by Putin.[45]

Official reaction in the US was initially conditioned by the same concern for Russia's fledgling free-market order that dictated approval of Yeltsin's war. Clinton raised human-rights issues on a handful of occasions, but demonstrated the insincerity of these gestures by hailing the 'liberation' of Grozny in early 2000. At the Auckland meeting of the Asia-Pacific Economic Cooperation Forum in mid-September 1999, Putin had assured Clinton that Russian forces would stop at the Terek, and even drew a map for him on a serviette. At the same meeting, he tried to play up the Islamist threat from Chechnya by telling the US ambassador to Moscow that Osama bin Laden, whom the US had tried

[43] Quoted on Newsru.com, 3 March 2006.
[44] Michael Reynolds, 'Turkish-Russian Relations and the Conflict in Chechnya', *Central Asia – Caucasus Analyst*, 30 January 2002.
[45] Anar Valiyev, 'Growing Anti-Chechen Sentiment in Azerbaijan', *Chechnya Weekly*, 18 May 2006.

to kill by bombing Sudan in 1996, had been in Chechnya 'several times that year'.[46] Of course, attempts to connect Chechnya to a wider battle against Islamism met with far more success after September 11. The Russian response to the attacks on the World Trade Center and Pentagon redrew Eurasia's geopolitical map: Putin gave the US permission to plant forward bases across Central Asia, Russia's former sphere of influence. Washington responded with the requisite silence on Chechnya, which it showed no signs of breaking even with the reappearance of Cold War rhetoric after the Ukrainian election crisis of late 2004.

The rapprochement with Russia, while it lasted, was a marked change of tack for many of the neo-cons, whose hostility to Russia meant support for Chechen independence from unlikely quarters. Members of the American Committee for Peace in Chechnya include Richard Perle, Kenneth Adelman, Elliott Abrams, Midge Decter and James Woolsey, as well as Zbigniew Brzezinski. Outside official circles, right-wingers such as Richard Pipes have also argued the Chechens' case, pointing out that authoritarianism is in the Russian DNA and that Putin would do well to learn the lessons de Gaulle drew from Algeria.[47] A similar Cold War animus motivates French *philosophe* André Glucksmann's consistent criticism of the Chechen War. His indignation does not, however, stretch to Western acts of aggression: he solidly backed the invasion of Iraq, and in 2006 called for the revival of a 'democratic, military and critical European-Atlantic alliance' to stave off the threat of Islamists, 'bloodthirsty Saddam Hussein nostalgics' and the 'sirens of isolationism' alike.[48]

Liberals, by contrast, have been divided between those who accept the devastation visited on Chechnya as a regrettable bump in Russia's difficult road to a stable democracy, and those who actively endorse Putin's war. There is almost universal agreement on the unacceptability of Chechen independence. The 'Brzezinski plan' put forward in 2002 merely provided for autonomy within Russia, and required Russia to

---

[46] Truscott, *Putin's Progress*, p. 247.

[47] John Laughland, 'The Chechens' American Friends', *Guardian*, 8 September 2004; Richard Pipes, 'Give the Chechens a Land of Their Own', *New York Times*, 9 September 2004.

[48] See Éric Aeschimann, 'Les meilleurs amis de l'Amérique', *Libération*, 9 May 2006; and André Glucksmann, 'Vietnamisierung oder Somalisierung?', *Der Standard*, 16 June 2006.

acknowledge only 'the right of the Chechens to political, though not national, self-determination'.[49] Similarly, after describing the horrors it has experienced over the last decade, Jonathan Steele concludes that Chechnya was a 'failed state', and argues that in order to persuade Putin to enter into talks with the Chechens, 'the first requirement is the exclusion of formal independence as a subject for negotiation'.[50] The same point has been made by Thomas de Waal, who said in July 2006 that Chechnya should not even be treated any longer as a conflict, but rather as a 'human-rights disaster area'.[51] De Waal has advocated independence for Abkhazia, on the grounds that refusing to the Abkhaz what is being granted to the Kosovars smacks of 'double standards'; but he seems unwilling to apply the same argument to Chechnya.[52]

Anatol Lieven, meanwhile, has moved from a warm, critical sympathy for the separatist cause to a vigorous defence of Putin's right to launch an invasion of Chechnya. In September 2004 he suggested Maskhadov needed to fight 'alongside Russian forces' against his Islamist compatriots.[53] Elsewhere Lieven has drawn a distinction between the legal basis for waging war – *jus ad bellum* – and the legality of combatants' conduct during the war itself – *jus in bello*. On the latter count, he condemns Russian atrocities, but at the same time urges 'more nuanced' assessments, labelling 'some of the criticism directed at Russia' as 'both unfair and ignorant of military realities'. The street-by-street defence of Grozny against vastly superior Russian weaponry and manpower, which won the separatists praise in his powerful *Chechnya: Tombstone of Russian Power* for their tactical agility, is here assailed as having provoked the Russian bombardment. That the city was virtually levelled should not, in Lieven's view, be blamed on Russia; for 'to accuse the

---

[49] Zbigniew Brzezinski, Alexander Haig and Max Kampelman, 'The Way to Chechen Peace', *Washington Post*, 21 June 2002.

[50] Jonathan Steele, 'Doing Well out of War', *London Review of Books*, 21 October 2004.

[51] Comments at a House of Lords meeting on Chechnya, 18 July 2006.

[52] Thomas de Waal, 'Abkhazia's Dream of Freedom', *openDemocracy*, 10 May 2006. On 2 June 2006, however, the Russian Foreign Minister Sergei Lavrov did make the connection: he called for referenda on self-determination in South Ossetia and Abkhazia, and proudly pointed to the example of Chechnya's 2003 constitutional referendum – a staggering piece of mendaciousness that only demonstrates how free a hand Putin has been given in Chechnya.

[53] Anatol Lieven, 'A Western Strategy for Chechnya', *International Herald Tribune*, 9 September 2004.

attacking side of committing a crime in its use of heavy firepower is to declare war itself a crime'.[54] With regard to *jus ad bellum*, he now describes Russia's right to wage war on Chechnya as 'incontestable', given that Chechnya is 'an internationally recognized part of Russia's territory in rebellion against its sovereign', and that Maskhadov's government 'proved incapable of controlling its territory'.

Russia's overwhelming responsibility in making Chechnya uncontrollable, and ensuring it continued to be so, has been discussed in chapter 4. We should note here that the disorders of which Lieven speaks were to a large extent matters of law enforcement; Putin's choice of known criminals as his allies reveals Russia's lack of interest in restoring legality in Chechnya, for which purpose massive military force was manifestly ill-suited. More importantly, Chechnya was not in rebellion against its sovereign: according to the 12 May 1997 treaty, it had de facto been recognized as a sovereign state by Russia. In the same treaty, Russia pledged to use all peaceful means to resolve disputes. Prior to Putin's invasion of 1999, no peaceful avenues were even explored, leaving Russia in breach of the 1997 treaty – and therefore, according to the stipulations of that document, in breach of international law. Far from being a justifiable war conducted unjustly, Putin's war on Chechnya trampled on the legal principles and treaty obligations to which the Russian state was bound by international law. Any claims to a moral basis would have been shattered by the conduct of Russian forces in Chechnya, which have inflicted such sustained violence on the local population that, even had their right to statehood been in doubt before 1999, the Chechens now have a plausible case for sovereignty as the best means of protecting themselves from annihilation as a people.

Common to much Western commentary on Russia since the turn of the century has been a recurrent focus on Putin – some decrying his authoritarian leanings, others approving of his drive to regain control over a state that was in danger of unravelling under Yeltsin. The main items of contention have not been the lives of Russians or Chechens, but above all the interests of Western investors. The arrest of YUKOS

---

[54] Lieven, 'Chechya and the Laws of War', in Trenin and Malashenko, *Russia's Restless Frontier*, pp. 209–24.

chairman Mikhail Khodorkovsky for tax evasion in 2003 and his subsequent imprisonment prompted an outpouring of articles discussing the harm thereby done to Russia's fragile democracy, while the concentration of key posts in Russian industry in the hands of government personnel has brought accusations of nationalization by stealth. Such were the principal concerns mooted when Russia took up the presidency of the G8 in 2006, and which dominated discussion thereafter.

Yet for all the column inches expended on Putin's economic policy and retrograde political leanings, it is in Chechnya that the true face of his regime is revealed, and it is above all by his sponsorship of wanton brutality there that Putin should be judged. His rise to power was founded on the flattening of Grozny and the deaths of countless civilians, on the unleashing of hatred to redress Russia's decline as a world power. With his term due to expire in 2008, Putin will likely name a successor who will continue along much the same path, and he will at the very least remain influential behind the scenes. Nevertheless, Russia's next president may be in a better position to negotiate than Putin, whose career was built on icy intransigence. Both Russia's and Chechnya's hopes for the future rest on the conclusion of his blood-soaked reign, and on bringing to an end a war which has disfigured Russia and once again devastated Chechnya. No democracy worthy of the name will be possible in either country until the killing stops – and until the Chechens are allowed freely to decide on their own status.

6.

The Uses of Islamism

The Russian authorities have long sought to portray their attack on Chechnya not as an attempt to crush the Chechens' aspirations to independence, but as part of a wider battle against Islamist insurgency. In July 2000, Putin referred to 'the formation of a sort of fundamentalist international, an arc of instability extending from the Philippines to Kosovo', adding that 'Europe should be grateful to us and offer its appreciation for our fight against terrorism even if we are, unfortunately, waging it on our own.'[1] Since the September 11 attacks, Western governments have been much more willing to give credence to Moscow's assertions of an 'Islamic threat'. The hysterical rhetoric and military aggressions of the US-led 'War on Terror' have only served to validate Putin's world-view, in which Russia is fighting forces menacing modern civilization itself; as he told assembled journalists in The Hague in November 2005, his opponents in Chechnya are 'beasts in the guise of human beings'.[2]

The slaughter of innocent civilians at Moscow's Dubrovka Theatre in October 2002 and in Beslan in September 2004, after the seizure

[1] Interview with *Paris Match*, quoted by Reuters, 7 July 2000.
[2] Interfax, 2 November 2005.

of hostages by groups loyal to Shamil Basaev, certainly revealed an appalling degeneration among elements in the Chechen resistance, whose borrowing of tactics and slogans from Islamist militant groups elsewhere has helped to further embed the Chechen struggle in the typology of terrorism. The recent spread of armed rebellion across the North Caucasus, meanwhile, has been credited to guerrillas allied to Chechen Islamists bent on carving a pan-Caucasian Islamic state out of Russia's southern periphery – precisely the danger on whose existence Russian official-dom has been insisting.

But to accept this picture is to misunderstand the character and composition of Islamic radicalism in Chechnya. In order to grasp the actual role it has played in the Chechen war, we need to examine the specific history of Islam in the country: its arrival and adaptation to local circumstances, its social and political functions under Russian and Soviet rule, and its intensifying use as mobilizing ideology since 1991. We can then turn to the extent of radicalizing influences from overseas. These have played an important part in Chechnya's fate, affecting the battle tactics and political complexion of the Chechen resistance move-ment. But they have not, I will argue, altered its core substance, which was and is directed towards achieving national self-determination. The kingdom of heaven is, for the Chechens, no substitute for the right to their own earthly republic.

Islam first arrived in the region with the conquest of Derbent on the coast of present-day Dagestan by the soldiers of the Ummayad caliph Hisham ibn Abd al-Malik in 733 AD. By the tenth century, Derbent – known in Arabic as Bab al-Abwab, the Gate of Gates – had become a formidable centre of Arab learning, dispatching Muslim missionaries inland to Islamize the scattered tribes of the Caucasus. There is no real agreement as to when the conversion of the Chechens and Ingush took place, but it was most likely a lengthy process that began around the sixteenth century in the lowlands and was not completed until at least the mid-nineteenth century. Prior to this, the Vainakhs – as the Chechens and Ingush collectively refer to themselves – venerated a pantheon of deities including gods of time, death, fire, hunting and a supreme god, Dela, whose name to this day stands in for the Arabic Allah. There were also animist strands, with goddesses of water, winds and snowstorms held to inhabit the land itself, along with forest spirits known as *alma*.[3] Many of these elements survive in Islamized form: tombs of Sufi saints are often located near springs, and the cult of ancestors continues in the significance allotted to death and burial.

A key role in the Islamization of Chechnya was played by Sufi brotherhoods, which arrived in the region in the late eighteenth century and were intimately linked with the anti-colonial struggle against the Russians. Sufism is a mystical tradition in Islam which spans Sunni and Shi'a rites and has taken a variety of social and political colorations – actively combating colonialism in Algeria, Java, Xinjiang, the Punjab and the Fergana Valley, collaborating with it to become the clerical establishment in Bukhara, Kokand and Khiva.[4] As noted in chapter 1, in the North Caucasus, it was the Naqshbandi brotherhood, originating in Bukhara in the fourteenth century, which first mobilized resistance to Russia's southward expansion. It is widely believed that Sheikh Mansur was the region's first Naqshbandi sheikh, and the leaders of the great rebellion of 1829–59 were all Naqshbandis. The attraction of the Naqshbandiyya lay in their appeal to pan-Caucasian solidarity and their egalitarianism, which gained them supporters in semi-feudal Dagestan. In Chechnya, they acquired adepts as a result of their success in battle against the Russians, and seemingly offered the best means of protecting Caucasian autonomy from incorporation into the Tsar's empire. Imam Shamil's imposition of a disciplinarian interpretation of *shari'a*, however, clashed with the long-standing customary laws or *adat* – the first in a series of collisions between Chechen particularities and Qur'anic literalism that continues to this day.

As defeat at the hands of the Tsar's armies neared for Shamil's Imamate, Kunta-Hadji Kishiev's quietistic version of the faith became increasingly popular. Its pacifism offered solace for a flagging resistance, and its use of music and dancing during the *zikr* made it more compatible with local culture than Shamil's austerity. A sheikh of the Qadiri Sufi order, founded in Baghdad by Abd al-Qadir al-Ghilani in the twelfth century, Kunta-Hadji had been expelled from Chechnya by Shamil,

---

[3] Anna Zelkina, *In Quest for God and Freedom: Sufi Responses to the Russian Advance in the North Caucasus*, London 2000, pp. 26, 33–7.
[4] Alexandre Bennigsen and Enders Wimbush, *Mystics and Commissars: Sufism in the Soviet Union*, London 1985, p. 3.

but returned in 1861. With the imprisonment and exile of Shamil and many of his key lieutenants, the Qadiriyya rapidly moved to fill the space the Naqshbandis once occupied. The Qadiris' initial acceptance of Russian rule soon gave way to active resistance: after considerable unrest in Chechnya in 1862–3, Kunta-Hadji was arrested in 1864, and died in a Russian prison three years later. Both Naqshbandis and Qadiris took part in the rebellion of 1877, but even after its repression the Qadiris maintained the numerical superiority over the Naqshbandis that they still retain.

The resilience of the Sufi orders in Chechnya is due to the convergence in the late nineteenth century between the organizational structures of the brotherhoods or *virds* on the one hand, and the Chechen clan system on the other. The boundaries of *taip* and *vird* mapped onto each other: leadership of Qadiri and Naqshbandi branches remained within families over generations, and belonging to a particular *taip* often in itself conferred membership of the relevant *vird*. One of the reasons it is difficult to assess the role currently played by the Sufi orders is that the overlap between *vird* and other allegiances is so extensive that Sufism is to all appearances interwoven with Chechen identity. The most significant result of this has been a conflation of the national and religious that has proved potent until the present day.[5]

However, the Naqshbandiyya and Qadiriyya had distinct social characters. The former was more decentralized and, its earlier record notwithstanding, by the late nineteenth century proved more adaptable to the circumstances of Tsarist rule; it counted Chechnya's wealthier residents among its adepts – landowners and industrialists for the most part, though several Naqshbandi sheikhs profited from the oil boom of the late nineteenth and early twentieth centuries.[6] The Qadiris, on the other hand, were far more rigorously structured, resulting in far better mechanisms both for clandestine activity and the preservation of religious and national traditions. They were particularly strong among popular layers, above all in rural areas.[7] These differences go a long way towards

[5] A. K. Alikberov, *Epokha klassicheskogo islama na Kavkaze*, Moscow 2003, p. 686.
[6] Moshe Gammer, *The Lone Wolf and the Bear: Three Centuries of Chechen Defiance of Russian Rule*, London 2006, p. 107.
[7] See Musa Iusupov, 'Islam v sotsial'no-politicheskoi zhizni Chechni', *Tsentral'naia Aziia i Kavkaz*, No. 2 (8), 2000, p. 167, and Bennigsen and Wimbush, *Mystics and Commissars*, pp. 22–3.

explaining the two orders' divergent responses to 1917 and its aftermath: while the Naqshbandis welcomed the February Revolution, they were hostile to the Bolshevik takeover and it was Naqshbandis who primarily supported Najmuddin of Hotso's Emirate during the Civil War. The followers of Kunta-Hadji, by contrast, were much more positively disposed towards the advent of Soviet power: Sheikh Ali Mitaev of the Bammat Girey *vird* was a member of the Chechen Revolutionary Committee, and some Party members were also Qadiris.[8]

Many of these 'Red Sufis', however, fell victim to a purportedly 'anti-religious' campaign which gathered pace from late 1923 onwards, and which also targeted prominent nationalist figures. Mitaev was arrested in 1924 and then executed, as were many non-believing Caucasian Bolsheviks, notably Najmuddin Samurskii, first secretary of the regional committee of the Dagestani CP. Both Qadiris and Naqshbandis participated in the numerous uprisings against Soviet power that flared up in Chechnya in the 1920s and 30s, and members of the Batal Hadji *vird* continued to wage guerrilla war until 1947, having somehow escaped the NKVD's net during the deportations of 1944.[9]

The period of enforced exile inevitably had a dramatic impact on the spiritual life of the Chechens. The Sufi orders, fusing religious and national traditions, kept functioning in Central Asia and were an important means through which the Chechens retained a sense of common nationhood. A new *vird* was even founded in exile, named Vis Hadji, which thereafter became the most active and radical branch of the Qadiriyya. But the personal networks on which the *virds* were founded had been seriously damaged by deaths and separations after 1944. The *silsila*, the chain through which spiritual authority was transmitted, was in many cases broken, and the otherworldly component of Sufi ritual began to cede ground to the ethno-national dimension. In the eyes of one scholar, it became 'an ethno-cultural tradition that lacked its vital spiritual component' altogether.[10] The trend was accelerated by Soviet repression after the deportation, forcing Sufi practices underground, where they turned inwards to face the core of a shared Chechen past.

---

[8] Bennigsen and Wimbush, *Mystics and Commissars*, p. 27.
[9] Bennigsen and Wimbush, *Mystics and Commissars*, p. 29.
[10] Galina Yemelianova, 'Sufism and Politics in the North Caucasus', *Nationalities Papers*, vol. 29, no. 4, 2001, p. 665.

This was a repository of sorrows with far more immediate force than the consolations of religion.

After the Chechens' return to their homeland in the 1950s, Sufi orders continued to operate clandestinely despite official persecution, circulating texts in *samizdat*, and tape recordings of sermons making repeated reference to Shamil and other heroes of the nineteenth-century resistance. Pilgrimages to *mazars*, the tombs of Sufi saints, had resumed in the 1950s, and those of sheikhs who had fought the Russians proved particularly popular. Soviet specialists noted with concern the 'frankly nationalistic character of the preachings during *zikr* ceremonies'.[11]

The late Soviet period saw a relaxation of constraints on religion in the North Caucasus which resulted in a ferment of debate and a renewal of public forms of worship. Between 1944 and 1978, there were no functioning mosques in Chechnya; between 1978 and 1991, some 200 were opened, built with donations from the faithful and funds provided by local entrepreneurs.[12] The new atmosphere of relative openness brought mounting criticism of the official clergy – the Spiritual Board of Muslims of the North Caucasus (DUMSK in the Russian acronym), established by Stalin in 1943 and based in Makhachkala, capital of Dagestan. Seen as collaborationist by the broad mass of the population – as with the Orthodox church, many of its clerics were known to be KGB operatives – the DUMSK was the target of complaints from a variety of sources, Sufi *virds* prominent among them. It was to fragment into several muftiates in 1989, as many of the constituent republics of the Russian Federation sought the attributes of statehood.

The crucial point to note here, however, is that the religious revival that gathered pace in the 1980s did not seek to achieve its goals on spiritual grounds alone, but instead allied with emerging democratic movements. In 1985, Alexandre Bennigsen and Enders Wimbush, specialists on Islam in the USSR, concluded that the Sufi brotherhoods 'have no political ideology and no political programme. On the other

---

[11] Bennigsen and Wimbush, *Mystics and Commissars*, p. 105, quoting S. Murtazalieva's 1981 article 'Bor'ba idei i svoboda sovesti'. See also pp. 64, 83, 92.

[12] Iusupov, 'Islam v sotsial'no-politicheskoi zhizni Chechni', p. 165. The frenzy of mosque-construction intensified after 1991: see Anatol Lieven, *Chechnya: Tombstone of Russian Power*, London 1998, pp. 24–5, on the curious neo-Gothic architecture of these buildings.

hand, they do possess an exceptionally effective organizational framework around which potential political dissent with Muslim religious colouring could coalesce and be directed.'[13] Precisely this combination of forces was to take shape during Chechnya's push for independence in 1990–1.

The synchrony between Chechen social and spiritual life to which I have already referred had the effect of turning religious rites into formal displays of ethno-national identity. In the Soviet period, these had been a means of asserting a common tradition in the face of official repression and the contradictory pressures of modernity. But with the collapse of Soviet authority and Dudaev's declaration of independence in 1991, the function of religion in public life underwent a far-reaching transformation.[14]

As noted in chapter 2, Dudaev's main support base was among rural Chechens, while lowlanders and city-dwellers tended to have a more positive view of the Soviet system, having acquired concrete benefits from it – education, healthcare, secure employment. The social distinctions between broadly pro- and anti-Dudaev sectors of the population often paralleled those between other categories, such as *taip* and *vird*. The few Chechens who had reached prominent positions in the political and economic elite tended to come from the lowlands, and from families with ties to the Naqshbandiyya. When the opposition began to organize demonstrations against Dudaev on a regular basis starting in 1991, he made overtures to the Qadiris and encouraged their involvement in public life. It was at this stage that the *zikr* began to be held on the streets of Grozny, rapidly becoming a symbol for the national movement.

Given the numerical weight of Dudaev's more traditionalist support base, religious slogans proved an irresistible tool for sidelining the opposition, and a vital means for Dudaev to mobilize his constituency in a crisis. During the stand-off between parliament and president of spring 1993, for instance, Dudaev announced that Islam would be the state religion. Dudaev's Islamicizing stance had a further, external function, as 'an ideological means of pressuring the political leadership of the Russian Federation'.[15] With Moscow ratcheting up pressure on Dudaev,

---

[13] Bennigsen and Wimbush, *Mystics and Commissars*, p. 112.
[14] Musa Iusupov's 'Islam v sotsial'no-politicheskoi zhizni Chechni' provides an excellent account; see also Yemelianova, 'Sufism and Politics in the North Caucasus'.
[15] Iusupov, 'Islam v sotsial'no-politicheskoi zhizni Chechni', p. 168.

the rhetorical recourse to Islam became more frequent. But the substance of political contention in Chechnya was still rooted in this world. In Anatol Lieven's account, 'it was only with the autumn of 1994, and the imminent threat of war, that the rhetoric of political Islam became insistent – and even then, it was I felt overwhelmingly a symbol and expression of national feeling rather than a detailed programme in its own right.'[16] The Russian invasion of 1994, in smashing Chechnya's physical structures and social life, was to alter drastically this configuration of spirit and matter.

The harsh circumstances of war are fertile ground for austere, millenarian brands of religion. Shamil had been proof of this in the nineteenth century, as had Thomas Müntzer during the Peasants' War in fifteenth-century Germany, and countless others in between; examples from the 1990s would include the Lord's Resistance Army in Uganda, Islamist warlords in Somalia and the Taliban's ascent to power amid the rubble of Afghanistan (though this last was mostly due to the backing of Pakistani intelligence). The battlefields of Chechnya were no exception to the rule. The radicalization that took place there in 1994–6 has been tendentiously portrayed as simply the product of outside influences, brought in by Arab *mujahideen* and propelled by Saudi money. A more accurate picture would trace its origins to an indigenous struggle between orthopractic forms of Islam and local traditions which predated the war. This confrontation was devastatingly sharpened by the onset of war, and its future direction was heavily influenced by the few foreigners who came to Chechnya's aid. But it was the war itself that was responsible for the success of a chiliastic brand of Islam which was ultimately to prove hugely destructive.

The term 'Wahhabi' is commonly used to denote Islamic radicals in Chechnya. Though it has wide currency among Chechens, Russians and Westerners alike, we should resist its application to the North Caucasus for two interlinked reasons: firstly, because it is inaccurate; and, second, because this inaccuracy works to further the agenda of those who would ascribe the region's problems solely to outside interference. To take the first point: the word Wahhabi derives from

---

[16] Lieven, *Chechnya*, p. 363.

Mohammed ibn Abd al-Wahhab, an Arabian Sunni preacher who in the mid-seventeenth century made a pact with the tribal chief Mohammed ibn Saud. Abd al-Wahhab provided the legitimating ideology for Saud's expansionist project, consecrating his family's conquest of neighbouring tribes as a holy war promoting a return to the supposed purity of early Islam – dubbed *salafiyya* after the 'righteous ones', the first followers of the Prophet. Wahhabism is inextricably linked to the political fortunes of the House of Saud; it is the social and spiritual complement to the worldly dealings of the Saudi state, and as such has little real meaning outside the Peninsula in which it originated.

Salafism, however, as a movement towards orthopraxy, is a much broader phenomenon. Its recent expansion can be tied to the rise of alternative currents in Islamic thought in the 1950s and 60s – notably the Muslim Brotherhood in Egypt – known as the *sahwa*, or 'awakening'. Many of its key figures fled repression by secular Arab regimes in Egypt, Syria or Iraq and arrived in Saudi Arabia, where they staffed the departments of Islamic universities in Mecca or Jeddah and took over the running of a number of well-resourced NGOs. Their critical view of the clergy's politically compliant role in Saudi Arabia put considerable pressure on the compact between Wahhab's followers and the Saudi monarchy. The solution was to export the ideology of the *sahwa* as a bulwark against communism – thus removing troublesome critics from the scene and ingratiating the Sauds with their patrons in Washington. The volunteers arriving to fight the Red Army in Afghanistan in the early 1980s – including Osama bin Laden – were then the bearers not of Wahhabism, but of a fusion of official Saudi Salafism and the ideas of figures such as Sayyid Qutb, executed in Nasser's Egypt, and the Palestinian Abdullah Azzam, both of whom advocated more active resistance to the colonization of the Muslim world by the West.[17]

In the North Caucasus, there had been indigenous proponents of a return to the sources of Islam during the late Soviet period. They were critical, on the one hand, of the official clerical establishment, seen as colluding with an atheistic regime, and on the other, of traditional local

[17] Gilles Kepel, *The War for Muslim Minds: Islam and the West*, Cambridge, MA 2004, pp. 159, 170–9; Jason Burke, *Al Qaeda: The True Story of Radical Islam*, London 2003, pp. 42–3, 60. See also Aziz al-Azmeh, *Islams and Modernities*, London 1996, chapter 7.

beliefs, seen as distortions of the true faith. Among these early Salafis was Adam Deniev, a member of the pan-Soviet Islamic Renaissance Party which was founded in Astrakhan in 1990 with a programme for the gradual Islamization of public life. Deniev attracted followers from the Ali Mitaev *vird*, as some Chechens sought to distance themselves from traditions they saw as both outmoded and corruptions of Islam.[18] Moreover, the years of Soviet rule had largely cut the USSR's Muslims off from the rest of the Islamic world. The general religious revival that accompanied the collapse of the Soviet Union brought with it a renewed curiosity about the contemporary practice and theory of Islam, creating fertile ground for preachers and educational materials eagerly provided by an array of Islamic foundations in the Gulf. While ostensibly bringing Russian Muslims up to date with developments and ideas in the wider Islamic world, in many cases these foundations propounded a specific, Salafi variant of Islam which sharply contrasted with local traditions.

The contrast was not without its attractions. A significant point worth noting here is that Salafism in the North Caucasus is a paradoxical product of modernization. For many, the superstitions and rituals of their forefathers no longer seemed appropriate to life in industrial society. Official Soviet ideology held little appeal by the time the USSR collapsed, and many of those not taken up in the surge of national sentiment sought other belief-systems and world-views. Salafism was streamlined and – however nebulously, since it lacked a cogent programme – promised social change: while advocating a return to the ways of the *salaf*, it also held out the possibility of 'overcoming the closure and elitism of Sufism, modernizing Islam [by] liberating it from patriarchal traditions', and offering instead 'new, contemporary forms of Muslim solidarity'.[19] Another factor in Salafism's appeal was surely

---

[18] Deniev had a murky career thereafter: he was accused of involvement in the killing of six Red Cross workers in December 1996, and in 1998 the Maskhadov government requested his extradition from Moscow; the request was not granted. During the second war, Deniev was 'generally loyal to the Russian authorities and especially loyal to the special services', claiming himself to be an FSB colonel; he was killed by a bomb in 2001. See Tanya Lokshina, ed., *The Imposition of a Fake Political Settlement in the Northern Caucasus: The 2003 Chechen Presidential Election*, Stuttgart 2005, pp. 158–9, and *Chechnya Weekly*, 17 April 2001.

[19] S. E. Berezhnoi, I. P. Dobaev and P. V. Krainiuchenko, *Islam i islamizm na iuge Rossii*, Rostov-on-Don 2003, pp. 104–6; see also Iusupov, 'Islam v sotsial'no-politicheskoi zhizni Chechni', p. 166.

its asceticism: in harsh economic conditions, a version of Islam that frowned upon costly traditional Caucasian wedding celebrations, for instance, might gather support – especially among young men who were having difficulty securing enough work to be able to think of marriage.

Nevertheless, Salafism was initially restricted to a handful of people in Chechnya. The fusion between the national and religious noted above had given rise to a refreshingly cavalier attitude to the dictates of scripture, as conveyed by the Chechen saying: 'Mohammed was an Arab, but Allah is Chechen.'[20] The real substance of the proverb – apart from its appealing arrogance – is a dogged insistence on ethno-national particularity, which outweighs the outward observances of faith. The same trait was to ensure the Salafis remained vastly in the minority. In 1989, the republic's few Salafis had united with the Qadiris to depose the DUMSK clergy, but the alliance unravelled when the Qadiris took control of the muftiate and effectively became the religious establishment for the democratic nationalist movement. The Salafis were marginalized and played no role in the push for independence; though they joined the opposition to Dudaev, they were not prominent in public life in the years immediately following the Chechen Revolution.[21]

However, the 1994–6 war altered the situation in several respects. Firstly, the native Salafis who now took up arms against the Russian invasion were joined after 1995 by scores of like-minded Arab volunteers. A key link in the recruitment of battle-hardened Arab veterans of Afghanistan was Sheikh Ali Fathi al-Shishani, a Jordanian from a Chechen ethnic background. He had returned to the ancestral homeland in the early 1990s and in 1993 founded a Salafi brotherhood or *jamaat*. He was the point of contact for the Saudi Khattab, who arrived in Chechnya in 1995 and was to become an important conduit for funds from the Gulf. Though small in number – probably no more than 300, out of a total resistance force of several thousand – Khattab's followers made an undoubted impact on the fighting. In this they were aided by their command of media techniques: Khattab, for instance, raised funds

[20] Quoted in Vanora Bennett, *Crying Wolf: The Return of War to Chechnya*, London 1998, p. 455.
[21] Yemelianova, 'Sufism and Politics in the North Caucasus', p. 667; Iusupov, 'Islam v sotsial'no-politicheskoi zhizni Chechni', p. 168.

by means of video presentations circulated to sympathetic mosques in the Gulf and as far afield as London.[22] The bulk of the Chechen resistance had no such means of addressing the outside world, which meant that the Salafis acquired disproportionate coverage and prestige – undoubtedly increasing, in the process, the appeal of the Salafism they espoused. The austere provisions of their faith also enforced a certain discipline among their troops, as it had done for Mohammed's armies in the seventh century.

Moreover, Salafis were able to attract far more funding than secular nationalist units – a situation which obtains to this day, and to which I will return. For the present, it should be noted that Islamists have therefore been among the best equipped components of the Chechen resistance, able to pay fighters a wage and to give compensation to the relatives of those killed – 'an obvious advantage in a country in which so many families are without legal means of support'.[23] They attracted the allegiance of prominent field commanders such as Shamil Basaev, Movladi Udugov and Salman Raduev, among others, amplifying the reputation of Islamism as these figures increased the proportion of Islamic slogans in their communiqués.

The military prowess of the Islamists earned them prominent positions in the state apparatus of independent Chechnya at the war's end. Maskhadov appointed several of them to key positions: Udugov became Foreign Minister and other Islamists gained control of the Ministries of Education and the Interior.[24] The latter was renamed the Ministry of Shari'a Security, and oversaw the *shari'a* courts that had been established in parallel to the secular ones in March 1995 by Dudaev – another Islamicizing political gesture – but were turned into Chechnya's official judicial bodies by the 1996 constitution brought in by acting president Yandarbiev. The Salafis set about attempting to impose the rigours of seventh-century Medina on the chaos of post-war Chechnya,

[22] Paul Tumelty, 'The Rise and Fall of Foreign Fighters in Chechnya', *Terrorism Monitor*, vol. 4, no. 2, 26 Jan 2006; Roddy Scott, 'Britons connected to Pankisi militants', *Jane's Intelligence Review*, April 2002. Khattab's real name was Samir Saleh Abdullah Al-Suwailem, divulged by his brother after Khattab was killed by Russian intelligence in March 2002.

[23] Mark Galeotti, 'Beslan Shows Growing Islamist Influence in Chechen War', *Jane's Intelligence Review*, October 2004.

[24] Mayrbek Vachagaev, 'The Role of Sufism in the Chechen Resistance', *Chechnya Weekly*, 28 April 2005.

thus entering into conflict with Chechen customary law and its people's syncretistic traditions. Sometimes the courts delivered farcical verdicts – for instance, in 1997 demanding a man pay a fine of sixty-three camels as compensation to the family of a person he had killed in a traffic accident.[25] On other occasions the outcome was sanguinary, with public executions carried out in central Grozny. The courts also clamped down on alcohol consumption and – for the first time in Chechen history – sought to impose restrictions on what women could wear in public. Sharp collisions over the actual forms of worship had begun during the war, notably in 1995 over the shrine of Kunta-Hadji's mother, seen by the Salafis as a proto-pagan lapse, but venerated by Chechens as among the holiest places in the land. In the war's aftermath, the rivalry between Salafism and Sufism became increasingly heated.

The broad mass of Chechens had no special sympathy for the Salafis' doctrinal severity. But the funding to which they had access – tiny by international standards, but significant in the shattered circumstances in which Chechens were living in 1997 – meant that they could provide a livelihood to hundreds of young men whose only occupation until then had been war. The Salafis also conducted some educational programmes, such as computer training classes, which were gratefully welcomed by many young Chechens. Money from the Gulf was crucial to the construction of dozens of mosques, controlled by the Salafis, which provided rare places for worship. Meanwhile their ability to command political support from Basaev, Udugov and Yandarbiev – as well as a substantial private army led by Raduev – strengthened their hand against Maskhadov, who was consistently attacked at the slightest hint of any concession to Moscow.

The Islamization of political life in Chechnya under Maskhadov was a response to these pressures; in the words of Musa Iusupov, it was 'provoked by the concrete circumstances of a struggle between groups over power and the distribution of spheres of influence', and at the same time 'by the position of Moscow, which was unwilling to hold a constructive dialogue with Grozny'.[26] Islamists played a prominent part in destabilizing Maskhadov, and bear a sizeable portion of the blame

---

[25] 'Court Formula: Camels for Life', *Moscow Times*, 4 January 1997. Camels are not native to the Caucasus; it is not clear where the accused was expected to find them.

[26] Iusupov, 'Islam v sotsial'no-politicheskoi zhizni Chechni', p. 170.

for the collapse of state authority between the wars. Though they criticized Maskhadov for seemingly being ready to compromise on sovereignty, it was their undermining of his rule that opened the way for the definitive assault on Chechen independence in 1999.

The Second Chechen War has widened the rift between traditional Chechen Islam and more recent Salafi strands. The appeal of the latter can only have been strengthened by the conduct of the official clergy. Muslim clerics forming part of any state-sanctioned body had always commanded scant respect in Chechnya; as elsewhere in the Islamic world, deference towards 'holy men' depends far more on their personal dignity and wisdom than on credentials established by the powers that be. In 2000, both Qadiri and Naqshbandi clerics united behind Moscow's puppet Kadyrov, resulting in a 'new wave of increasing disrespect for their muftis' on the part of ordinary Chechens. Russian experts on the North Caucasus reported in 2003 that 'in the majority of regions the officially functioning clergy is in close contact with local administrations, law enforcement and military officials.' In response to this, separatist fighters had killed seventeen imams in 2001–2.[27] The link between national resistance and Salafism, tenuous during the previous war, became less so after 1999.

This was rendered all the more significant by the lack of official Muslim solidarity for Chechnya. Of course, little could be expected from Russia's government-approved mullahs. In March 2000, Talgat Tadzhuddin of the Central Spiritual Board of Muslims, one of two squabbling directorates of official Islam, said that 'the war in Chechnya is not against Islam, but for the restoration of law and order'; in November 1999 he asserted that 'the actions of the authorities fully correspond to international and religious laws'.[28] These sentiments have generally been echoed by his rival at the Russian Council of Muftis, Ravil Gainutdin. The response from governments of the Islamic world to the invasion of Chechnya has been a deafening silence. As a result, the only sources of material support for the Chechens have been unofficial channels, some

---

[27] Yemelianova, 'Sufism and Politics in the North Caucasus', p. 681; Politkovskaya, *Small Corner of Hell*, p. 142; Berezhnoi et al., *Islam i islamizm na iuge Rossii*, pp. 115–6.
[28] Quoted in Shireen Hunter, *Islam in Russia: The Politics of Identity and Security*, Armonk, NY 2004, pp. 108, 105.

from the Chechen diaspora in Turkey and Jordan, and a good deal from NGOs and foundations dominated by Salafists in the Gulf.

Since September 11, the Russian authorities have focused their rhetorical strategy on linking Chechen rebels to al-Qaeda, and to the network of Islamist NGOs which became the target of Western scrutiny at the onset of the 'War on Terror'. The intention is not only to convey the impression that Russians, Americans and Europeans are all fighting the same *jihadi* adversary, but that the particularly harsh measures inflicted on Chechnya can be justified as the opening engagement of the same battle. Countless Russian statements have been issued affirming a long-standing al-Qaeda presence in Chechnya, pointing to links between Chechens and Taliban fighters, listing huge donations from foundations in Saudi Arabia, Kuwait, Jordan; time and again these have simply been echoed by Western officialdom without concern for their truthfulness.

The real extent of international backing for the Chechen resistance is, by its clandestine nature, impossible to determine. A range of figures and sources have been put forward – $20m from the Jordanian Muslim Brotherhood in late 1999, $13.5m from the Kuwaiti Islamic Centre, anywhere between $5m and $10m from Osama bin Laden himself. However, Aleksei Malashenko, the leading Russian expert on Islamism in the North Caucasus, argues that 'the reported level of funding for Chechnya is simply too high', while the British security analyst Mark Galeotti agrees that 'these figures are grossly exaggerated'.[29] A counter-indication might be taken from the 2002 trial of the Syrian businessman Enaam Arnaout, head of the Chicago-based charity Benevolence International Foundation. Accused of funding the activities of terrorist groups and individuals – including bin Laden – in Afghanistan, Bosnia, Chechnya, Sudan and elsewhere, Arnaout pleaded guilty to one charge of racketeering in 2003. The assistance he was alleged to have provided the Chechens amounted to $685,000 in the first four months of 2000, a portable X-ray machine, and a shipment of hand- and toewarmers, as used by fishermen or hunters.[30]

---

[29] Dmitri Trenin and Aleksei Malashenko, *Russia's Restless Frontier: The Chechnya Factor in Post-Soviet Russia*, Washington, D.C. 2004, pp. 93–4; Galeotti, 'Al-Qaeda and the Chechens', *Jane's Intelligence Review*, December 2001.

[30] United States v Benevolence International Foundation, Inc. and Enaam M. Arnaout, affidavit of FBI Special Agent Robert Walker, filed 29 April 2002 in Cook County Court, Illinois; available on FindLaw website.

It is, however, the case that a number of foreign fighters are present in Chechnya and, as previously noted, that they are among the best armed and supplied forces ranged against the Russian army. But their numbers have also been overstated – in part because Moscow has gladly chosen to take the recent trend among many Chechen fighters to take Arabic *noms de guerre* as proof of Arab origins. Military analysts have at various times estimated the total number of foreign fighters to be anywhere between 200 and 400; in March 2002 pro-Moscow forces in Chechnya declared there were 250–300 foreigners operating there. Given this, Malashenko has observed that they would 'account for 1–2 per cent of the total rebel strength and, therefore, cannot decisively influence the course of the war'.[31] Numerical inferiority is not the only reason for this: as outsiders, 'they have little in common with the vast majority of the Chechen fighting force, either culturally or linguistically'.[32]

What of purported links to al-Qaeda? It is likely that many of the *mujahideen* who arrived in Chechnya after 1995 had passed through any one of the constellation of camps in Afghanistan and Pakistan's North West Frontier Province during the 1980s and early 1990s – over which bin Laden had at most a marginal influence at the time. Jason Burke presents perhaps the most plausible picture of al-Qaeda as consisting of three components: a small 'core' of committed activists; a wider layer of contacts who would approach the 'core' with plans, seeking its approval and logistical backing; and an extensive but much looser network of sympathizers over whom bin Laden exercised absolutely no organizational control or ideological direction. On this model, Chechnya has had no proven contact with the 'core'. Though one of bin Laden's aides boasted in August 2000 of having sent 400 fighters to Chechnya and donated $5–$10m to the separatist cause,[33] these claims should obviously not be taken at face value: they are above all intended to give an inflated sense of al-Qaeda's reach, and cannot be substantiated in any way. In terms of personnel, although Ayman al-Zawahiri, held to be bin Laden's second-in-command, reportedly

[31] Berezhnoi et al., *Islam i islamizm na iuge Rossii*, p. 119; Galeotti, 'Al-Qaeda and the Chechens'; Trenin and Malashenko, *Russia's Restless Frontier*, p. 97.

[32] Scott, 'Britons Connected to Pankisi Militants'.

[33] Galeotti, 'Al-Qaeda and the Chechens'. Burke, *Al-Qaeda*, p. 146, says bin Laden dispatched some fighters to Chechnya 'via an office set up in Azerbaijan' during the 1994–6 war, though bin Laden himself was in Sudan at the time.

attempted to go to Chechnya in 1996, he was arrested by the Russian authorities in Dagestan and later released.

Indeed, despite bin Laden's repeated references to Chechnya since 1995 as yet another instance of barbarity inflicted on the Muslim world by what he terms the 'Judeo-Christian alliance', there is little indication of what substance, if any, lies behind these rhetorical gestures.[34] Two of the September 11 hijackers are thought to have possibly fought in Chechnya, though the evidence for this is slim; another four had told their families they were going to fight in Chechnya, but for one reason or another could not find a route there.[35] The pattern of unsuccessful attempts to promote *jihad* in Chechnya is consistent: 'a review of the autobiographies of some Salafi-Jihadists in various parts of the world indicates that after 2001 a large number of young men tried to go to Chechnya but failed'.[36]

Conversely, reference is often made to Chechens having fought or trained in Afghanistan, as part of an internationalist Islamist effort against first the Red Army, then the Northern Alliance and, as of autumn 2001, the US. In January 2001, the Pakistani ambassador to Kabul made an inventory of the foreign militants in Afghanistan which included 500 Chechens – though this seems a remarkably high number considering that the active core of the separatists' forces was estimated at the time to amount to no more than 3,000 people; could the Chechens really afford, in the midst of a full-scale Russian invasion, to send so many men to fight someone else's battles?[37] The route from the Caucasus to the Hindu Kush purportedly lies through Uzbekistan: according to the leading Central Asia reporter Ahmed Rashid, the Islamic Movement of Uzbekistan, which has been involved in a low-intensity war with the Karimov regime since 1998, and which contributed fighters to the Taliban cause in late 2001, included Chechens among its ranks.[38]

---

[34] See *Messages to the World. The Statements of Osama Bin Laden*, edited and introduced by Bruce Lawrence, London 2005.

[35] Burke, *Al-Qaeda*, pp. 237, 246–7. The two supposed 'veterans' of Chechnya are Khalid al-Midhar and Nawaf al-Hazmi; the four who failed to get there are Wail and Waleed al-Shehri, and Ahmed and Hamza al-Ghamdi.

[36] Murad Batal al-Shishani, 'Abu Omar al-Saif: His Life and After His Death', *Chechnya Weekly*, 19 January 2006.

[37] Tim Judah, 'The Taliban Papers', *Survival*, vol. 44, no. 1, Spring 2002, p. 74.

[38] Ahmed Rashid, *Jihad: The Rise of Militant Islam in Central Asia*, New Haven 2002, pp. 9, 171, 174, 176. See also Burke, *Al-Qaeda*, p. 192.

However, information as to when they joined the IMU and how many of them there are is entirely absent from his account, as from others. This is not to deny that Chechens were ever present at all; but we should be wary of leaping to the Islamist conclusions so actively promoted in Moscow, Tashkent and Washington. For all the Russian claims that Chechens were among those captured by the Northern Alliance in their sweep towards Kabul, not a single Chechen has surfaced from among those detained: of the eight 'Russian Taliban' detained in Guantánamo Bay, six were from Tatarstan and two from Kabardino-Balkaria.[39]

The connection between Chechnya and the targets of the West's 'War on Terror', then, is clearly not as solid as the Russians insist. It is less a matter of integrated flows of personnel, finances and weaponry – which would presuppose a level of transnational organizational coherence neither al-Qaeda nor any other Islamist group has – but at most a case of ad hoc arrangements and alliances. With no assistance forthcoming from the outside world in the 1994–6 war, nor in the period of independence, nor since the Russian invasion of 1999, the Chechen resistance has relied on funding from Islamists and the Chechen diaspora. The latter can be counted upon to continue supplying cash, but the former have to be cultivated, and the Chechens have adapted their discourse to satisfy these patrons. But their target remains the Russian occupation: they have not professed any particular hostility to Western civilization, nor even shown much interest in Western military aggression in the Middle East. The principal concern of the Chechens is not a putative pan-Islamic insurrection, but the war that has ripped apart their country, and the need to secure what assistance they can to prevent their annihilation as a people.

The vast imbalance in military strength between the two sides in 1994–6 was if anything more pronounced after 1999. The second war has brought with it a terrifying tactical innovation designed to address this problem – suicide bombings, which since 2000 have targeted military installations in Mozdok, Gudermes, Znamenskoe and elsewhere, as well

---

[39] Seven were released in February 2004; one of the Tatars, Imam Airat Vakhitov, had visited Chechnya once in 1998. See Andrew McGregor, 'A Sour Freedom: The Return of Russia's Guantanamo Bay Prisoners', *Chechnya Weekly*, 1 June 2006.

as public spaces in Moscow. These have drawn their human material from the deepening well of desperation created by the two wars: hundreds of people without families, either to support or be supported by; hundreds of family members to be avenged. It has been suggested that the high incidence of female suicide bombers may be connected with widespread rape by Russian troops, though this aspect of the war is still less reported than the rest.

Pointing to a commonality of methods between elements of the Chechen resistance and groups such as Hamas and Hezbollah, Russian officialdom has spoken of a 'Palestinization' of Chechnya. The largely unmentioned obverse, or better, precursor of this has been an 'Israelization' of Russian strategy. The mass of checkpoints designed to prevent the population from moving freely; the killing of unarmed civilians; the impunity enjoyed by the occupying forces; the deliberate economic immiseration and overall humiliation visited on the inhabitants of the occupied territory – all these features are common to the West Bank and Chechnya today. Aping the Israelis' approach to Hamas, Russia has repeatedly resorted to targeted assassination, notably with the killing of former president Yandarbiev in Qatar by car bomb in February 2004. They have also borrowed from Likud's lexicon the slogan that 'there is no partner for peace', on several occasions refusing talks with Maskhadov, before killing him too in March 2005.

The Russian authorities, and many foreign observers, claimed that Maskhadov's hold over his field commanders was by this time weak, and that there would have been little point in negotiating with him. The month-long total ceasefire he imposed from February 2005 until his death proves otherwise. He was eliminated not because he was irrelevant, but because he was a serious potential interlocutor. In a continuation of the policy of assassination, in June 2006 Ramzan Kadyrov's militia captured and killed Maskhadov's successor Abdul-Khalim Sadulaev, putting his half-naked, chained body on display. As Israel has done in the West Bank, Gaza and Lebanon, moreover, the Russians have conducted raids on Chechen refugee camps in Ingushetia, seeing them as breeding grounds and hiding places for resistance fighters. These repeated incursions have served only to enrage both the refugees and the local population, between whom Russian soldiers have proved unable or unwilling to distinguish, and are among the reasons for the wider escalation of the conflict that forms the subject of the next chapter.

The asymmetries of force between Russian army and Chechen resistance have also prompted a grim return to the tactic Shamil Basaev used to such effect in Budennovsk: hostage-taking, designed to have a spectacular impact on Russian public opinion. Basaev claimed responsibility for several of the worst outrages in recent years, including the seizures of the Dubrovka theatre in October 2002 and of the school at Beslan in September 2004. Horrors such as these have not roused the Russian public into pushing its government to withdraw from Chechnya. Rather, they have blackened the reputation of the Chechen resistance and given credence to those on either side who claim no negotiations are possible, and that no quarter is to be given. The Dubrovka siege took place at a moment when the popularity of the war was rapidly waning in Russia, and proposals for a negotiated settlement were being mooted: talks had been held in Liechtenstein between Duma deputies and Maskhadov's representative Zakaev in August 2002, and there were contacts between Putin's human-rights envoy to Chechnya and members of the separatist parliament only ten days before the hostage-taking.[40]

The carnage that ensued when Russian forces stormed the building swept such possibilities aside. The hostage-takers must bear the blame for endangering the lives of so many innocent civilians. But the Russian authorities too must share the grim burden. Prior to the assault, they pumped into the auditorium a gas they have refused to identify – probably a form of the opiate fentanyl. Though the goal was ostensibly the preservation of lives, the provision of first aid was so poorly organized and the doctors given so little clue as to what had poisoned the victims that, as Russian doctors confidentially told Duma deputies, 'up to half the hostages who died did so because of too little medical care at the scene'.[41] The final death toll may have been over 200.

The Russian authorities have shown little patience with those questioning their tactics or their version of events. In the aftermath of the siege, a media law was introduced barring coverage of such incidents – starving terrorism of the oxygen of publicity, but also denying the

[40] John Dunlop, *The 2002 Dubrovka and 2004 Beslan Hostage Crises: A Critique of Russian Counter-Terrorism*, Stuttgart 2006, pp. 107–11.
[41] Peter Truscott, *Putin's Progress*, London 2004, p. 336.

public access to any information other than that provided by security forces. This is all the more troubling considering the number of irregularities and misrepresentations in the official account. During the Dubrovka crisis Putin once again connected Chechnya with 'international terrorism', linking the theatre siege with the recent bombings in the Philippines and Indonesia by stating they were all planned by 'the same people'.[42] The reality is that Dubrovka was planned and executed by Chechens, who declared themselves 'prepared for self-sacrifice, for the sake of Allah and the independence of Chechnya'.[43]

The nominal leader of the hostage-takers was Movsar Baraev, nephew of the notorious kidnapper Arbi Baraev, who had done so much to destabilize Maskhadov. Though Maskhadov was swift to condemn the hostage-taking, Moscow chose to hold him responsible, ruling out any future negotiations. The closure of any avenue towards peace talks was a priority for representatives of Russia's 'power ministries', who feared a repetition of the Khasavyurt Accords of 1996, regarded as a humiliation for Russian arms. For their part, the hostage-takers may have wanted to marginalize Maskhadov and strengthen their own position by securing further financial backing from the Gulf: the group called itself the Riyadh as-Salihin (Gardens of the Righteous) Brigade, and Arabic slogans were prominently displayed. Chechen women appeared among the hostage-takers wearing the *chador*, not at all traditional in Chechnya. The bloodletting in Moscow was a victory for those on both sides bent on mutual destruction.[44] But as events in Beslan nearly two years later were to show, their implacable enmity had not been exhausted.

Even before Beslan or Dubrovka, the prominent role played by Shamil Basaev in the Chechen resistance was the basis for much of the opprobrium heaped upon it in both Russia and the West. Ever since the

---

[42] Newsru.com, 24 October 2002.

[43] From video fragments screened on al-Jazeera, quoted in Gazeta.ru, 24 October 2002, cited by Dunlop, *Dubrovka and Beslan*, p. 134.

[44] John Dunlop has gone so far as to label the events at Dubrovka a 'joint venture' between Russian intelligence and Islamists grouped around Shamil Basaev. He presents troubling evidence, for instance, of the involvement of Arman Menkeev, a former Russian Army Intelligence major, in the preparation of the bombs for the theatre; Menkeev was arrested in November 2002, but then released, despite 400kg of plastic explosive being found at the house where he was staying outside Moscow. Dunlop, *Dubrovka and Beslan*, pp. 115–17, 153.

Budennovsk hostage-taking, he had been Russia's demon of choice, increasingly portrayed as a bloodthirsty fanatic whose goal was the establishment of a theocratic state. His trajectory is more complex, and reveals a great deal about the Islamic dimension of the Chechen struggle. A dropout from agricultural college in Moscow and sometime computer salesman, Basaev was on the barricades in 1991, defending Yeltsin against the August putsch, and fought as a guerrilla – he was an ardent admirer of Che Guevara – in Abkhazia and Nagorno-Karabakh in 1992–3. His experience there stood him in good stead when he returned to stand alongside Dudaev, above all when organizing the defence of Grozny in 1994–5.

It was the Russian onslaught which followed that was the catalyst for his adoption of Islamist rhetoric and terroristic methods. Eleven members of his family were killed in a bombing raid on his home town of Vedeno, adding revenge to the list of grievances against an invader whose strength massively outweighed that of its opponents – making the methods of 'asymmetric warfare' a morally repugnant, but logical choice. As noted earlier, Islamist funds were plentiful, and the battle experience of men such as Khattab invaluable. Given the lack of international assistance, or even of verbal protest over Russian actions, it is not surprising that Basaev forged alliances with the few who showed themselves willing and able to help. But his principal commitment was not to Islamist dogma: in an interview with Andrei Babitsky in July 2005, Basaev claimed that 'Freedom is primary . . . Shari'a comes second.'[45]

The same holds true for other prominent Chechen Islamists. In March 2005, the Muslim cleric Abdul-Khalim Sadulaev became acting president after the killing of Maskhadov by Russian forces, and immediately declared a multiplication of fronts against Russia – raising the standard of pan-Caucasian Islamic unity, and reviving notions of a Caucasian federation carved out of Russia's southern fringe. His elevation completed, in foreign eyes, the triumph of the Islamists: in February 2006, for instance, Sadulaev declared that 'the source of all decisions made is the Qur'an and Sunna'.[46] But the widening of the war was

[45] Aired by ABC television on 28 July 2005.
[46] Quoted in *Chechnya Weekly*, 16 February 2006.

above all a military move, aimed at forcing the Russian authorities to re-direct troops and resources away from Chechnya in order to weaken the occupation there. The prime goal remained sovereignty, not an imamate, and early in 2006 Sadulaev intervened in a dispute between secular nationalists and Islamists by supporting the former's insistence on national independence.[47]

Sadulaev's capture and killing by pro-Moscow Chechens in June 2006 led to the appointment as leader of long-standing field commander Dokku Umarov. Born in 1964, Umarov was educated at Grozny's oil institute. An adept of the Kunta-Hadji Sufi order, he forms a link with the mainstream of the Chechen religious tradition and national movement. His early pronouncements tended, accordingly, to stress the national dimension over religious aspects of the struggle, and to point to secular instruments for determining his nation's fate: 'Russia and the Chechen Republic must build their mutual relations on the basis of universally recognized principles and norms of international law.'[48]

The overlaying of Islamist rhetoric onto the arguments of Chechen nationalism has modified the tactics used and the language in which they are couched, which since 1995 has taken on an increasingly millenarian hue. But as the sociologist Mark Juergensmeyer has remarked, in the midst of conflict, 'to be without such images of war is almost to be without hope itself'.[49] The thunder of apocalypse has not altered the war's substance, which remains the question of sovereignty. The succession of leaders from Dudaev onwards – Yandarbiev, Maskhadov, Sadulaev, Umarov – reveals an oscillation between the rhetorical poles of nationalism and Islam that is driven by a desperate need to secure what scraps of support or even attention the listless world holds out. The Chechen resistance is first of all Chechen, with Islam as a component of that identity. But it will take on whatever appearance gives it the best chance of survival. Its opportunism is born of necessity, and nourished by a global indifference to the loss of thousands of Chechen lives.

[47] See Andrei Smirnov, 'Sadulaev's New Decrees Reveal Divisions Within the Separatist Movement', *Chechnya Weekly*, 9 February 2006.
[48] Statement of 23 June 2006, cited in *Chechnya Weekly*, 29 June 2006.
[49] Quoted in Burke, *Al-Qaeda*, p. 26.

7.

After Beslan

And now, what will become of us without the barbarians?
Those people were a kind of solution.
                    Constantine Cavafy, 'Waiting for the Barbarians'

The horrors of Beslan, where 330 people were killed in September 2004 after Russian forces stormed a school full of hostages being held by gunmen loyal to Shamil Basaev, raised fears that the war in Chechnya could overspill the boundaries of that battered republic, putting the entire region at risk of an even more deadly conflagration. The Russian security services' opponents now include not only Chechen resistance fighters, but a panoply of armed Islamist groups spread across the Muslim territories of southern Russia, whose activities have increased in scope and scale in recent years. As we will see, in Dagestan the clash between state authorities and Islamism began even before the first war in Chechnya, and in the region more generally has roots in a wider systemic crisis of the post-Soviet order. Nevertheless, the ongoing conflict in Chechnya is the epicentre of the social, political, economic and now military earthquake that is shaking the North Caucasus, and it is Russian policy there that has set the tone for Moscow's dealings with the surrounding area. This chapter tracks the evolution of the crisis in the region, laying out the extent to which the war in Chechnya has augmented existing problems. The 'regionalization' the Russian authorities so feared has arrived, and it is an escalation entirely of their own making. Defusing it, I argue, will require not only significant shifts in policy, but the establishment of a stable and just peace in Chechnya.

The event that permitted Putin to portray the invasion of Chechnya in September 1999 as a retaliatory strike was Basaev and Khattab's incursion into Dagestan that August. As noted in chapter 4, they had avowedly undertaken the raid to support Islamists in the villages of Chabanmakhi, Karamakhi and Kadar. Armed clashes between Dagestani Islamists and the federal authorities had in fact taken place as early as 1997, and though the story of Islamic radicalism in Dagestan has become intermeshed with the war in Chechnya, its initial trajectory was significantly different.

Dagestan always had a considerably richer Islamic culture than Chechnya, owing to its earlier conversion and long heritage as a place of Qur'anic learning. With an area of 50,300 square kilometres and a population of around 2.5 million, it is over three times the size of Chechnya, and has over double the population. Yet the practice and institutions of Islam are far more active here than mere proportionality would dictate: in 2000, it had 1,099 Muslim organizations, registered and unregistered, to Chechnya's 150, and 1,200 functioning mosques to Chechnya's 400 (though this last disparity can to a large extent be ascribed to war damage).[1] Moreover, the radicalization of Islam began far earlier in Dagestan: it was here that the first Salafi preachers arrived in the mid-1980s, and a Dagestani preacher, Akhmadkadi Akhtaev, was prominent among the founders of the Islamic Renaissance Party in 1990.

Specialists differ on the subsequent gradations of Islamism in Dagestan. Galina Yemelianova identifies two main tendencies – a rural radical one, and a more malleable urban one based in the capital, Makhachkala; Igor Dobaev divides the movement into three currents: gradualist, Salafi and ultra-radical.[2] However, it is clear that the advocates of an incremental, political path towards the Islamization of the republic

---

[1] Shireen Hunter, *Islam in Russia: The Politics of Identity and Security*, Armonk, NY 2004, pp. 50, 65.
[2] Galina Yemelianova, 'Sufism and Politics in the North Caucasus', *Nationalities Papers*, vol. 29, no. 4, 2001, pp. 665–6; I. P. Dobaev, 'Islam i kvaziislamskie organizatsii na Iuge Rossii', in S. E. Berezhnoi, I. P. Dobaev and P. V. Krainiuchenko, *Islam i islamizm na iuge Rossii*, Rostov-on-Don 2003, pp. 23–5.

met with considerable opposition from Dagestan's official clergy and political elite – thus increasing the appeal of more radical groups to a disaffected population.

Dagestan's fragile ethnic balance has long been underwritten by subsidies from the central authorities in Moscow. In rural areas, ethnic identity can often be subsumed into village communes or broader categories based on shared mountain traditions; but in the cities and at the national level, tensions between Dagestan's many *ethnies* come to the fore – especially given the hold exerted on official positions by the two largest, the Avars and Dargins. Still more significant, however, is the phenomenal concentration of wealth and power even within these ethnic subdivisions. In the 1990s, according to Georgi Derluguian, Dagestan 'came to be dominated by approximately two hundred powerful families, or six to seven thousand people, who dispose of nearly 85 per cent of the local wealth.' These leading families 'secured their powers through extended patronage networks entangling another 200,000 people as more or less handsomely paid retainers or in clientelistic relations'.[3] The republic is so riddled with corruption that in 2005, Mukhu Aliev, then chairman of the People's Assembly of Dagestan, but appointed its president in February 2006, admitted that 'there is not a single post to which one could be appointed without a bribe'; a low-level police position reportedly cost $3,000 to $5,000, that of a district administration chief $150,000, while one could become a minister in the republic's government for $450,000 – $500,000.[4]

In post-Soviet conditions of economic collapse and de-industrialization, unemployment skyrocketed, reaching 30 per cent in 1999, though the true figure is undoubtedly higher. Poverty levels were astronomical: in 1995, 71 per cent of Dagestan's population had an income below the official subsistence level, compared to 25 per cent across the Russian Federation; by 1998, it remained at 58 per cent, compared to 21 per cent nationwide.[5] Those on the inside of Dagestan's neo-patrimonial order strove to reinforce it; the tens of thousands on the outside grew increasingly dissatisfied with their lot. Islamist groups were an outlet

---

[3] Derluguian, 'Che Guevaras in Turbans', *New Left Review*, 1/237, September–October 1999, p. 12.

[4] *Rossiiskaia gazeta*, 7 July 2005; Liz Fuller, 'Daghestan: Anatomy of a Permanent Crisis', *Radio Free Europe/Radio Liberty*, 13 July 2005.

[5] Hunter, *Islam in Russia*, pp. 99–100.

for criticism of official corruption and misrule, as well as of the complicity of the official clergy. The Islamists' calls for equality and social justice, gesturing beyond ethnic particularities to a shared Muslim identity, inevitably acquired greater and greater resonance. Moreover, as discussed with regard to Chechnya, Salafism joined the flow of deeper social dynamics, being described by one expert as a 'mechanism for the democratization of Dagestani society through cleansing its Islamic life of mysticism, superstition and patriarchal elements'.[6] In sum, the roots of Dagestani Salafism are to be found in 'the socio-economic realities of the republic, in the unbearably onerous burden of pseudo-traditional customs, and in disillusionment with the spiritual authorities'.[7]

The Salafis grew in strength and influence after the 1994–6 war in Chechnya, where small numbers of Dagestani volunteers had fought in Islamist 'international brigades', and returned home having successfully defied Moscow. They provided the most vocal opposition to the republican establishment, whose reflexive response was repression. In September 1996, at the behest of the official clergy of the Spiritual Board of Muslims of Dagestan (DUMD), 'Wahhabism and other extremism' were banned – effectively resulting in a clampdown on any manifestations of Islam the DUMD found inconvenient. Still, in 1997 the DUMD could accuse Dagestan's political leaders of 'insufficient hostility' to an ill-defined 'Wahhabism'.[8]

It was at this time that some of the more radicalized Salafi groups opted for a strategy of withdrawal from mainstream Dagestani society, setting up so-called *shari'a* enclaves in remote mountain districts in the south-east of the republic. Their strategy of seizing islands of territory, with a view to forming a base from which to Islamicize the rest of the country, reprises that carried out by the Tajik Islamist leader Ahmad Shah Massoud in Afghanistan and by al-Gamaa al-Islamiyya in Egypt – which in turn has certain echoes with Mao's theories of guerrilla

[6] Yemelianova, 'Sufism and Politics in the North Caucasus', p. 667.

[7] Dobaev, 'Islam i kvaziislamskie organizatsii na Iuge Rossii', p. 21. Disillusionment with the mullahs may have been reinforced by economic motives: according to some researchers, the official clergy of Dagestan 'has striven to establish a monopoly over the lucrative business of arranging pilgrimages to Mecca and prevent other firms and organizations from offering such services'. *Johnson's Russia List Research and Analytical Supplement* no. 32, 1 November 2005.

[8] A. A. Iarlykapov, *Problema vakhkhabizma na Severnom Kavkaze*, Moscow 2001, p. 6; Yemelianova, 'Sufism and Politics in the North Caucasus', p. 686.

warfare.[9] Clashes between the Islamic Jamaat of Dagestan and local law enforcement and federal troops began in 1997; in the summer of 1998, the villages of Chabanmakhi, Karamakhi and Kadar were declared '*shari'a* zones' by the IJD, which immediately led to a stepping-up of military and political pressure in the area.

The connections forged between Chechen and Dagestani Salafis during the 1994–6 war proved vital to the survival of the latter. The IJD, whose leader Bagauddin Kebedov had at first tried to officially register the organization as a legitimate political group, moved its headquarters to Chechnya in 1997, 'in response to repression by the republican authorities'.[10] The arrival of Kebedov briefly strengthened the position of Salafis in Chechnya, adding energy, personnel and activist experience. But during the stand-off between Islamists and forces loyal to Maskhadov in the summer of 1998, Kebedov was declared *persona non grata* by the Maskhadov government, and many Dagestanis returned to the struggle with their own authorities, which continued to the accompaniment of increasingly hysterical rhetoric: in June 2000, a leading DUMD mufti said that 'Wahhabis can only be straightened out with a bullet'.[11]

The position of the Russian authorities in 1998 forms a curious contrast to this, and to Moscow's attitude since then. When the first clashes between Islamists in the three '*shari'a*' villages and Dagestani troops took place, a truce was negotiated by none other than Sergei Stepashin, then Russian Interior Minister, who visited the area in September 1998 and arranged for supplies to be delivered to the villages.[12] In July 1998, a meeting attended by the Justice Minister, the head of the FSB, the Nationalities Minister and Stepashin himself had concluded that 'the Wahhabist tendency is not extremist'.[13] The official position was to swing to the opposite pole within months, as Putin declared

[9] Jason Burke, *Al Qaeda: The True Story of Radical Islam*, London 2003, pp. 68, 312–13.
[10] Hunter, *Islam in Russia*, p. 89; Dobaev, 'Islam i kvaziislamskie organizatsii na Iuge Rossii', pp. 23–5.
[11] Iarlykapov, *Problema vakhkhabizma*, p. 9.
[12] Matthew Evangelista, *The Chechen Wars: Will Russia Go the Way of the Soviet Union?*, Washington, D.C. 2002, p. 65; Hunter, *Islam in Russia*, p. 89. Evangelista cites an unnamed Chechen mufti who claims the supplies included weapons – Stepashin backing the Salafis in a Machiavellian scheme to sow discord in Dagestan and instability in Chechnya to justify a new invasion.
[13] *Izvestiia*, 22 July 1998, cited in V. Kh. Akaev, *Sufizm i vakhkhabizm na Severnom Kavkaze*, Moscow 1999, p. 14.

Salafis in both Dagestan and Chechnya to be 'terrorists' who could only be dealt with by unleashing war on an entire nation.

The 'anti-terrorist' operation initially had a certain amount of popular support in Dagestan, where many locals – predominantly Andi villagers – were among those taking up arms to repulse Basaev and Khattab.[14] But the subsequent assault on Chechnya regained its people much of the sympathy Basaev had squandered. Moreover, with the underlying socio-economic problems of the republic left unaddressed and its iniquitous political hierarchy intact, opposition continued to coalesce around the groups most active against the existing order. The authorities' hostility to 'Wahhabism' was, and is, often underpinned by blind ignorance and indiscriminate brutality: anyone bearded or teetotal is liable to be dragged in for questioning by the police, and there have been dozens of reported cases of torture. The authoritarian reflexes of Russian power in Dagestan have in fact served to loosen its grip on the territory. In the mountain village of Gimri – home to Imam Shamil in the nineteenth century – federal law has been replaced by local interpretations of *shari'a*; visiting journalists noted that 'residents here have unabashed contempt for the regional government'.[15]

The contempt has often arisen in response to police bribe-taking and ill-treatment of prisoners, and local anger has frequently spilled over into physical hostility to law enforcement officers. Guerrilla activity by Islamists is in some cases merely a continuation of protest by other means. But rather than counteract the abuses, the Russian authorities have responded by increasing troop levels in the republic. The Russian Army has not had the desired deterrent effect: in 2005 and 2006 there were more attacks on security personnel in Dagestan than in Chechnya. Every day brings reports of bomb attacks and attempted or successful assassinations of government personnel, of MVD assaults on apartment blocks in search of 'Wahhabites', of gunfights not only in the remote mountains but in Makhachkala. From 2003 to 2005, more than 970 Russian soldiers and civilians were killed by Islamist attacks. The Russian Duma deputy Aleksandr

---

[14] Mikhail Roshchin, 'Islam in the North Caucasus: Dagestan', paper presented at Jamestown Foundation conference, 14 September 2006, available on the Foundation's website.

[15] *Los Angeles Times*, 23 October 2005.

Khinshtein observed in spring 2006 that 'news from the republic sounds like front-line reports'.[16]

The storm looming over Dagestan, to Chechnya's east, is also casting its shadow over the four North Caucasian republics to its west. Tensions had erupted between Ingush and Ossetians in 1992 over the Prigorodny region, annexed to North Ossetia after being emptied of its Ingush inhabitants by the deportations of 1944. Many of the Ingush who returned as of the late 1950s were forcibly displaced from the district once again in 1992; 40,000 of them still lived in tent camps at the time of the Beslan atrocity.[17] The choice of Beslan as a target was undoubtedly dictated by a desire to stir up these inter-ethnic grievances. The gym at School No. 1 itself had been used in 1992 as a holding pen for Ingush expelled from their homes. Chechens might also have had motives for vengeance against the town: planes dropping bombs on Chechnya in 1994–6 had flown from Beslan's airbase.[18]

In this regard, the ethnic composition of the hostage-takers at Beslan is highly significant. Though Moscow initially said the band were largely Chechens, plus several Arabs and one black African, the sole surviving hostage-taker said at his trial hearings that there was one Arab, one Ossetian, four or five Chechens, and that the rest of the group were Ingush.[19] There are several more discrepancies between the official version of events and the accounts of survivors – notably concerning the number of hostage-takers: while the Russian authorities insist there were thirty-two, only one of whom survived, eyewitnesses counted at least fifty, and reported five being captured alive who have subsequently not been seen again.[20] Some unexplained facts have been taken to indicate

---

[16] *Los Angeles Times,* 23 October 2005; *Moskovskii komsomolets,* 26 April 2006.

[17] Liz Fuller, 'Are Ingushetia, North Ossetia on the Verge of New Hostilities?', *Radio Free Europe/Radio Liberty,* 28 March 2006.

[18] Fred Weir, 'Russia Struggles to Keep Grip on Caucasus', *Christian Science Monitor,* 13 September 2005; Alan Tskhurbayev and Valery Dzutsev, 'Fear and Tension in Siege Town', *IWPR Caucasus Reporting Service,* 2 September 2004.

[19] John Dunlop, *The 2002 Dubrovka and 2004 Beslan Hostage Crises: A Critique of Russian Counter-Terrorism,* Stuttgart 2006, pp. 42–3, 63–4. In an interview with *Time* magazine, Putin claimed nine were Arabs and one an African Muslim, though a month later his defence minister had revised this down to only five 'citizens of Arab states'; the African was dropped. *Time Europe,* 20 September 2004, *RIA Novosti,* 14 October 2004.

[20] *New York Times,* 26 August 2005.

more sinister machinations – for instance, many of the hostage-takers had previously been imprisoned or detained by police, but were released at various times before the seizure of the school.[21] Still more disturbing were the deliberate falsehoods propagated by officials during the crisis: government spokesmen understated the number of hostages by several hundred; the FSB insisted that a tape released by the hostage-takers on 1 September supposedly containing their demands was blank, but it was broadcast by NTV six days later.[22]

These details, of course, do nothing to change the infernal outcome. As in the Dubrovka siege, prime responsibility for the deaths of the hostages – 186 of them children – must lie with the hostage-takers themselves, whose callous disregard for the lives of civilians all but extinguished public sympathy for the Chechen cause in much of the world. Nonetheless, as at Dubrovka, the conduct of the Russian authorities during the crisis was integral to the chaotic sequence of events that sent the death toll spiralling. A day and a half passed before negotiations were begun, in which time several different federal agencies set up headquarters in the town and made preparations for an assault.[23] The preservation of lives cannot have been the principal consideration: Russian Special Forces directed massive firepower on a room still full of children, and used rocket-propelled incendiary projectile launchers to set the roof of the building alight; over half the hostages who died 'perished under the collapsed roof'.[24]

As with the apartment bombings of 1999, the rubble at Beslan was cleared away too quickly to permit proper forensic investigation. The entire truth may never emerge: a full reckoning would require testimony from officials all the way up the chain of command, many of whom have resolutely refused to contribute even to the sanitized reports of the Duma. The secretiveness, and in many cases mendaciousness, of the Russian government's response prompted strong criticism, not only from eyewitnesses and the relatives of those killed, but also from the commission established to investigate the events by the North Ossetian

---

[21] Dunlop, *Dubrovka and Beslan*, p. 51.
[22] Dunlop, *Dubrovka and Beslan*, p. 55.
[23] Interview with Ruslan Aushev, *Novaia gazeta*, 6–9 September 2004. Aushev, formerly president of Ingushetia, was the only person to enter the school during the crisis, and secured the release of 26 hostages.
[24] Dunlop, *Dubrovka and Beslan*, p. 17.

parliament. The latter has refused to assign blame solely to those local police who are widely believed to have accepted bribes to let the heavily armed hostage-takers into the republic, contending that the FSB and MVD were also at fault for their poor coordination and their readiness to deploy maximum force. At the end of August 2006, meanwhile, one member of the Russian parliamentary commission released his own report which diverged sharply from that of the Duma commission itself. Yuri Savelev's 700-page document concluded that the first shots came from outside the gym, and that the storming of the school was not spontaneous – laying responsibility for the hostages' deaths not on the terrorists, but on the security services.[25]

Relatives of the victims have directed their anger at Russian official-dom not only for the corruption of law enforcement, but for their heavy-handedness in storming the school, and for their dishonest handling of the events and attempts to silence those challenging the view from Moscow. The trial of the one surviving hostage-taker, Nur-Pashi Kulaev, was described as a 'showcase of contempt for the govern-ment', with those attending the hearings bitterly criticizing the authorities' performance during and after the crisis.[26] In the words of one Beslan resident, 'It is not so much the facts about heavy weaponry being used – established during the trial – and the failure of rescue procedures, as the persistence with which the authorities have concealed everything. That has provided more proof that they are responsible for people's deaths.' Ella Kesaeva, chairwoman of the Voice of Beslan committee, insisted in May 2006, when Kulaev was found guilty and sentenced to life imprisonment, that 'we won't stop with Kulaev. It is the job of the prosecutor's office to bring to justice the other guilty parties, the generals who gave the orders to shoot at our children.'[27]

It was, of course, Shamil Basaev who gave the order to take the chil-dren captive in the first place; and it was he who masterminded the Dubrovka hostage-taking, as well as a string of other atrocities against

[25] 'Iurii Savel'ev: zalozhniki v Beslane pogibli po vine silovikov', *Kavkazskii Uzel*, 28 August 2006.

[26] *New York Times*, 26 August 2005.

[27] Alan Tskhurbayev, 'Discontent with Beslan Trial', *IWPR Caucasus Reporting Service*, 25 May 2006. The FSB general in charge of the storming of the school was Vladimir Pronichev, who had also overseen the assault on the Dubrovka theatre.

civilians. His death in July 2006 – another event where the FSB's version, claiming credit, conflicts with that of local law enforcement, pointing to an accidental explosion – robbed the survivors and the bereaved of their chance for justice. Until his own death Maskhadov insisted that, once peace was established, Basaev would stand trial for his crimes, as part of a wider effort at redressing wrongs. Moscow had little interest in such a reconciliation, preferring the route of force: after Beslan, a bounty was placed on the heads of both Basaev and Maskhadov, and the last legitimately elected president of the Chechen people was assassinated in March 2005. The Putin regime's predilection for bombs, secrecy and summary justice has not only brought ruin to Chechnya; it has also caused enormous harm to the surrounding region and Russia as a whole, entrenching a culture of suspicion, official impunity and blind militarism. The pathological fixation of Russia's rulers with state security bears no relation to the needs of the people they are supposedly protecting; the longer it continues, the greater the distance between government and populace, and the weaker the basis of the power they so jealously guard.

The conclusion Putin drew from the Beslan atrocity was that 'We showed weakness, and the weak are trampled upon.'[28] His response was to tighten the noose of centralization still further by ending the election of regional governors altogether, in favour of hand-picked appointees. The strategy had already been tried out in Ingushetia in 2002, when Putin engineered the exit of the elected president, Ruslan Aushev, and his replacement with an FSB cadre, Murat Ziazikov. Aushev was not only widely popular, but had provided assistance to tens of thousands of Chechen refugees, who effectively doubled the population of his republic. Once installed, Ziazikov swiftly moved to close down several tent camps, forcing many of the refugees back into the war-zone where, despite Russian assurances of a return to normality, an even worse fate generally awaited them. The clampdown on Chechens, combined with the choking-off of organized political opposition to Moscow's will, prompted many Ingush to take up arms. It is worth noting that, like the Beslan hostage-taking, the raids on government offices in the Ingush

---

[28] BBC Monitoring, 4 September 2004.

capital Nazran in June 2004, in which ninety-two were killed, were conducted primarily by Ingush.

Armed opposition has also flared up in Kabardino-Balkaria: in October 2005, attacks were carried out on a range of targets – including the FSB and MVD offices – in the republic's capital Nal'chik. Official reports claimed ninety-two of the insurgents had been killed, along with twenty-four policemen and ten civilians; eyewitnesses and relatives visiting the morgue suggested that the real figures should be much higher, and that a significant number of innocent civilians were killed by a police force that failed to differentiate attackers from bystanders.[29] Only a handful of the perpetrators were Chechens; the rest were young local Islamists, revolting against official persecution of their faith, and against what Georgi Derluguian has described as the 'neo-feudalism' of local elites.[30]

As in Dagestan, power and wealth in the other Muslim republics of the North Caucasus has been concentrated in the hands of a thin layer of post-Soviet cronies, who have generally proved unwilling either to disburse more equitably the funds provided by Moscow, or to submit to full democratic accountability. Challenges to their rule from political Islamist movements have been met with repression – the closure of mosques, medressehs and publications, the harassment and detention of anyone suspected of 'Wahhabism'. The official measures against 'extremism' in the North Caucasus that accompanied the 'anti-terrorist' operation in Chechnya have in many cases degenerated into an ignorant, Islamophobic attack on civil liberties, pushing the Islamists further underground on the one hand, and vastly increasing public sympathy for them on the other. As the mother of one of those killed in Nal'chik in October 2005 put it, 'Wasn't it the authorities who drove them to this by detaining them constantly, taking them to police stations and torturing them?'[31] Anger among those the Russian government claims to be protecting has been fuelled by the fact that official brutality has not only been directed at Islamists: in 2004, the journalist Fatima Tlisova

---

[29] *Chechnya Weekly*, 20 October 2005. The bodies of those killed were by and large not released for burial, in accordance with Russian 'anti-terrorist' laws.

[30] Georgi Derluguian, 'Nal'chik kak rossiiskii Andizhan?', *Izvestiia*, 18 October 2005.

[31] *IWPR Caucasus Reporting Service*, 20 October 2005.

reported on the story of Rasul Tsakoev, a 26-year-old man who was arrested by police, tortured and then dumped outside his village: he died of his injuries two days later. His parents said their son did not belong to a radical group. After the story was printed, Tlisova was bundled into a car by a group of police officers, who took her down to a riverbank, burned her fingers with cigarettes and told her to stop reporting.[32]

There are plenty of socio-economic grounds for discontent: the North Caucasus remains one of the country's poorest regions, with the lowest wages and official unemployment rates several times higher than the national average – 21 per cent in Dagestan; 53 per cent in Ingushetia; 10 per cent in North Ossetia; 22 per cent in Kabardino-Balkaria; and 19 per cent in Karachaevo-Cherkessia, compared to 9 per cent nationwide. In 1998, poverty levels reached 52 per cent in Karachaevo-Cherkessia, 44 per cent in Kabardino-Balkaria, 34 per cent in North Ossetia and an incredible 76 per cent in Ingushetia, compared to a national figure of 21 per cent.[33] In the summer of 2005, Putin's envoy to the Southern Federal District, Dmitri Kozak, compiled a report that painted a dismal picture of the North Caucasus as a region gripped by systemic corruption, economic depression and social and political instability.[34] The Caucasus expert Robert Bruce Ware has concluded that 'the region is seeing the development of hierarchies of power and subordination that resemble those of Russian colonial domination in the early 19th century'. But where the Tsars and Soviets stabilized the North Caucasus by offering its inhabitants either a compromise on religious freedoms, or the material benefits of education and employment, Russia's present rulers have yet to devise an equivalent compact.[35]

In early 2006, on Kozak's recommendations, the political balance of Dagestan was shaken up, the president of thirteen years and many officials replaced, and attempts initiated to curb patronage. But these

[32] Thomas de Waal, 'Diary', *London Review of Books*, 3 November 2005.
[33] *The Territories of the Russian Federation 2004*, London and New York 2004, pp. 30–5; Hunter, *Islam in Russia*, p. 99.
[34] Extracts are quoted by Aleksandr Khinshtein, 'Prodaem Kavkaz. Torg umesten', *Moskovskii komsomolets*, 16 June 2005.
[35] Robert Bruce Ware, 'Stepping on the Same Rake: A Historical Analysis of Russian Recentralization in the North Caucasus', *New Europe Review*, vol. 2, no. 4 (2005).

were adjustments to the existing order, rather than a fundamental realignment of the social, economic and political system that has worked to impoverish and antagonize Russia's southern periphery. This is only confirmed by the identity of Kozak's adviser on security: Ramzan Kadyrov. Early in 2006, Defence Minister Sergei Ivanov conceded that 'we have no mechanism to solve the social and economic problems' of the region.[36] This devastating admission captures the nature of Russian policy there: loyalty is expected of its inhabitants, to whom nothing is being offered but prison or poverty.

Faced with socio-economic misery, the closure of a political system dominated by immovable elites, and a government clampdown on basic Islamic practices founded on ill-informed assumptions and repressive instincts, further dissent against Russian rule is increasingly likely to be channelled in the direction of armed movements. These are growing in numbers and daring across the region, underscoring the failure of Moscow's authoritarian response. Its aggression in Chechnya has provided the fuel for a lasting insurgency there, while the authorities' crackdown on Islamic activism elsewhere has allowed the two struggles to become joined.

Yet for all their claims that Chechen separatism has given way to a pan-Caucasian Islamism, the cause in which resistance has been mobilized in Chechnya remains that of national independence, an issue distinct from those afflicting other parts of the region. A more rational Russian policy for the North Caucasus would seek to undercut Islamist rebellion elsewhere by removing one of its principal rallying points: the suppression of Chechen sovereignty. Such a change of strategy seems extremely unlikely, given Putin's need to bolster his authoritarian rule by pointing to the dangers of a fictive international Islamist conspiracy – a smokescreen that he has extended to occlude all the ills for which his government has no remedy. Behind it live people of flesh and blood, whose real needs and aspirations will always be of less value to Putin's Russia than the shadows cast by imaginary barbarians.

[36] Interview with *Frankfurter Allgemeine*, quoted in *Chechnya Weekly*, 9 February 2006.

8.

An Invisible Catastrophe

According to the pronouncements of the Russian authorities, life in Chechnya is well on the path back to normality. Reconstruction is proceeding apace, economic activity has resumed, and the separatist insurgency is a matter of weeks from ultimate defeat. In a series of elections and referenda held since 2003, Chechens have chosen their own leaders and approved a constitution confirming their desire to form part of the Russian Federation.

The bitter reality is far removed from these official fabrications. Grozny is still largely a city of rubble, and most of its inhabitants have no running water or electricity. They live under curfew, and in constant fear of sniper-fire or, worse, of abduction by one of several pro-Moscow armed factions which roar around the republic at night, bursting into houses and taking away men and women who are often never seen again. Fear is all-pervasive. In the mountainous south, the resistance continues to engage the Russian army in inconclusive battles; elsewhere in the republic, the war has mutated into a vicious counter-insurgency waged against the entire nation by militias loyal to Moscow – foremost among them the gunmen of Ramzan Kadyrov, the most powerful man in Chechnya and, despite the selection of Alu Alkhanov to succeed the assassinated Akhmad Kadyrov as puppet president in 2004, its de facto ruler. Behind the façade of the political institutions Putin has set in place through a string of fraudulent elections sits a predatory regime, extorting tribute from its subjects when not terrorizing them through arbitrary arrests, torture and summary executions.

This chapter seeks to provide a balance sheet of Putin's 'Chechen-ization' strategy, laying out the main features of the pro-Moscow regime, the conditions in which Chechens are now forced to live, and the prospects facing the republic. Both the present and the immediate future are bleak, with little sign of a shift in Russia's policy of awarding control of Chechnya to an unstable clique of quislings and criminals. Imposed on the populace by vote-rigging and intimidation, the regime in Grozny has no democratic legitimacy, and no project for its country other than a spree of unchecked violence and extortion. Any bearable future for Chechnya will depend not on its further entrenchment, but on its removal from the scene – and a withdrawal by the occupying power, in order to permit the Chechens freely to decide their own destiny.

In June 2000, Akhmad Kadyrov became the latest in a long line of puppet rulers Russia has tried to impose on the Chechens. As Russian casualties mounted and a military victory continued to prove elusive, he became the figurehead for Putin's strategy of 'Chechenization'. A referendum held in March 2003, from which the bulk of the population stayed away, paved the way for another electoral sham in October 2003 which proclaimed Kadyrov president. In June of that year he had come a poor fourth even in a Russian-organized opinion poll, but his main competitors were either bought off with offers of posts in Russia or else excluded from the race on spurious technicalities.[1] The remaining candidates were all but invisible; one of them was in fact an employee in Kadyrov's press office. But Kadyrov's path to the presidency still needed to be secured by extensive fraud: remote mountain villages posted improbable turnout figures of 90 per cent, while the tally for Kadyrov's home town of Tsentoroi was an outstanding 100 per cent.[2] In some

---

[1] Tanya Lokshina, ed., *The Imposition of a Fake Political Settlement in the Northern Caucasus: The 2003 Chechen Presidential Election*, Stuttgart 2005, p. 44. Kadyrov had the approval of only 13 per cent of those polled.

[2] Lokshina, *Imposition of a Fake Settlement*, p. 178.

districts, the number of votes even exceeded the number of voters.

The groundwork for the fraud had been laid by the 2002 Russian census, which put the total population of Chechnya at 1,103,686 – despite the fact that before the invasion in 1999 Russian officials had claimed the population was only 350,000. The cash-strapped Maskhadov government had conducted its own census in 1998–9 which, despite the lack of computers and incomplete data, gave a credible figure of around 800,000. Having understated the population by over half in 1999, then, the Russian authorities were now claiming that in three years of constant warfare, with the thousands of deaths and displacements that entailed, the population of Chechnya had grown by over 750,000 – or, if they were to accept the Chechens' own figure, around 300,000. These 'dead souls' were all, of course, loyal Kadyrov voters.[3]

Despite all this, observers from the Commonwealth of Independent States approved the election, and Said al-Barami of the Arab League said it was 'legitimate, free and democratic'. The US ambassador feebly suggested that it was 'not clear that the election can be considered legitimate', while the EU, noting the many irregularities, intimidation and exclusion of candidates, lack of meaningful political choice or independent media coverage, expressed its 'hope that the political settlement process in Chechnya continues'.[4] The UN's invertebrate response to the forcible imposition of Kadyrov has been described in chapter 5. These reactions once again demonstrated to Russia that it could abuse, punish and kill Chechens without facing any international consequences; the rest of the world has effectively connived at its crimes by failing to raise the protests that mere human decency demands.

Confident that the world would not lift a finger against its placeman, Moscow set about handing him greater and greater power. Kadyrov's private army was incorporated into the Russian Interior Ministry's structures in 2004, in effect legitimating their extra-judicial activities: brute force was to be Chechnya's only law. In April 2001 he had signed a decree banning any congresses, meetings or other mass events 'until the

---

[3] Aleksandr Cherkasov, 'Book of Numbers: Book of the Lost', in Lokshina, *Imposition of a Fake Settlement*, pp. 190–7.
[4] Lokshina, *Imposition of a Fake Settlement*, p. 172, 180–1; Declaration of EU Presidency of 8 October 2003, No. 13393/03 (Presse 297).

situation in the republic is fully stabilized' – lest anyone consider making their discontent apparent. Nonetheless, the mothers of the disappeared continued to gather every Monday and Wednesday at the government building in Grozny, waiting to see Kadyrov.[5] But the former mufti had other priorities besides the fate of his countrymen – such as adding to his private fortune. Since his assassination in a bomb explosion at the Victory Day parade on 9 May 2004, a number of projects have been paid for by the Akhmad Kadyrov Fund, whose vast resources are of unclear origin. Coincidentally, as noted in chapter 5, Putin's human-rights envoy to Chechnya admitted than no more than 10 per cent of the $500m allocated to the republic in 2001 had actually been spent, and in 2002, FSB director Nikolai Patrushev admitted that $22m had been 'misused' that year.[6]

The killing of Kadyrov by the separatists delivered a blow to the 'Chechenization' strategy. The Kremlin swiftly organized new elections in August 2004, duly won by Alu Alkhanov, who officially scored 74 per cent, on a turnout of 80 per cent. Yet real power rests with Ramzan Kadyrov. Lacking any popular legitimacy, he has been garlanded with medals and honours in a vain attempt to increase his stature. Putin awarded Ramzan Kadyrov the status of Hero of Russia in December 2004, leading Kadyrov to put up giant advertising hoardings depicting the ceremony. Others showed members of his militias and bore the legend 'You Are Not Born a Hero, You Become One' – prompting local wits to retort, 'You do not become a bastard, you are born one'.[7] A grotesque cult of personality has also been created around Akhmad Kadyrov: Grozny's central square now boasts a three-metre high statue of him by the Kremlin's favourite sculptor, Zurab Tsereteli; unveiled in August 2005, it bears the mendacious inscription 'Chechnya's First President', and is kept under 24-hour armed guard.[8] Grozny's central thoroughfare was renamed after Kadyrov, and orders were given for the

[5] Lokshina, *Imposition of a Fake Settlement*, pp. 64–6, 251.
[6] Dmitri Trenin and Aleksei Malashenko, with Anatol Lieven, *Russia's Restless Frontier: The Chechnya Factor in Post-Soviet Russia*, Washington, D.C. 2004, p. 38.
[7] *Le Monde*, 21 July 2005. The war has given rise to much bleak humour: the Chechen website www.sobar.org recounts the 'shortest ever Chechen joke' – 'the Russians have left!'
[8] *IWPR Caucasus Reporting Service*, 1 September 2005; Anne Nivat, 'Ravalement de façade en Tchétchénie', *Le Monde diplomatique*, May 2006.

same to be done in all major towns in the republic. A museum was even set up to commemorate his life and good works – while Chechnya's national museum languishes in ruins, 90 per cent of its priceless collections stolen or destroyed by bombs.[9]

Alongside these propaganda exercises, there has been a continuing political charade, culminating in November 2005 in the election of a tame parliament. Out of 357 candidates, 213 worked directly for the pro-Moscow government – 126 of them were acting officials, and most of the rest were relatives of theirs.[10] All critics of current Russian policy were excluded, even those opposed to independence and with long-standing loyalty to Moscow, such as Umar Avtorkhanov and Bislan Gantemirov, both previously funded and armed as opponents of Dudaev and Maskhadov. The Russian authorities did score something of a coup by securing the participation of Magomed Khanbiev, former defence minister under Maskhadov and brother of the current separatist health minister. Khanbiev had surrendered to pro-Moscow forces in 2004, seemingly because most of his family had been kidnapped; he told Reuters, 'I still believe in independence for the republic', and that he was standing for the Union of Right Forces (SPS), the only party which had not 'thrown filth at my people'.[11] But he could not publicly campaign on such a platform – Article 1 of the 2002 law 'On countering extremist activities' labelled any proposal to affect the territorial integrity of Russia as 'extremism', punishable by imprisonment. In Chechnya, the sentence for advocating independence is generally administered through summary justice: contrast Khanbiev's fate with that of separatist fighter Shamil-Khadzhi Muskiev, whose severed head was impaled for display on a bridge outside Tsotsin-Yurt in mid-September 2005.[12]

As with previous elections organized by Moscow, the actual turnout in November 2005 was low: the human-rights NGO Memorial estimated it at no more than 10 per cent in the first half of the day, reaching 25 per cent in some villages. The official figure, of course, was higher – over 60 per cent – and the Russian government newspaper *Rossiiskaia gazeta* asserted that 'everyone noticed that the general mood

[9] *IWPR Caucasus Reporting Service*, 16 September 2005.
[10] *Kavkazskii Uzel*, 24 October 2005.
[11] Reuters, 15 November 2005.
[12] *Los Angeles Times*, 5 November 2005.

was festive, joyful and smiling'.[13] The *Economist*, by contrast, reported that 'weapons often outnumbered the voters'.[14] Indeed, soldiers played a prominent role, and not only in guarding polling stations. The 33,000 occupying troops eligible to vote formed 5 per cent of the electorate, and had 19 dedicated polling stations. The astonishing result was that in Itum-Kale district, still the scene of some of the fiercest resistance to the occupation, one Colonel Aleksandr Radvan was returned as a member of the Chechen parliament.[15]

A second significant feature of the 2005 elections was the tightening grip of the United Russia party. Dominant in the Duma in Moscow, it is headed in Chechnya by Ruslan Yamadaev, a former separatist field commander who switched allegiances in 1999, he and his brothers converting their militia into the 'Vostok' (East) Battalion, officially subordinated to Russian Military Intelligence (GRU). In Russia, the party has gradually come to resemble the Communist Party: its members are in positions of power across the country, creating a formidable network of 'administrative resources' with which to advance the careers of colleagues – and block off challengers. In Chechnya, the same structures have far more sinister applications: the party's 29,000 members gain access to health benefits and salaries unavailable to the general populace. Moreover, by late 2005 a party membership card had become the only document that could guarantee safe passage through checkpoints and immunity from abduction.[16] Unsurprisingly, United Russia won over 60 per cent of the votes in the 2005 parliamentary elections, five times more than its nearest rivals, the SPS and the Communists. The EU's spokeswoman murmured a few concerns, but once again gave assent to the transparent fraud being perpetrated in Chechnya, announcing that 'we welcome the fact that elections took place without violence' – ignoring the fact that they had been conducted in the midst of an ongoing war, which had killed 6 Russian soldiers in the previous week alone.[17]

The increased influence of Yamadaev, with active backing from Moscow, betrayed a certain anxiety in official quarters about the concen-

---

[13] Cited by BBC Monitoring, 28 November 2005.
[14] *Economist*, 3–9 December 2005.
[15] *IWPR Caucasus Reporting Service*, 29 November 2005.
[16] International Helsinki Federation for Human Rights, 'In a Climate of Fear: "Political Process" and Parliamentary Elections in Chechnya', November 2005.
[17] AFP, 28 and 22 November 2005.

tration of power in the hands of Ramzan Kadyrov. For behind the façade of the 'political process', Putin's 'Chechenization' strategy had rapidly become one of 'Kadyrovization'. In March 2006, Sergei Abramov, the Russian-appointed Prime Minister of Chechnya, was shoved aside to enable Kadyrov to take up the post – a similar fate perhaps awaiting President Alkhanov. Kadyrov has sought to boost his public profile by demanding that Chechnya be made a free economic zone to aid recovery – which will coincidentally give a boost to his own business interests, including a lucrative chain of petrol stations branded 'Leader'. He has also attempted to establish his Islamic credentials by a series of pronouncements banning, in turn, slot-machines, alcohol, and women appearing bare-headed in official institutions or on TV. He has announced the construction of Europe's largest mosque in Grozny, and called for compulsory instruction in the Qur'an in schools. Such gestures have not resulted in the popular approval he obviously craves. In August 2005 a pro-Moscow official admitted that 90 per cent of the population disliked the administration.[18]

Among the many reasons for Kadyrov's lack of popular support is the racketeering which has come to characterize his rule. The civilian populace is regularly shaken down – several schools reported *kadyrovtsy* demanding fifty roubles from each teacher 'to fund the referendum' in 2003; similar donations were extracted to pay for the statue to Akhmad Kadyrov, and for Ramzan's birthday celebrations.[19] Neither are officials exempt: on the contrary, public servants are actively required to pay regular tribute to ensure continued tenure. According to Anna Politkovskaya, 'all functionaries in Chechnya and all *siloviki* pay tribute to those above – to the Kadyrov clan; the higher the functionary, the larger the sum'. As an instance of this, she reports the abduction in 2005 of the pro-Moscow minister of labour and social development by *kadyrovtsy*, they demanded $200,000, which the official paid in cash – strongly implying that he too had been dipping into the public purse.[20]

[18] Lenta.ru, 25 August 2005. In an interview with the BBC, Kadyrov made a comment about his pet lion cub which seems metaphorically to sum up his relationship to the general population: 'it will either kill me or learn to be obedient'. BBC website, 26 November 2005.

[19] IHF, 'In a Climate of Fear'.

[20] Anna Politkovskaya, 'Zindan dlia tainogo golosovaniia', *Novaia gazeta*, 17 November 2005.

Riddled with corruption, Kadyrov's neo-feudal, gangster regime is held in place by fear and bullets alone.

As Russian troops have gradually handed over responsibility for policing the occupation to their Chechen proxies, the militias loyal to Kadyrov have steadily multiplied in size and number. Estimates range anywhere between 4,000 and 12,000 men in total, spread across formations known as the 'Security Service', the 'Oil Regiment', the 'Second Road Patrol Regiment' and the 'Anti-Terrorist Centre' – the latter re-organized into 'North' and 'South' battalions in mid-2006. In addition to these, there are the Yamadaev brothers' 'Vostok' battalion, and the 'Zapad' (West) battalion commanded by Said-Magomed Kakiev, prominent in the opposition to Dudaev and in pro-Moscow forces in the 1994–6 war. These various factions are riven by infighting and rivalries that often explode into gunfights, and considerable tensions between them make for an unstable political scene. But they are united by a common function. It is not that of fighting the insurgency, for which, as of mid-2006, over 60,000 Russian troops were still required.[21] Rather, they are tasked with beating their countrymen into submitting to Moscow's line.

'Chechenization' has resulted in the institutionalization of kidnapping, and the establishment of an entire parallel penal system, a shadowy counterpart to the Russian army's 'filtration camps'. The scale of abductions is dizzying in a country as small as Chechnya. In October 2004, the puppet president Alkhanov admitted that up to seven people were disappearing every day. By 2006 the rate had declined slightly, but Memorial nonetheless confirmed that since 2002, a total of 1,893 Chechens had been kidnapped, of whom 653 had been found alive, and 186 dead; the vast majority however – 1,023 people – remained missing.[22] Moreover, it should be stressed that

---

[21] John Dunlop gives a breakdown of 23,000 from the Ministry of Defence, 24,000 from the MVD, 17,000 regular police, 3,000 FSB border guards and an unspecified number from the FSB and Justice Ministry. 'Putin, Kozak and Russian Policy toward the North Caucasus', paper presented at Jamestown Foundation conference, 14 September 2006, available on the Foundation's website.

[22] *Vremia Novostei*, 26 October 2004; Interfax, 12 May 2006. The figures appear to leave thirty-one people unaccounted for. It should be noted that a drop in statistical frequency does not necessarily mean an actual decrease in the number of abductions: many of those interviewed by the NGO are too frightened to give details, and have often been threatened into silence.

these are only the documented cases for the 25–30 per cent of the country Memorial covers; including the period 1999–2002 and extrapolating to the rest of the country, Memorial has suggested a figure of between 3,000 and 5,000 disappearances for the duration of Putin's 'anti-terrorist' operation.

Those who disappear are sometimes summarily executed, and offered up as proof of success in the battle against 'insurgents'. But the majority vanish into the network of prisons and torture cells that has taken root across the republic, held until their relatives raise exorbitant ransoms. Prisons can take the form of pits dug into the ground, known as *zindans*, or of 'metal storage containers put into pits and filled with water'; some are converted pedestrian subways. Each of the pro-Moscow factions has its own places of detention: there are several in Kadyrov's home village of Tsentoroi, including one in the basement of a two-storey building that also houses Kadyrov's private gym; *kadyrovtsy* also hold captives in Gudermes, Urus-Martan and Geldagan, while the 'Vostok' and 'Zapad' battalions have prisons in Gudermes, Grozny and Urus-Martan. The FSB also has a few scattered across the republic.[23] This is far from a comprehensive list. And all of these, it bears repeating, operate in addition to the official prisons and detention camps through which thousands of Chechens, male and female, have passed since 1999 – and from which many have never returned.

Torture is endemic. Survivors report beatings with spades, rubber hoses, butts of revolvers, clubs or water bottles filled with sand; some were repeatedly burned with blowtorches, another had his ear sliced off. Many have had electric current passed through them – in several cases by Kadyrov himself, whom several witnesses accuse of participating in torture. Those who emerge from these horrors frequently have broken ribs, jaws or limbs, and many have persistent kidney problems or end up permanently disabled or disfigured.[24] The traditional prohibitions on Chechen killing Chechen are now a thing of the past. Indeed, the

---

[23] International Helsinki Federation report, 'Unofficial Places of Detention in the Chechen Republic', 12 May 2006.

[24] IHF, 'Unofficial Places of Detention'; Mark Franchetti, 'In the Torture Cell of Chechnya's Tyrant', *Sunday Times*, 30 April 2006; *IWPR Caucasus Reporting Service*, 15 June 2006. Anna Politkovskaya's last piece was to be on the torture of civilians by *kadyrovtsy*; an unfinished version was printed in *Novaia gazeta* as 'Naznachaem tebia terroristom' on 12 October 2006.

damage inflicted by Moscow's proxies on their countrymen forms an indelible tattoo of violence, which can only be erased by death or by vengeance, giving further impetus to what is fast becoming a civil war.

Many observers, in Russia and in the West, have been sharply critical both of Russia's sham political process and of the abuses committed by pro-Moscow militias. They point to a need to establish the rule of law, and demand that Chechnya's present masters rein in those responsible for the worst excesses. Once due process has been enshrined and the culture of impunity ended, these critics argue, then some stability might be achieved; this is the best that can be hoped for in such dismal circumstances, and might eventually allow for an end to the fighting, a genuine recovery and, at some future date, more open political discussions. The priority, they insist, is the security of individuals, in the name of which the question of independence should be set aside.[25]

This is to misunderstand the fundamental nature of the Kadyrov regime, and of the conflict itself. For beneath Russia's propagandistic claims of international Islamist conspiracy, of foreign-funded *jihadi* terrorism or simple banditry, there still lies a national struggle for self-determination. The extent of its appeal today cannot be measured by elections organized by Moscow which, quite apart from being fraudulent, automatically exclude anyone with separatist sympathies. Opinion polls conducted under military occupation are worthless. To be fair, after more than a decade of almost constant conflict, we cannot be sure that independence has the backing of an absolute majority of the population. But as in 1994–6, without material support from a substantial proportion of the populace, it would have been impossible for the separatists to conduct a continuous guerrilla war against one of the world's largest armies, as they have for over seven years now. The senseless rampages of pro-Moscow militias therefore possess a terrifying rationality. They must strike fear into every family because every family contains someone connected in some way to the resistance. They must detain people in pits and torture them for information because it would otherwise be withheld; it would be withheld because Kadyrov is a ruler

---

[25] Thomas de Waal, for instance, writes that the Chechens 'would almost certainly give up the hope of independence for a peaceful existence in the Russian state – if only the Russians would guarantee them basic rights' ('Europe's darkest corner', *Guardian*, 30 August 2004).

whom no one in Chechnya chose, engaged in a bloody battle against his own people. It is the logic of a colonial war, in which every civilian is a target.

Living conditions in Chechnya remain desperate. According to local experts, up to 85 per cent of Grozny's housing has been destroyed by the two wars since 1994.[26] Many thousands remain homeless: the authorities admit to 48,000 who were displaced from their homes at the beginning of the war and remain without a permanent residence, but international agencies believe the figure could be as high as 180,000.[27] The bulk of the refugees were forcibly removed from tent camps and settlements in Ingushetia, where Murat Ziazikov whittled the number of displaced Chechens in his republic down from 140,000 in 2001 to around 30,000 in 2005 simply by shutting the camps down and driving their inhabitants back across the border. According to UNHCR figures, most of the refugees in Chechnya are distributed across fifty or so crowded and unsanitary 'temporary accommodation centres'; 24,000 live in such conditions in Grozny alone.[28] In April 2006, Kadyrov described these centres as 'breeding grounds' for crime, drugs and prostitution, and initiated a drive to shut them down – without, however, providing any alternative form of shelter.[29]

Housing remains in short supply. Despite some showpiece reconstruction in the city's centre, the pattern remains one of large-scale devastation, with the pace of rebuilding agonizingly slow. Between 2000 and 2005, the city administration only put up 53 buildings altogether – though an estimated 17,400 had been destroyed since 1994. Moscow's stinginess is partly to blame for this – over 2001–5, it set aside a total of 64 billion roubles for reconstruction in Grozny, compared to 40 billion spent on St Petersburg's 300th anniversary celebrations.[30] Much of the money budgeted remains unspent, or else has been pocketed by

---

26 *IWPR Caucasus Reporting Service*, 6 April 2006.
27 Norwegian Refugee Council, Internal Displacement Monitoring Centre report, 10 October 2006, cited in *Chechnya Weekly*, 19 October 2006.
28 *Kavkazskii Uzel*, 19 April 2006; Internal Displacement Monitoring Centre, March 2005; *IWPR Caucasus Reporting Service*, 30 June 2006.
29 *Ekho Moskvy*, 19 April 2006.
30 *IWPR Caucasus Reporting Service*, 6 October 2005; Paul Goble, 'Chechen Tragedy by Numbers', *Window on Eurasia*, 22 August 2005.

officials in Russia and Chechnya. What new apartments there are lie beyond the reach of most Chechens: a three-bedroom flat in central Grozny's Oil Worker Square, for instance, costs twenty-five times what an average white-collar employee makes in a year.[31]

In the absence of state activity, private entrepreneurs have rushed to fill the vacuum, putting up ramshackle buildings which contravene regulations and, in the few cases where these are residential blocks, prove uninhabitable in colder weather. The economy as a whole has the same short-term, small-scale character. Markets staffed by shuttle traders are once more up and running, as are cafes, hairdressers and a range of enterprises dealing in day-to-day goods. The lack of basic amenities also provides a living for many – for instance, those selling water by the bucketful to households without their own supplies; many wells have been poisoned by oil leaks or toxic waste, and the city lacks running water or functioning sewers – though, of course, the square housing Kadyrov's statue boasts a fountain.[32]

Those who can secure a livelihood are very much in the minority. Officially, as of 2005, only 150,000 have any kind of job, out of a total economically active population of 550,000 – meaning that unemployment was running at 73 per cent.[33] Wages reflect the hierarchy of force in Chechnya: *kadyrovtsy* were reportedly paid 14,000 roubles a month, which is double the earnings of a pro-Moscow functionary, and nearly ten times that of an agricultural worker. In the countryside itself there are scant means of subsistence: 'besides a few roadside shacks and some shepherds, there is little economy to speak of outside Grozny, and unemployment is almost total'.[34]

The lack of employment leaves Chechen men with few options but to join either the separatists or one of the pro-Moscow militias. For there are risks even in seeking other work: all men between the ages of ten and sixty are classified as potential fighters, and hence liable to be arrested or abducted without warning. To avoid these dangers, many men simply stay at home, leaving the women to go out and earn a living – a humiliating role reversal according to Chechnya's patriarchal

[31] Walter Mayr, 'Die Trasse des Todes', *Der Spiegel*, 24 October 2005.
[32] *IWPR Caucasus Reporting Service*, 2 March 2006; *Le Monde*, 21 July 2005.
[33] Timur Aliev, 'Chechnya: The Draft', *Chechen Society*, 30 August 2005.
[34] *The Economist*, 3–9 December 2005.

traditions.[35] The occupation has scrambled Chechen social codes in a variety of ways, including not only relations between the sexes but also traditions of hospitality. With Moscow pitting Chechens against each other, trust has been corroded into oblivion, replaced only by fear and the desperate, cynical reflexes of self-preservation.

War and occupation have placed enormous strains on Chechens' physical and mental health. An entire generation has grown up knowing nothing but the sounds of shelling and gunfire, and scores of adults are in a deep state of trauma. Those physically wounded by bombardment at the beginning of the war found it difficult to get medical help, with what hospitals there were coming under fire. Since then, curfews and sniper-fire have made it difficult to get medical treatment at night. Apart from the depredations of Kadyrov's militias, there are countless other life-threatening hazards, such as thousands of unexploded mines; by April 2006, UNICEF estimated that nearly 700 people, including 132 children, had been killed and nearly 3,000 injured by landmines since 1994.[36] Those not maimed by ordnance face a battery of health risks, including dysentery and tuberculosis, as well as poisoning by toxic materials or oil fumes. Not only those working in pirate oil processing operations are affected: the burning of vast quantities of petroleum products around Grozny, for instance, means that 'whenever it rains something black and greasy falls out of the sky instead of water'.[37]

Much of the danger to Chechens' health is due to the devastating environmental toll of the two wars – much of the arable land has been ruined, and in many places the groundwater has been poisoned. There is also significant evidence that, as in 1994–6, Russian forces have used chemical weapons and other toxic substances in Chechnya. The Chechen doctor Khassan Baiev reports treating 'many patients with mysterious skin eruptions', possibly caused by defoliants.[38] In the summer of 2000, a silvery-purple cloud appeared after an explosion in Starye Atagi, following which twenty-three people came down with symptoms of poisoning; three subse-

---

[35] For interviews with several Chechen women discussing these and other questions at length, see Petra Prochazkova, *Aluminium Queen*, Prague 2002, available at www.berkat.cz.

[36] Cited in *Chechnya Weekly*, 20 April 2006.

[37] Prochazkova, *Aluminium Queen*, p. 162.

[38] Khassan Baiev, *The Oath*, London 2003, p. 251.

[39] Anna Politkovskaya, 'Poison in the Air', Guardian, 1 March 2006.

quently died.[39] In December 2005, in a case that reveals a great deal about Russian official priorities in Chechnya and elsewhere, over eighty people from Chechnya's northern Shchelkovskii region, most of them children, were hospitalized suffering from seizures whose cause was unknown.[40] After initial diagnoses by local doctors suggested poisoning by a toxic substance in a school, Russian officials moved to counter this by announcing a verdict of mass hysteria – motivated in part by 'mercenary interests' seeking compensation.[41] Instead of being properly tested and treated, several of the children were interned in mental hospitals – the better to guard, no doubt, the ghastly secret of what Russia's army had done to them. Chechens have not only been placed at the mercy of a tyrant's death-squads; they have also, it seems, become 'biomaterial for experiments'.[42]

Putin's war to rid Chechnya of 'bandits' has served to elevate a cluster of criminals whose main function is to terrorize the civilian population. As a political strategy, it has been a failure: one fraudulent poll after another has produced a regime with no popular support or legitimacy, in which even the Russians' racketeers and collaborators of choice have been unable to agree on how to divide the spoils. For instance, a gunfight took place between *kadyrovtsy* and Alkhanov's men in April 2006, and the situation was only defused by the intervention of the other pro-Russian warlords, Yamadaev and Kakiev. Some analysts see the latter as necessary counter-weights to Kadyrov, who every so often seems to strain at Moscow's leash. Often this takes the form of demanding increased federal subsidies, but in late 2005 he suggested that Chechnya extend its boundaries; in April 2006, deputies loyal to him proposed the amalgamation of Chechnya and Ingushetia, and possibly Dagestan too – prompting furious objections from Ingush and Dagestani officials.[43] The more power accrues to him, the less controllable Kadyrov will become – and he is already powerful enough to cause Moscow serious problems if he so wishes. The monster of Putin's making may have outgrown the

[40] *Chechnya Weekly*, 30 March 2006.
[41] Itar-Tass, 2 March 2006. The person voicing this opinion was the chief psychiatrist at the Serbskii Institute, famous during the Soviet period for certifying dissidents insane at the prompting of the Kremlin.
[42] Politkovskaya, 'Poison in the Air'.
[43] Interfax, 24 April 2006. Increased tensions with the Ingush exploded into a shootout between Chechen pro-Moscow security personnel and Ingush police in September 2006, in which 8 were killed: *IWPR Caucasus Reporting Service*, 21 September 2006.

master's grip. Indeed, there are those who worry that 'Kadyrovization' may result in the effective sectioning off of Chechnya as Kadyrov's private realm – de facto independence under a Russian flag.[44]

But Kadyrov is incapable of taking on the separatists himself. His regime depends on the presence of Russian troops, just as Russian forces depend on Kadyrov, Yamadaev and Kakiev to squeeze the civilian population for intelligence on the separatists' movements. Offers of amnesty, coercion through the abduction of relatives of fighters and simple battle-exhaustion have thinned the ranks of the resistance in recent years – as have the deaths of a series of leaders and senior field commanders: most prominently, Maskhadov, Sadulaev, Basaev and Ruslan Gelaev. Dokku Umarov, who became acting president in June 2006, is among the last survivors from the generation who led the fighting in 1994–6. His title is significant: according to the Ichkerian constitution, Maskhadov's term was to expire in 2002, and any separatist leader since then therefore only occupies the post temporarily, pending new elections. Umarov is one of the few figures with a public reputation outside the resistance itself, and were he to be assassinated like his predecessors, there are relatively few men left who could speak with any authority on behalf of such a decentralized movement.

However, it is unlikely that a conclusive military defeat would follow. The resistance is not large: estimates range either side of 2,000 active fighters, facing around 60,000 Russian troops and perhaps 10,000 pro-Moscow militiamen. The secret of its durability lies in its structure, based on small cells of a dozen or so men scattered across several fronts. According to defence analyst Paul Tumelty, despite the high rate of attrition in its upper ranks, at the middle and lower levels the resistance units 'exhibit a coherent and stable configuration throughout Chechnya's fronts, sectors and areas', maintaining 'a permanent and relatively stable number of active fighters' across the territory. Volunteers are turned away and asked to wait in the much larger reserve. When an active fighter is killed, 'the unit is immediately replenished, thus maintaining a core level of fighters engaged in resistance.'[45]

---

[44] Political analyst Sergei Markedonov, cited in *IWPR Caucasus Reporting Service*, 20 July 2006.
[45] Paul Tumelty, 'Chechnya: A Strategy for Independence', *Chechnya Weekly*, 3 August 2005.

Such a structure makes large-scale operations, along the lines of the 1996 re-capture of Grozny, extremely improbable. But with strong roots in the local population and an assured stream of reserves and recruits, it provides a solid basis for prolonged guerrilla warfare, of a kind that will cause yet more Russian casualties, making it increasingly difficult for the authorities to maintain that the war is over. At the end of January 2006, Putin triumphantly declared that the 'anti-terrorist operation' in Chechnya had been concluded. Statements from his own generals flatly contradicted him: after a meeting of top brass at Khankala airbase a fortnight earlier, MVD General Nikolai Rogozhkin said that the 'importance and difficulty of the military missions will increase this year'.[46] Though it is a war neither side can win, the Chechens score a tactical victory with every moment they stave off defeat; the Russians are defeated as long as they cannot claim victory.

Putin has managed to convince much of the world that his war in Chechnya is a struggle against religious extremism and criminal chaos. The credulousness and cowardice of the 'international community' have facilitated a chilling conjuring trick, in which the aspirations of an entire people to self-determination have been made to disappear, and the violence inflicted upon them has been hidden behind a cloud of euphemisms and falsifications. Yet the cause for which war is being waged in Chechnya was and remains that of independence. In a less guarded moment, Putin himself implicitly admitted as much, comparing his campaign in Chechnya 'to the security service operation in the Baltics . . . aimed at eradicating anti-Soviet resistance lasting from 1944 to the mid-1950s'.[47] The analogy is telling: the Baltic states were forcibly incorporated into the USSR in 1940, an annexation that was internationally condemned as illegitimate. No such response has greeted Putin's attempted reconquest of Chechnya.

Yet 'no legitimate Chechen authority has ever signed any formal treaty accepting Russian or Soviet authority'.[48] On the only occasions when the Chechens have genuinely been offered the chance – in 1991

---

[46] Both quoted in *Chechnya Weekly*, 13 April 2006.
[47] Trenin and Malashenko, *Russia's Restless Frontier*, p. 119.
[48] Roman Khalilov, 'Moral Justifications of Secession: the Case of Chechnya', *Central Asian Survey*, vol. 22, no. 4 (December 2003), p. 410.

and 1997 – the great majority of them have given democratic approval
to the idea of sovereign statehood. War-weariness, cynicism and a desire
for peace at any price may have undermined its appeal, as, for many,
might the experience of de facto independence under Maskhadov and
Dudaev. But such speculations are impossible to verify amid the larcenous brutality of Kadyrov and continuing occupation by Russian soldiers.
The present situation is not a legitimate or stable alternative to allowing
the Chechens freely to express their preference, and it is a disgrace that
the majority of world opinion should continue to connive at the strangulation of their basic right as a people.

As the preceding chapters will, I hope, have made clear, the Chechens
have solid legal grounds for their bid for sovereignty, and an overwhelming moral case for their own state. Over the course of centuries,
they have experienced colonization, repression, discrimination and
marginalization at the hands of both Russian and Soviet authorities,
before falling victim to a wholesale deportation that fits every available
definition of genocide. The pattern is so consistent that a mere change
of government was no assurance that it would alter: hence the gathering
momentum for a sovereign Chechen state as the Soviet Union crumbled.
Russia deployed terrifying military force to halt this movement in 1994,
and again in 1999 after smashing any possibility of a viable state in the
interim. It has since imposed a vicious client regime and conducted
travesties of democratic elections, in a savage reprise of the Soviet fiction
of 'voluntary union' – a fake 'political process' that has excluded anyone
actively advocating sovereignty for Chechnya not because the issue is
dead, but precisely because it remains live.

In years to come, historians may come to see the struggle over
Chechnya as perhaps the most striking feature of the post-Soviet political
landscape: a tiny nation has played a determining role in the fortunes
of its incomparably larger neighbour. The Chechens have defeated the
Russian army, crippled the Yeltsin presidency, provided the springboard
for Putin's ascent to power, and today present the principal threat to
Russia's stability. The same historians will also be astounded by the
continued complacency of Western governments and citizens alike,
whose inertia has helped Russia's rulers to prosecute an unnecessary,
illegitimate and unwinnable war that has killed thousands of its own
citizens, and utterly failed in its stated goals. For the bombs and tyranny

Russia has unleashed on Chechnya since 1994 can only have increased the Chechens' desire to separate from the orchestrators of their destruction. Russia's current policy is designed forever to prevent them from making such a choice. But there can be no peace until it is once again possible for the Chechens freely and democratically to determine their own future. Their right to govern themselves should be the starting point for any discussions aimed at bringing to an end their ongoing tragedy.

Appendix

Russian Arguments for Chechen Independence

Introduction to Illarionov and Lvin

In February 1995 *Moscow News* published an article by two leading Russian economists, Andrei Illarionov and Boris Lvin, which argued, in a succinct set of theses, that Russia should recognize Chechnya's independence on grounds ranging from the historical, economic and geographical to the legal, moral and ethical. The lucidity with which the arguments are posed is matched only by the text's urgency and its strong sense of the moral damage being wrought on Russia by its conduct of the war. *Moscow News*, a weekly paper published in Russian, English and several other languages, had served as a voice for the liberal intelligentsia during the *glasnost* years. It was this constituency that raised the strongest initial protests against Yeltsin's invasion of Chechnya in December 1994; *Moscow News* ran many critical reports from Grozny in the war's early stages.

The article's authors were both born in 1961 and educated in Leningrad. At the time of its publication, Illarionov was director of the Institute for Economic Analysis in Moscow, and Lvin an employee of the IMF in Washington. Lvin moved to the World Bank in 1998, while Illarionov became chief economic adviser to Vladimir Putin in April 2000; a role in which he continued until his resignation in December

2005 over the government's drift towards authoritarianism – telling a press conference on 21 December that Russia was 'no longer a democratic country'. In October 2006 he took up a fellowship at the Cato Institute.

Perhaps the most striking feature of Illarionov and Lvin's article is that its publication in today's Russia would be all but unthinkable. The state-sponsored obfuscations of the 'anti-terrorist operation' have served to marginalize completely the matter of Chechen independence, as well as fostering widespread hostility to Chechens as a whole. Indeed, neither author appears to have spoken out against Putin's war on Chechnya, which – as they predicted – has ensured 'the best conditions for the suppression of democracy in Russia itself'. The contrast between the liberals' earlier anger over Chechnya and recent silence is indicative of a broader transformation of Russian opinion: while in 1994 bloodshed had been an unacceptable shock, a decade later it has become routine, part of the background hum of state activity.

Yet the arguments Illarionov and Lvin set out are fully as valid now as they were over a decade ago. Across the years of slaughter and destruction visited on the Chechens, the fundamental question they posed in 1995 – 'What can be obtained by a military victory and the appointment of an occupation puppet regime?' – has been drowned out by bombs, gunfire, kidnapping, torture. Every new casualty raises the question once more; every new casualty is itself the answer.

Andrei Illarionov and Boris Lvin

Should Russia Recognize Chechnya's Independence?

Historical

1. Chechnya has never been a voluntary member of Russia. No Chechen leader has ever signed a treaty on voluntarily joining Russia. The Chechens fought for their freedom under Sheikh Mansur in the 18th century and during the Caucasian War. which lasted for almost 50 years in the 19th century. The entire history of the Chechen people 'in the Russian epoch' is a chain of anti-Russian uprisings: in 1877, in 1918–1920, in 1920–1930, during the Second World War and in 1991. It is an endless list of punitive expeditions, colonial suppression, various forms of punishment, deportations, and new waves of the national-liberation movement.

2. Formally 'pacified' Chechnya remained within Russia for 132 years, exactly as long as Poland, which also refused to tolerate the loss of independence. This is much shorter than the amount of time that many other states on the territory of the former USSR spent in the Russian embrace. Their independence has already been internationally recognized.

3. The present 'winter war' in the Caucasus painfully resembles another 'winter war.' In December of 1939 Kuusinen, a leader of the All-Union Communist Party (Bolsheviks) was forming a 'workers' and peasants' government of the Democratic Republic of Finland' in the town of Terijoki, which was burned down by Soviet artillery. He called on the Red Army 'to complete cleansing the territory of Finland from white Finn gangs.' As is being done now in Grozny, 'Stalin's falcons' bombed Helsinki's residential quarters in 1939 and hunted 'gunmen' who pushed baby carriages. Like today, the generals of that time complained of 'incorrect' methods of resistance that were being employed by the Finnish side. While the Soviet Union was expelled from the League of Nations (the only case in all of its history) for this undisguised act of aggression, today Russia is not allowed to enter the Council of Europe.

4. It is impossible to persuade any nation to abandon their efforts to gain independence from an aggressor or colonialist: neither the Americans or Indians from Great Britain, nor the Algerians or Vietnamese from France, nor the Angolans or Mozambicans from Portugal.

Economic

1. Chechnya, along with Daghestan, has always been the most subsidized republic within the Russian Federation. The Grozny oil reserves have been practically exhausted. Even from a most cynical point of view a few Chechen mountain ridges are worth neither the efforts spent to possess them nor the lost human lives.

2. Reparations for the damage inflicted on Chechnya will have to be paid by the Russian people. The continuation of the war only increases this price. Only its termination provides a chance to reduce inflation and a theoretical possibility for Russia's economic recovery.

3. Even if Chechnya is independent de jure, because of its geographical situation it is doomed to most intensive economic contacts with Russia.

Geographical

1. Russia has never had any need for Chechnya. In the 19th century Russia's strategic goal was Persian possessions. Russia went to the Caucasus in order to capture Persian Transcaucasia – Georgia and the Baku, Sheki, Talysh, Karabakh and Erivan khanates, which occupied the territory of present Azerbaijan and Armenia. However, the way to get there was either through Sochi – for which Russia almost exterminated the Adyghe peoples of the Caucasus and deported more than a million Circassians to Turkey and other Middle Eastern countries – or through Derbent, for which Daghestan had to be conquered. Since Daghestan depended economically on Chechnya, pressure was put on the latter.

   These 'geopolitics' can now be dismissed. Chechnya's strategic importance for Russia has dropped to zero.

2. Arguments on the necessity to protect Russian transit through Chechnya by military force have as much legal power as the idea of protecting Russian transit through the Kaliningrad Region by occupying Lithuania and of transit to Germany by occupying Poland. Precisely the same pretext – the protection of German transit through the 'Polish corridor' – was employed by Hitler for unleashing the Second World War.

3. Chechnya has an outlet to Russia's external border, and its independence appears to be more viable than that of Tatarstan or any other enclave territory.

National-ethnic

1. The Chechens number more than one million people, over 800,000 of whom live in Chechnya proper. There are more Chechens in Chechnya than there are Estonians in Estonia.

2. The population of Chechnya is now already nationally very homogeneous. According to the 1989 census, Chechens made up 69 percent of the population of the present Chechen Republic; by 1994 they accounted for more than 76 percent and make up no less than 80 percent today. No other national minority of Russia is as large and as compactly settled as Chechnya.

The current war will only enhance this homogeneity. However, the number of Chechens in Chechnya would have grown without the war. Unlike the Russians and most other nations, the rate of natural increase of the population here is among the highest within the former USSR.

3. The Chechens have vigorously resisted Russification and have preserved a high degree of national identity. More than 98 percent of Chechens consider the Chechen language to be their mother tongue, which, along with Russians and Tuvans, is the highest figure in Russia.

Legal

1. National parliamentary and presidential elections were held in Chechnya on October 27, 1991. The elections were attended by 458,144 people, or 72 percent of the total number of voters. Dzhokhar Dudayev won the votes of 412,671 persons – 90.1 percent of those who took part in the elections, or 63.1 per cent of the total number of the electors. Thus the legitimacy of the Chechen authorities is in any case not below that of the Russian authorities. Although the Chechen parliament was subsequently disbanded by Dudayev, this fact is by no means an exception on the territory of the former USSR.

2. Dudayev proclaimed the sovereignty of the Chechen Republic as of November 1, 1991, acting on the strength of the Law on State Sovereignty and the expression of the will of the republic's citizens. From that moment Chechnya actually existed as an independent state for over three years. Not once did Chechnya take part in any Russian voting, either in elections or the referendum. Nor did it send its representatives to Russian bodies of power.

Chechnya's sovereignty was tacitly recognized by Moscow. For more than three years the Russian administration did not appear on Chechen territory. Russian authorities levied no taxes on Chechen enterprises and did not finance the Chechen budget. Chechnya was the first territory of the former Soviet Union from which Russian troops were withdrawn. It was only later that they left Azerbaijan, Lithuania and Estonia.

3. The absence of other states' legal recognition of Chechnya is also not a valid argument. Although Stalin's annexation of the Baltic states was always criticized in the West, their formal recognition of the independence of the Baltic countries came only after the corresponding decision of the Union authorities in August of 1991. The history of states that were not recognized for a long time, but which were actually independent, is very rich; it stretches from the German Democratic Republic to Taiwan, North Korea, Northern Cyprus and Serbian Krajina. The post-Soviet problems with Karabakh, Abkhazia, Transdnestr and Chechnya are only a small portion of this history.

4. In the former USSR the borderline between the status of a 'Union' republic, which had the right 'to leave' the Union and that of an 'autonomous' republic, which had no such right, was never impassable. Kazakhstan was at first an autonomy within the Russian Federation; Moldova was once also an autonomy within Ukraine. Karelia used to be a Union republic, while the Baltic republics and Tuva were independent states.

5. The official Russian authorities deliberately replace the question of Chechnya's independence with that of its state organization, of the nature of the regime within it and its correspondence to the principles of democracy and law. Neither the Viet Cong in Vietnam, nor the Bolshevik regime in Russia had anything to do with democracy. However the crimes committed by them did not justify denying the people of the countries the right to independence.

Criminal

1. The Chechen authorities are regularly accused of crimes against the population, especially the Russian-speaking people. However, before the current war the emigration of the Russian-speaking population from Chechnya was no more intense than that from Kalmykia, Tuva and Saha-Yakutia. In Grozny itself there remained a 200,000-strong Russian-speaking population which did not hasten to leave it.

2. Chechens' participation in criminal activity on the territory of Russia proper is undoubtedly the same as that of other peoples of our

country and the 'near abroad.' However, the main reason for the unprecedented scope of this activity was not the actions of Chechen, but of Russian authorities, which imposed an economic blockade on Chechnya. As a result, the republic's population was deprived of legal earnings and was forced to resort to illegal operations. There is no doubt, however, that the machinations with oil, arms, smuggling and financial documents could not, in principle, be carried out without the participation of 'partners' from Moscow, Stavropol, Krasnodar, etc.

The Chechen mafia was born of the Russian economic blockade, just as the Romanian and Bulgarian mafia was born of the UN-imposed blockade of Yugoslavia. The overwhelming majority of Chechens are related to the Chechen mafia in the same way as most Italians are to the 'cosa nostra'.

3. The crimes committed by the federal authorities in Chechnya are incomparable to even the most incredible real or imagined actions of the Chechens. The extermination of thousands of utterly innocent citizens on the territory of Chechnya is unambiguously characterized as genocide by international and national law.

4. In connection with Dudayev's 'criminal regime', mention should be made of a very important fact which has for some reason been ignored by the public. Dudayev's government recognized the self-determination of the Ingush people and agreed that the Ingush Republic should withdraw from the Chechen-Ingush Autonomous Republic and remain in Russia. There must be weighty political reasons for such behavior by Dudayev, but is there another government in the world that has voluntarily given up its national minority? The only possible exception is the Havel-Klaus government in former Czechoslovakia.

Russia's Unity and Security

1. The current dirty war in Chechnya is a detonator of Russia's state unity and national security. He who wants to get more closely acquainted with terrorism should support the preservation of Russian power over a country enveloped in the fires of an uprising.

There will be no real terrorism while the war lasts. Terrorism is a weapon of the desperate; the last argument of people who have been defeated on the battlefield but do not admit their defeat. Russia will thus get its own Ulster and Bosnia, Corsica and the Basque Provinces, Palestine and Kashmir, Eritrea and Biafra all 'in the same package'.

If Chechnya remains within Russia, the Bickford fuse of centripedal movement, fired from the Chechen spark, will ignite other national areas. Pavel Miliukov once said that Russia perished in October 1917 because of the slogan 'one and indivisible'.

Political

1. The continuation of the punitive expedition in Chechnya ensures the best conditions for the suppression of democracy in Russia itself, for strengthening the punitive function of the state, which is often aimed not at crime but at its own citizens. Chechnya already has screening camps, which can well be called concentration camps.
2. The continuation of the war releases the most vile vices. Today round-ups on national grounds, conducted all over the country, already arouse almost no indignation or protest. Russia is sinking into racism at a time when South Africa is getting out of it.

Moral and Ethical

1. The punitive expedition cannot reach 'pacification'. It can give rise to only one reaction. Just as the responsibility for the Nazi crimes was shared by all Germans after the Second World War, the responsibility for the Chechen punitive expedition is inevitably extended to all of Russia, to the entire Russian people.
2. The Chechen adventure is Russia's disgrace. It is said that when the US Supreme Court passed decision on the case of Dred Scott, which obliged the northern states to return slaves to their former owners, a meeting of an American town adopted this resolution: 'We despise this decision, we hate it, we spit on it and trample on it.' The dirty

war in Chechnya, accompanied by monstrous and foul lies, deserves only such an attitude.

What can be obtained by a military victory and the appointment of an occupation puppet regime? The Chechens' submission? No. Their loyalty? No. Constitutional order? No again. Security in Chechnya and in the Northern Caucasus? Economic revival? The Chechens' rejection of attempts for national independence? All this is very doubtful.

What will be the result of the cessation of hostilities, the withdrawal of the Russian troops from Chechnya and the unconditional recognition of the independence of the Chechen Republic? First of all, and this is more than enough, the result will be the saving of thousands and tens of thousands of lives, Russian and Chechen; the establishment of normal diplomatic and business relations between Russia and Chechnya; the saving of immense material resources. It will also lead to a chance for success of the Russian economic reforms, a colossal moral victory with very strong trump cards in all negotiations with our neighbors about national minorities, the preservation of the fundamentals of democracy in Russia. Finally, it will allow for the prevention of Russia's disintegration, the redemption of national disgrace and the saving of national honor.

Will Russia find its Mendes-France who found courage to recognize Vietnam's independence? Will it have its de Gaulle who agreed, after eight years of bloody war and the death of more than a million people, to recognize Algeria's independence? Or perhaps it will find a Lord Mountbatten of its own, who managed to leave British India in such a way that he is still regarded as a benefactor both of India and Pakistan.

Moscow News, February 24–March 2, 1995

Glossary and abbreviations

ASSR— Autonomous Soviet Socialist Republic: sub-unit of the Russian Soviet Federative Socialist Republic (RSFSR)

CIS—Commonwealth of Independent States: a loose grouping of 11 former Soviet republics, formed as the USSR was collapsing in December 1991

DUMD—*Dukhovnoe upravlenie musul'man Dagestana* (Russian), Spiritual Board of Muslims of Dagestan: official Islamic clerical body, established in 1990

DUMSK—*Dukhovnoe upravlenie musul'man Severnogo Kavkaza* (Russian), Spiritual Board of Muslims of the North Caucasus: official Soviet-era Islamic clerical body

FSB — *Federal'naia sluzhba bezopasnosti* (Russian), Federal Security Service: successor agency to the KGB and FSK (see below)

FSK—*Federal'naia sluzhba kontrrazvedki* (Russian), Federal Counter-Intelligence Service: post-Soviet successor agency to the KGB, formed in 1993, renamed FSB in 1995

ghazavat —holy war (from Arabic, pl. of raid, incursion)

GPU—*Gosudarstvennoe politicheskoe upravlenie* (Russian), State Political Directorate: Soviet secret police from 1922–34, when it was incorporated into the NKVD

GRU—*Glavnoe razvedyvatel'noe upravlenie* (Russian), Main Intelligence Directorate: Russian military intelligence

IJD—Islamic Jamaat of Dagestan: Salafist militant group, in armed opposition to Russian authorities since 1997

IMU—Islamic Movement of Uzbekistan: militant Islamist group founded in the early 1990s, aiming at overthrow of Kasimov government.

kadyrovtsy—militias loyal to Akhmad Kadyrov, pro-Moscow president of Chechnya from 2003–4, or to his son Ramzan, currently the republic's Kremlin-approved prime minister

MVD—*Ministerstvo vnutrennykh del* (Russian), Ministry of Internal Affairs

NKVD—*Narodnyi komissariat vnutrennykh del* (Russian), People's Commissariat of Internal Affairs: Soviet secret police, intelligence and security service from 1934–46

RSFSR—Russian Soviet Federative Socialist Republic, the largest of the fifteen republics composing the Soviet Union

siloviki—from Russian *sila,* force: term applied to representatives of 'force structures' in the Russian government, a broad faction consisting of former and current security and armed services personnel

stanitsa—Cossack settlement

taip—clan (Chechen)

Vainakh—lit. 'our people': joint designation for Chechens, Ingush, Kists and Bats

VDP—Vainakh Democratic Party: driving force behind push for Chechen independence in 1991

vird—Sufi brotherhood

zachistka —'clean-up' operation (Russian)

zikr—incantatory Sufi ritual, involving either prayer alone or music and a circular dance, depending on the Sufi order

Index